双语名著无障碍阅读丛书
第一级

远古传奇
Just So Stories

[英国] 吉卜林 著
吕薇 译

中国出版集团公司
中国对外翻译出版有限公司

图书在版编目（CIP）数据

远古传奇：英汉对照 /（英）吉卜林著；吕薇译. —北京：中国对外翻译出版有限公司，2012.7

（双语名著无障碍阅读丛书）

ISBN 978-7-5001-3459-6

Ⅰ.①远… Ⅱ.①吉… ②吕… Ⅲ.①英语—汉语—对照读物 ②儿童故事—作品集—英国—现代 Ⅳ.①H319.4:I

中国版本图书馆 CIP 数据核字（2012）第 149830 号

出版发行 / 中国对外翻译出版有限公司
地　　址 / 北京市西城区车公庄大街甲 4 号物华大厦六层
电　　话 /（010）68359827　68359303（发行部）　68359287（编辑部）
邮　　编 / 100044
传　　真 /（010）68357870
电子邮箱 / book@ctpc.com.cn
网　　址 / http://www.ctpc.com.cn

出版策划 / 张高里　凌从严
执行策划 / 胡晓凯
责任编辑 / 张琳洁
封面设计 / 奇文堂·潘峰

排　　版 / 北京巴蜀阳光图文设计有限公司
印　　刷 / 环球印刷（北京）有限公司
经　　销 / 新华书店

规　　格 / 700×960 毫米　1/16
印　　张 / 17.5
字　　数 / 220 千字
版　　次 / 2012 年 7 月第 1 版
印　　次 / 2012 年 7 月第 1 次

ISBN 978-7-5001-3459-6　　　　定价：25.00 元

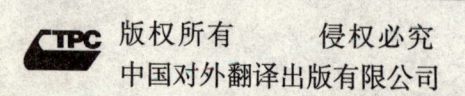

版权所有　　侵权必究
中国对外翻译出版有限公司

出版前言

多年以来，中国对外翻译出版有限公司凭借国内一流的翻译和出版实力及资源，精心策划、出版了大批双语读物，在海内外读者中和业界内产生了良好、深远的影响，形成了自己鲜明的出版特色。

二十世纪八九十年代出版的英汉（汉英）对照"一百丛书"，声名远扬，成为一套最权威、最有特色且又实用的双语读物，影响了一代又一代英语学习者和中华传统文化研究者、爱好者；还有"英若诚名剧译丛"、"中华传统文化精粹丛书"、"美丽英文书系"，这些优秀的双语读物，有的畅销，有的常销不衰反复再版，有的被选为大学英语阅读教材，受到广大读者的喜爱，获得了良好的社会效益和经济效益。

"双语名著无障碍阅读丛书"是中译专门为中学生和英语学习者精心打造的又一品牌，是一个新的双语读物系列，具有以下特点：

选题创新——该系列图书是国内第一套为中小学生量身打造的双语名著读物，所选篇目均为教育部颁布的语文新课标必读书目，或为中学生以及同等文化水平的社会读者喜闻乐见的世界名著，重新编译为英汉（汉英）

对照的双语读本。这些书既给青少年读者提供了成长过程中不可或缺的精神食粮，又让他们领略到原著的精髓和魅力，对他们更好地学习英文大有裨益；同时，丛书中入选的《论语》、《茶馆》、《家》等汉英对照读物，亦是热爱中国传统文化的中外读者所共知的经典名篇，能使读者充分享受阅读经典的无限乐趣。

无障碍阅读——中学生阅读世界文学名著的原著会遇到很多生词和文化难点。针对这一情况，我们给每一本读物原文中的较难词汇和不易理解之处都加上了注释，在内文的版式设计上也采取英汉（或汉英）对照方式，扫清了学生阅读时的障碍。

优良品质——中译双语读物多年来在读者中享有良好口碑，这得益于作者和出版者对于图书质量的不懈追求。"双语名著无障碍阅读丛书"继承了中译双语读物的优良传统——精选的篇目、优秀的译文、方便实用的注解，秉承着对每一个读者负责的精神，竭力打造精品图书。

愿这套丛书成为广大读者的良师益友，愿读者在英语学习和传统文化学习两方面都取得新的突破。

译 序

一直认为，寓言和童话是儿童的专利，然而，在那个夏日午后，一本附着奇怪插图的英文原版书在我面前打开，短短几分钟后，自己便深深地沉浸在另外一个世界里——那里有茂密的原始森林，有短鼻子的小象、披着光滑皮外套的犀牛、会跺脚的蝴蝶，还有和爸爸一起打猎的原始部落的小女孩……离奇而丰富的想象，细腻且生动的描写，讲述着很久很久以前人类与动物的种种变故。我流连在这个五彩缤纷而又光怪陆离的神奇王国里，全然忘却了自己已经处在波澜不惊的成人世界；一起被抛在脑后的，还有窗外熙熙攘攘、车水马龙的现实社会。

这本书就是——《远古传奇》（Just so Stories）。

于是译文便在笔下顺畅地流淌出来。翻译的过程不再枯燥，渐渐演变成一种享受，因为怀着与普通读者一样急于知道结果的心情。我一直惊诧于本书的作者——一位成年作家——是从哪里汲取撰写童话的灵感，又是从哪里获得了如此不可思议的想象力？

现在让我们来了解一下作者吧。洛德亚得·约契尔·

吉卜林（1865—1936年）是一位诗人、短篇小说家、新闻记者。他于1865年出生在孟买，父亲约翰·洛克伍德·吉卜林是《印度的野兽与人》的文字和插图作者，母亲艾莉是印刷设计师爱德华·波恩·琼斯的嫂子。1871年，吉卜林和他的小姐姐被带回了英国，与家住南海的一位上了年纪的亲戚在一起生活了五年。这五年他过得并不开心。后来，他把这段经历写入了一篇名为《黑羊咩咩》的短篇故事里，文中流露出一丝苦涩。1878年，吉卜林进入联合服务大学，这是一所专为服役军官的儿子们开设的小型公立学校。在那里，他开始写诗，并于1881年自行出版了诗集。离开学校后，吉卜林来到了印度，在1881至1889年间从事新闻记者的工作。这一期间他撰写了大量作品——故事、插图和诗歌，一时间享誉英伦三岛。1889年他定居伦敦时已颇有名望。后来他又创作了三篇作品，进一步提高了他的声望。他于1892年出版了第二本诗集《军营歌谣》，其中包括他最著名的几首诗《曼德勒》、《枪声喧嚣》和《丹妮·丹维尔》。1892年，吉卜林与卡洛琳·巴尔蒂斯结婚，婚后他们在佛蒙特州居住了四年。在那里，吉卜林创作出最广为人知的作品《丛林故事》，1894年一经出版便获得了巨大成功。1896年，他回到英格兰，并于1920年最终定居在赛萨克斯的贝特曼。1901年《吉姆》一书出版，人们一般称此书为吉卜林的代表作。不久，他又出版了一部面向少儿读者的作品《远古传奇》，获得了巨大成功。

吉卜林一直享有民间"桂冠诗人"的美誉（他却拒绝了英国国内的类似褒奖）。1907年，他成为第一位获得诺贝尔奖的英国作家。1936年，吉卜林与世长辞。他被埋葬在威斯敏斯特教堂。一部未完成的自传作品《我的一二事》在他死后出版。

《远古传奇》（1902年）是吉卜林创作的儿童作品中最有名的故事集之一。在吉卜林所有的著作当中，他自己最喜欢的就是这本《远古传奇》。每一个故事都称得上是吉卜林的代表作。他对动物的热爱仿佛与生俱来，并从中获得巨大的灵感。本书所收集的"大象的孩子"、"花豹身上的斑点是怎么长出来的"、"独来独往的猫"和其他寓言故事最初是吉卜林讲给他孩子的女护理员听的。前者讲得津津有味，后者听得如痴如醉。这些故事按照主题和描述的环境，从动物讲到字母的起源，从史前山洞讲到非洲热带丛林。本书文笔风趣生动，辅以诗歌和顺口溜，再加上谜一样的插图，体现了作者高超的创造力。打开书，便感觉吉卜林仿佛无所不在，他可能就在书中的某个角落或某幅插图里，狡黠地眨着眼睛，眨出一个又一个神奇……

在翻译的过程中，我不断地被作者特有的文笔魅力所吸引，甚至被深深地感动。记得在翻译"字母的起源"故事后面所附的小诗时，我的眼前仿佛出现了一幅画面："她穿着鹿皮鞋、鹿皮外套／飞舞着／无畏美丽自由自在／手中潮湿的小木块燃烧着／让飘散的烟雾／告诉爸

· v ·

爸她的去向／远方很远很远／她喊爸爸的声音都听不见／特奎曼正独自走来／寻找他的女儿／那个对他来说意味着一切的小姑娘……"我被这种自然流露的父女真情打动了，微笑着默诵诗句，眼里闪着泪光。

　　作为本书的翻译，我始终尽力用最传神的语言把吉卜林的故事原汁原味地呈现给读者。但因水平有限，文中不足之处，敬请读者指正。

译　者

目录
CONTENTS

How the Whale Got His Throat ………………… 002
鲸鱼的喉咙是怎么回事

How the Camel Got His Hump ………………… 016
骆驼背上的驼峰是怎么长出来的

How the Leopard Got His Spots ………………… 042
花豹身上的斑点是怎么长出来的

The Elephant's Child ………………………………… 062
大象的孩子

The Sing-Song of Old Man Kangaroo …………… 086
一只老雄袋鼠的冗长乏味的故事

The Beginning of the Armadillos ………………… 100
犰狳的起源

How the First Letter was Written ………………… 124
第一封信是怎么写出来的

目录 CONTENTS

How the Alphabet was Made ············· 150
字母表是怎么创造出来的

The Crab that Played with the Sea ············· 182
与大海游戏的螃蟹

The Cat that Walked by Himself ············· 212
独来独往的猫

The Butterfly that Stamped ············· 242
跺脚的蝴蝶

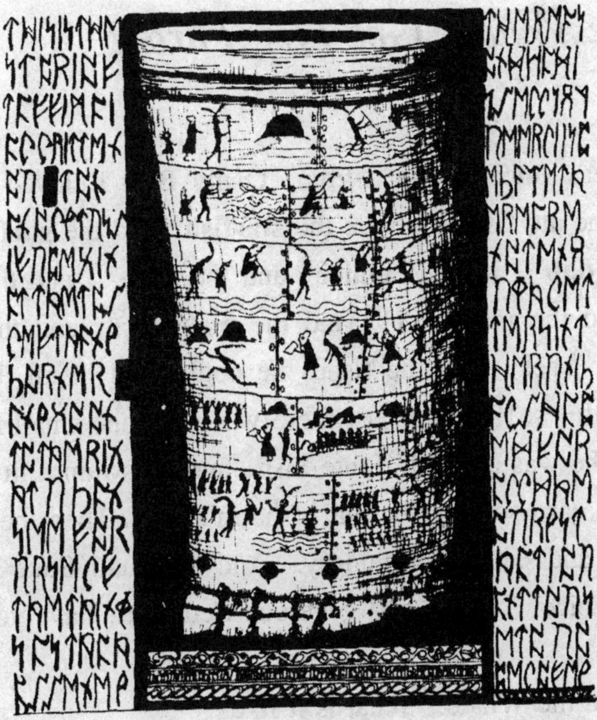

How the Whale Got His Throat

In the sea, **once**① upon a time, O my Best Beloved, there was a Whale, and he ate fishes. He ate the **starfish**② and the **garfish**③, and the crab and the **dab**④, and the **plaice**⑤ and the **dace**⑥, and the **skate**⑦ and his mate, and the **mackereel**⑧ and the **pickerel**⑨, and the really truly **twirly-whirly**⑩ **eel**⑪. All the fishes he could find in all the sea he ate with his mouth—so! Till at last there was only one small fish left in all the sea, and he was a small 'Stute Fish, and he swam a little behind the Whale's right ear, so as to be out of harm's way. Then the Whale stood up on his tail and said, 'I'm hungry.' And the small 'Stute Fish said in a small 'stute voice, 'Noble and generous Cetacean, have you ever tasted Man?'

'No,' said the Whale. 'What is it like?'

'Nice,' said the small 'Stute Fish. 'Nice but **nubbly**⑫.'

'Then fetch me some,' said the Whale, and he made the sea **froth**⑬ up with his tail.

'One at a time is enough,' said the 'Stute Fish. 'If you swim to **latitude**⑭ Fifty North, **longitude**⑮ Forty West (that is magic), you will find, sitting on a raft, in the middle of the sea, with nothing on but a pair of blue **canvas**⑯ **breeches**⑰, a pair of **suspenders**⑱ (you must *not* forget the suspenders, Best Beloved), and a **jack-knife**⑲, one ship-

鲸鱼的喉咙是怎么回事

① onceuponatime *n* 从前
② starfish /'stɑ:fɪʃ/ *n*. 海星
③ garfish /'gɑ:fɪʃ/ *n*. 长嘴硬鳞鱼
④ dab /dæb/ *n* 比目鱼
⑤ plaice /pleɪs/ *n*. 鲽(鱼)
⑥ dace /deɪs/ *n*. 鲦鱼
⑦ skate /skeɪt, skɪt/ *n* 鳐鱼
⑧ mackerel /'mækrəl/ *n* 鲭
⑨ pickerel /'pɪkərəl/ *n*. 小梭鱼
⑩ twirly-whirly /twə:lɪ-(h)wəlɪ/ *a* 快速旋转的
⑪ eel /i:l/ *n*. 鳗鱼
⑫ nubbly /'nʌblɪ/ *a*. 多瘤的,粗糙的
⑬ froth /frɒθ, frɔ:θ/ *v*. 使生泡沫
⑭ latitude /'lætɪtjuːd/ *n* 纬度
⑮ longitude /'lɒndʒɪtjuːd/ *n*. 经度
⑯ canvas /'kænvəs/ *n* 帆布
⑰ breech /bri:tʃ/ *n*. 马裤
⑱ suspender /sə'spendə(r)/ *n*. 吊裤带
⑲ jack-knife *n*. 折刀

亲爱的读者,我来给大家讲一个故事:很久很久以前,大海里有一条鲸鱼。无论海星、螃蟹、颌针鱼、比目鱼,还是鲽鱼、雅罗鱼、鳐鱼、鲭鱼、小狗鱼,甚至连那盘绕缠绵的鳗鲡,统统都成了它的美餐。它几乎吃掉了大海里所有能找到的鱼——最后只剩下一条伶俐的小鱼。这条小鱼总是在鲸鱼右耳边游动,这样就不会有危险了。一天,鲸鱼直起身子,说:"我饿了。"这条小鱼用细嫩的声音回答道:"尊贵而宽容的鲸鱼先生,您尝过人的味道吗?"

"没有,"鲸鱼说,"味道怎么样?"

"好极了,"小鱼说,"就是吃起来麻烦点儿,人的身体枝枝杈杈的。"

于是鲸鱼命令道:"快去给我找几个人来。"它摆摆尾巴,海面上顿时掀起了狂涛巨浪。

"每次您吃一个人就足够了,"小鱼说,"如果您能游到北纬50度、西经40度(这可有点神秘),您就会在海中央看到一个人。他坐在一只木筏上,只穿了一条帆布吊带裤(亲爱的读者,你可要记住这条吊带),手里拿着一把大折刀。

wrecked① **Mariner**②, who, it is only fair to tell you, is a man of infinite-**resource**③-and-**sagacity**④.'

So the Whale swam and swam to latitude Fifty North, longitude Forty West, as fast as he could swim, and on a raft, in the middle of the sea, with nothing to wear except a pair of blue canvas breeches, a pair of suspenders (you must particularly remember the suspenders, Best Beloved), and a jack-knife, he found one single, solitary shipwrecked Mariner, trailing his toes in the water. (He had his mummy's leave to **paddle**⑤, or else he would never have done it because he was a man of infinite-resource-and-sagacity.)

Then the Whale opened his mouth back and back and back till it nearly touched his tail, and he **swallowed**⑥ the shipwrecked Mariner, and the raft he was sitting on, and his blue canvas breeches, and the suspenders (which you must not forget), and the jack-knife—He swallowed them all down into his warm, dark, inside cupboards, and then he **smacked**⑦ his lips—so, and turned round three times on his tail.

But as soon as the Mariner, who was a man of infinite-resource-and-sagacity, found himself truly inside the Whale's warm, dark, inside cupboards, he **stumped**⑧ and he jumped and he **thumped**⑨ and he **bumped**⑩, and he **pranced**⑪ and he danced, and he **banged**⑫ and he **clanged**⑬, and he hit and he bit, and he **leaped**⑭ and he **creeped**⑮, and he **prowled**⑯ and he howled, and he **hopped**⑰ and he dropped, and he cried and he sighed, and he **crawled**⑱ and he **bawled**⑲, and he stepped and he lepped, and he danced **hornpipes**⑳ where he shouldn't, and the Whale felt most unhappy indeed. (Have you forgotten the suspenders?)

So he said to the 'Stute Fish, 'This man is very nubbly, and besides he is making me **hiccough**㉑. What shall I do?'

'Tell him to come out,' said the 'Stute Fish.

So the Whale called down his own throat to the shipwrecked

① wrecked /'rekɪd/ a. (船)失事的
② mariner /'mærɪnə/ n. 海员
③ resource /rɪ'sɔːs/ n. 才智
④ sagacity /sə'gæsɪtɪ/ n. 精明

⑤ paddle /'pædl/ v. 划桨

⑥ swallow /'swɒləʊ/ vt. 吞下

⑦ smack /smæk/ vt. 咂（嘴）

⑧ stump /stʌmp/ v. 碰踢
⑨ thump /θʌmp/ v. 用拳头打
⑩ bump /bʌmp/ v. 碰撞
⑪ prance /prɑːns/ v. 腾跃
⑫ bang /bæŋ/ v. 重击
⑬ clang /klæŋ/ v. 发出叮当声
⑭ leap /liːp/ v. 跳跃
⑮ creep /kriːp/ v. 爬
⑯ prowl /praʊl/ v. 潜行
⑰ hop /hɒp/ v. 单脚跳
⑱ crawl /krɔːl/ v. 爬行
⑲ bawl /bɔːl/ v. 大叫
⑳ hornpipe /'hɔːnpaɪp/ n. 角笛舞
㉑ hiccough /'hɪkəp/ v. 打嗝

他是一名水手，刚遇到海难，船沉了。而且，为公平起见，我还得提醒您，他可是个足智多谋的家伙。"

于是鲸鱼便使出了吃奶的劲儿拼命地游啊游啊，游到了北纬50度，西经40度这个地方。果然，在大海中央，它看到了一个水手，他的船沉了，他正孤独地坐在一只木筏上，只穿着一条粗帆布吊带裤（亲爱的读者，你可别忘了这条吊带），手里摆弄着一把大折刀，徒劳地用脚划着水（他向妈妈请了假，到海上划船——也许他本不该这样做，因为他是足智多谋的人）。

这时，鲸鱼把嘴巴向后张到最大，几乎快碰到了自己的尾巴。它把这个水手连同他的木筏、粗帆布吊带裤（你没有忘记那条吊带吧）和那把大折刀统统吞进了自己的肚子里，吞进它温暖、黑暗的胃里。然后，它咂咂嘴，直起身子转了三圈。

足智多谋的水手突然发现自己被吞进了鲸鱼的体内，这里很温暖，周围漆黑一片。他便开始又捶又撞、又蹦又踢、又撕又咬，连爬带骂。他一会儿来回踏步，一会儿叹息怒吼，一会儿居然跳起了号角舞。鲸鱼被惹急了，它真的生气了。（你还记着那条吊带吗？）

于是它对那条小鱼说："这个人真麻烦，害得我直打嗝。我该怎么对付他？"

小鱼说："那就让他出来吧。"

于是鲸鱼对着自己的喉咙往下喊："喂，水手，老实点儿，出来吧，我都开始打嗝了。"

Mariner, 'Come out and **behave yourself**①. I've got the hiccoughs.'

'Nay, nay!' said the Mariner. 'Not so, but far otherwise. Take me to my natal-shore and the white-cliffs-of-Albion, and I'll think about it.' And he began to dance more than ever.

'You had better take him home,' said the 'Stute Fish to the Whale. 'I ought to have warned you that he is a man of infinite-resource-and-sagacity.'

So the Whale swam and swam and swam, with both **flippers**② and his tail, as hard as he could for the hiccoughs; and at last he saw the Mariner's natal-shore and the white-cliffs-of-Albion, and he rushed halfway up the beach, and opened his mouth wide and wide and wide, and said, 'Change here for Winchester, Ashuelot, Nashua, keene, and stations on the Fitch-burg Road;' and just as he said 'Fitch' the Mariner waked out of his mouth. But while the Whale had been swimming, the Mariner, who was indeed a person of infinite-resource-and-sagacity, had taken his jack-knife and cut up the **raft**③ into a little square **grating**④ all running **criss-cross**⑤, and he had tied it firm with his suspenders (now you know why you were not to forget the suspenders!), and he dragged that grating good and tight into the Whale's throat, and there it stuck! Then he **recited**⑥ the following sloka, which, as you have not heard it, I will now proceed to **relate**⑦—

> **By means of**⑧ a grating
> I have stopped your ating.

For the Mariner he was also an Hi-ber-ni-an. And he stepped out on the **shingle**⑨, and went home to his mother, who had given him leave to **trail**⑩ his toes in the water; and he married and lived happily ever afterward. So did the Whale. But from that day on, the grating in his

远古传奇

① behave oneself 行为规矩些

② flipper /'flɪpə/ n. 鳍

③ raft /ra:ft/ n. 筏,木排
④ grating /'greɪtɪŋ/ n. 格子
⑤ criss-cross n. 十字架

⑥ recite /rɪ'saɪt/ v. 诵读,朗读
⑦ relate /rɪ'leɪt/ v. 讲,叙述

⑧ by means of 用,凭借

⑨ shingle /'ʃɪŋgl/ n. 砂石海滩
⑩ trail /treɪl/ v. 开辟,追随

"不,不!"水手答道,"现在我还不想出来。但如果你能把我带回我家乡的海岸英格兰的白色悬崖,我倒是可以考虑考虑。"他跳得更起劲了。

小鱼对鲸鱼说:"您最好把他送回家。我警告过您他是个足智多谋的家伙。"

于是,鲸鱼一边大声地打着嗝,一边用鳍和尾巴拼命地划水,最后总算游到了水手的故乡,看到了白色的悬崖。鲸鱼把半个身子冲上海滩,把嘴巴张得大大的,说:"从这儿换车去威斯敏斯特、阿舒洛特、纳舒、肯尼,还有费奇伯格路上的其他站点。"足智多谋的水手在它说"费奇"这个词时从鲸鱼嘴巴里走出来。水手趁鲸鱼游水的时候,用大折刀把木筏切开,摆成十字格型,并用裤子的吊带把十字架紧紧地系住(现在你知道为什么不能忘记吊带的原因了吧!)。他把十字架使劲地拽出来,不偏不倚,正好卡在鲸鱼的喉咙上!然后他便喊起了口号,因为你听不到,听我来学给你听——

放上了木头,
不再让你吃喝。

这个水手也是爱尔兰人。他走到海滩上,径直回家去找同意他下水的妈妈。后来他结了婚,过着幸福的生活。鲸鱼也是一样。不过从那一天起,喉咙里卡着的十字架使鲸鱼不能仰头咳嗽或低头吞咽,除了一些非常非常小的鱼以外,它什么也不能吃。这就是为什么现在鲸鱼不吃大人或

· 007 ·

throat, which he could neither cough up nor **swallow down**①, prevented him eating anything except very, very small fish; and that is the reason why whales nowadays never eat men or boys or little girls.

The small 'Stute Fish went and hid himself in the mud under the Door-sills of the **Equator**②. He was afraid that the whale might be angry with him.

The Sailor took the jack-knife home. He was wearing the blue canvas breeches when he waked out on the shingle. The suspenders were left behind, you see, to tie the grating with; and that is the end of that tale.

① swallow down 吞下

② equator /ɪˈkweɪtə/ n. 赤道

小孩子的原因。

  那条小鱼呢？它游走了，藏在赤道附近的海底山脊下。它害怕鲸鱼会迁怒于它。

  水手带着那把大折刀回了家。走上海滩时，他还穿着那条蓝帆布裤子。但吊带不见了，因为水手用它绑成了一个木架，卡在鲸鱼的喉咙里。故事结束了。

This is the picture of the Whale sawllowing the Mariner with his infinite-resource-and-sagacity, and the raft and the jack-kinfe and his suspenders, which you must not forget. The **buttony**①-things are the Mariner's suspenders, and you can see the knife close by them. He is sitting on the raft but it has **tilted**② up **sideways**③, so you don't see much of it. The **whity**④ thing by the Marner's left hand is a piece of wood that he was trying to **row**⑤ the raft with when the Whale **came along**⑥. The piece of wood is called the jaws-of-a-**gaff**⑦. The Mariner left it outside when he went in. The Whale's name was Smiler, and the Mariner was called Mr. Henry Albert Bivvens, A. B. The little 'Stute Fish is hiding under the Whale's **tummy**⑧, or else I would have drawn him. The reason that the sea looks so **ooshy-skooshy**⑨ is because the Whale is sucking it all into his mouth so as to **suck in**⑩ Mr. Henry Albert Bivvens and the raft and the jack-knife and the suspenders. You must never for get the suspenders.

这幅画描绘了鲸鱼把足智多谋的水手吞进嘴里的情景。被鲸鱼吞进嘴里的还有木筏、大折刀和水手的吊带，你可不能忘了这条吊带。带扣子的那个东西就是吊带，在它旁边你能找到那把大折刀。水手本来正坐在木筏上，但木筏歪斜到一边去了，所以你恐怕看不见。水手左边白色的东西是一片木头（叫渔叉嘴），鲸鱼刚来的时候，他正用这木片划水。水手被吞进去的时候，木片被丢在了外面。鲸鱼名叫斯迈尔，水手的名字叫亨利·阿尔伯特·比维斯。那条小鱼就藏在鲸鱼的肚子下面，否则我就能把它画出来了。海上掀起了可怕的巨浪，那是因为鲸鱼为了把水手、木筏、折刀和吊带吞进去，就张大了嘴巴，把所有的东西都吞进去了。你可千万别忘记那条吊带呀。

① buttony /'bʌtənɪ/ a. 钮扣状的,多钮扣的
② tilt /tɪlt/ v. 倾斜
③ sideways /'saɪdweɪz/ ad. 向侧面地
④ whity /'(h)waɪtɪ/ a. 发白的
⑤ row /rau/ v. 划,划船
⑥ come along vt. 一道走
⑦ gaff /gæf/ n. 大鱼钩
⑧ tummy /'tʌmɪ/ n. 胃,肚子
⑨ ooshy-skooshy a. 海浪翻腾的
⑩ suck in vt. 吞没,利用

Just So Stories

Here is the Whale looking for the little 'Stute Fish, who is hiding under the Door-sills of the Equator. The little 'Stute Fish's name was Pingle. He is hiding among the roots of the big **seaweed**① that grows in front of the Doors of the Equator. I have drawn the Doors of the Equator. They are shut. They are always kept shut, because a door ought always to be kept shut. The **ropy**②-thing right across is the Equator itself; and the things that look like rocks are the two giant Moar and Koar, that keep the Equator **in order**③. They drew the shadow-pictures on the doors of the Equator, and they **carved**④ all those **twisty**⑤ fishes under the Doors. The **beaky**⑥-fish are called beaked **Dolphins**⑦, and the other fish with the **queer**⑧ heads are called Hammer-headed **Sharks**⑨. The Whale never found the little 'Stute Fish till he **got over**⑩ his temper, and then they became good friends agaim.

此图描绘了鲸鱼寻找那条小鱼时的情景。小鱼名叫佩格尔,它躲在赤道大门前的海藻根部。我已经打开了赤道之门。那门是关着的,通常总是关着,门本来就应当总是关着。图中部绳子样的东西是赤道,两位巨人(看上去像岩石)分别是穆尔和科尔,他们管理赤道地区的事务。他们在赤道大门上描绘了一些阴影图形,并在门下雕刻了一幅缠绕的鱼群的图画。那些鸟嘴形的鱼是钩形海豚,头部古怪的鱼叫做锤形鲨鱼。鲸鱼怒气消了以后才找到那条小鱼,它们又成为了好朋友。

① seaweed /ˈsiːwiːd/ n. 海草，海藻

② ropy /ˈrəupɪ/ a. 绳状的
③ in order 整齐（秩序井然）
④ carve /kɑːv/ v. 雕刻，切
⑤ twisty /ˈtwɪstɪ/ a. 扭曲的
⑥ beaky 像鸟嘴的
⑦ dolphin /ˈdɔlfɪn/ n. 海豚
⑧ queer /kwɪə/ a. 奇怪的
⑨ shark /ʃɑːk/ n. 鲨鱼
⑩ get over /get ˈəuvə/ v. 从...中恢复过来

When the **cabin**① **port-holes**② are dark and green
Because of the seas outside;
When the ship goes *wop*③ (with a **wiggle**④ between)
And the **steward**⑤ falls into the soup-**tureen**⑥,
And the **trunks**⑦ begin to **slide**⑧;
When Nursey **lies**⑨ on the floor in a **heap**⑩,
And Mummy tells you to let her sleep,
And you aren't waked or washed or dressed,
Why, then you will know(if you haven't guessed)
You're 'Fifty North and Forty West!'

① cabin /ˈkæbɪn/ n. 船舱
② port-holes /ˈpɔːthəʊl/ n. 舷窗
③ wop /wɒp/ n. 美国的南欧移民
④ wiggle /ˈwɪɡl/ n. 摆动
⑤ steward /ˈstjuəd/ n. 乘务员
⑥ tureen /təˈriːn/ n. 有盖汤盘
⑦ trunk /trʌŋk/ n. 行李箱
⑧ slide /slaɪd/ v. 滑,跌落
⑨ lie /laɪ/ v. 躺着
⑩ heap /hiːp/ n. 堆

船浮在海面，窗口慢慢变黑，闪着绿光；
船一下下撞击着，
间或摇摇摆摆；
侍者跌进了汤锅，
皮箱开始滑动，
奶妈躺在地铺上，
妈妈打着哈欠请你让她睡觉，
你还没醒、没洗脸、没穿衣服，
那时你就知道了（如果没猜到）
——你到了北纬50度、西经40度那个地方！

How the Camel Got His Hump

Now this is the next tale, and it tells how the Camel got his big **hump**①.

In the beginning of years, when the world was so new and all, and the animals were just beginning to work for Man, there was a Camel, and he lived in the middle of a **Howling**② Desert because he did not want to work; and besides, he was a Howler himself. So he ate sticks and **thorns**③ and **tamarisks**④ and **milkweed**⑤ and **prickles**⑥, most **scruciating**⑦ idle; and when anybody spoke to him he said '**Humph**⑧!' Just 'Humph!' and no more.

Presently the Horse came to him on Monday morning, with a **saddle**⑨ on his back and a **bit**⑩ in his mouth, and said, 'Camel, O Camel, come out and **trot**⑪ like the rest of us.'

'Humph!' said the Camel; and the Horse went away and told the Man.

Presently the Dog came to him, with a stick in his mouth, and said, 'Camel, O Camel, come and fetch and carry like the rest of us.'

'Humph!' said the Camel; and the Dog went away and told the Man.

Presently the Ox came to him, with the **yoke**⑫ on his neck and said, 'Camel, O Camel, come and **plough**⑬ like the rest of us.'

'Humph!' said the Camel; and the Ox went away and told the Man.

At the end of the day the Man called the Horse and the Dog and the Ox together, and said, 'Three, O Three, I'm very sorry for you (with

骆驼背上的驼峰是怎么长出来的

① hump /hʌmp/ n. 圆形隆起物,瘤
② howling /ˈhaʊlɪŋ/ a. 寂寥的
③ thorn /θɔːn/ n. 刺,荆棘
④ tamarisk /ˈtæmərɪsk/ n. 柽柳
⑤ milkweed /ˈmɪlkwiːd/ n. 乳草属植物
⑥ prickle /ˈprɪkl/ n.（动物或植物上的）刺,棘
⑦ scruciating= excruciating /ɪkˈskruːʃɪeɪtɪŋ/ a. 极度的,非常的
⑧ humph /hʌmf/ int. 哼
⑨ saddle /ˈsædl/ n. 鞍
⑩ bit /bɪt/ n. 马嚼子
⑪ trot /trɒt/ v. 快步走,小跑步走

⑫ yoke /jəʊk/ n. 轭,套
⑬ plough /plaʊ/ v. 用犁耕田,耕犁

现在我来讲第二个故事：骆驼背上的驼峰是怎么长出来的。

世界刚诞生的时候，一切一切都是崭新的，动物们刚刚开始为人干活儿。然而，在荒凉的沙漠中有一头骆驼，除了时不时叫两声以外，它什么活儿也不想干。它每天吃枯枝、红柳、乳草和荆棘，整日无所事事地闲逛。如果有人跟它说话，它用鼻子"哼"一声就不再言语了。

星期一的早晨，马来找它。马的背上驮着鞍子，嘴上戴着嚼子，它对骆驼说："骆驼啊骆驼，来和我们一起忙碌奔跑吧！"

骆驼不屑地"哼"了一声。于是马走了，把这件事告诉了人。

狗来找它。狗的嘴里叼着一根手杖，对骆驼说："骆驼啊骆驼，来和我们一起送取物品吧！"

骆驼不屑地"哼"了一声。于是狗走了，把这件事告诉了人。

牛来找它。牛的脖子上套着轭，对骆驼说："骆驼啊骆驼，来和我们一起耕地吧！"

骆驼又不屑地"哼"了一声。于是牛也走

the world so new-and-all); but that Humph-thing in the Desert can't work, or he would have been here by now, so I am going to leave him alone, and you must work double-time to make up for it.'

That made the Three very angry (with the world so new-and-all), and they held a **palaver**①, and an **indaba**②, and a **punchayet**③, and a **pow-wow**④ on the edge of the Desert; and the Camel came chewing milkweed most scruciating idle, and laughed at them. Then he said 'Humph!' and went away again.

Presently there came along the Djinn in charge of All Deserts, rolling in a cloud of dust (Djinns always travel that way because it is **Magic**⑤), and he stopped to palaver and pow-wow with the Three.

'Djinn of All Deserts,' said the Horse, 'is it right for any one to be idle, with the world so new-and-all?'

'Certainly not,' said the Djinn.

'Well,' said the Horse, 'there's a thing in the middle of your Howling Desert (and he's a Howler himself) with a long neck and long legs, and he hasn't done **a stroke**⑥ of work since Monday morning. He won't trot.'

'Whew!' said the Djinn, **whistling**⑦, 'that's my Camel, for all the gold in Arabia! What does he say about it?'

'He says "Humph!"' said the Dog; 'and he won't fetch and carry.'

'Does he say anything else?'

'Only "Humph!"; and he won't plough,' said the Ox.

very good, said the Djinn. 'I'll humph him if you will kindly wait a minnie.'

The Djinn rolled himself up in his dust-**cloak**⑧, and took **a bearing**⑨ across the desert, and found the Camel most scruciatingly idle, looking at his own **reflection**⑩ in a pool of water.

'My long and **bubbling**⑪ friend,' said the Djinn, 'what's this I

① palaver /pəˈlɑːvə/ n. 交涉
② indaba /ɪnˈdɑːbɑː/ n. 部族的会议
③ panchayet /pʌnˈtʃaɪət/ n. (印度的)村委员会
④ pow-wow n. 北美土著人聚集会议
⑤ magic /ˈmædʒɪk/ n. 魔法,魔术

⑥ a stroke of work 一点工作

⑦ whistle /(h)wɪsl/ v. 吹口哨

⑧ cloak /kləʊk/ n. 斗篷
⑨ bearing /ˈbeərɪŋ/ n. 方位
⑩ reflection /rɪˈflekʃən/ n. 倒影
⑪ bubble /ˈbʌbl/ v. 洋溢;兴高采烈

了,把这件事告诉了人。

太阳下山的时候,人把马、狗和牛召集到一起,对它们说:"我为你们三个感到非常抱歉(世间万物都是崭新的),但是沙漠里那个只会'哼'的家伙不愿意干活儿,否则它现在就该在这里了。我决定不管它,由它去吧。因此,你们三个必须加倍干活儿弥补它的空缺。"

三个动物听了非常生气(世间万物都是崭新的),于是来到沙漠边缘开会商量这件事。骆驼一边悠闲地嚼着草,一边嘲笑它们。然后它"哼"了一声,扭头走了。

这时卷起了层层黄沙,沙漠之王来了(他是神,所以来来往往总是这样)。他停住脚步,开始与三种动物交谈起来。

"沙漠之王啊,"马说道,"世界刚刚诞生,难道应该整天无所事事吗?"

"当然不应该,"沙漠之王回答道。

"那么,"马说,"在你管辖的荒凉的沙漠中有一种会叫的动物,它长着长长的脖子和长长的腿,但从星期一开始,一丁点儿活儿也没干过。"

沙漠之王吹了声口哨:"嘘——!天哪,那是我的骆驼,堪比阿拉伯所有的黄金、它是怎么说的?"

"它'哼'了一声,"狗说,"它也不想取送东西。"

"它还说别的了吗?"

"它只会'哼',也不想耕地,"牛又补充道。

"很好,"沙漠之王说,"你们耐心等一会儿,我去'哼'它一回。"

沙漠之王一抖风沙袍,在沙漠中确定了一下

· 019 ·

hear of① your doing no work, with the world so new-and-all?'

'Humph!' said the Camel.

The Djinn sat down, with his chin in his hand, and began to think a Great Magic, while the Camel looked at his own reflection in the pool of water.

'You've given the Three **extra**② work ever since Monday morning, all on **account of**③ your 'scruciating idleness,' said the Djinn; and he went on thinking Magics, with his chin in his hand.

'Humph!' said the Camel.

'I shouldn't say that again if I were you,' said the Djinn; 'you might say it once too often. Bubbles, I want you to work.'

And the Camel said 'Humph!' again; but **no sooner**④ had he said it than he saw his back, that he **was so proud of**⑤, **puffing**⑥ up and puffing up into a great big **lolloping**⑦ **humph**⑧.

'Do you see that?' said the Djinn. 'That's your very own humph that you've brought upon your very own self by not working. To-day is Thursday, and you've done no work since Monday, when the work began. Now you are going to work.'

'How can I,' said the Camel, 'with this humph on my back?'

'That's made a purpose,' said the Djinn, 'all because you missed those three days. You will be able to work now for three days without eating, because you can **live on**⑨ your humph; and don't you ever say I never did anything for you. **Come out of**⑩ the Desert and go to the Three, and behave. Humph yourself!'

And the Camel humphed himself, humph and all, and went away to join the Three. And from that day to this the Camel always **wears**⑪ a humph (we call it 'hump' now, not to hurt his feelings); but he has never yet **caught up with**⑫ the three days that he missed **at the beginning**⑬ of the world, and he has never yet learned how to behave.

① hear of 听说

② extra /ˈekstrə/ a. 额外的
③ on account of 因为

④ no sooner…than 一…就…
⑤ be proud of 为…骄傲
⑥ puff /pʌf/ v. 喷出
⑦ lollop /ˈlɒləp/ v. 摇晃着走
⑧ humph /hʌmf/ 此处为大包的意思

⑨ live on 靠…生活
⑩ come out of 从…出来

⑪ wear /wɪə/ v. 穿着,戴

⑫ catch up with 赶上
⑬ at the beginning of 在…初

方位。他发现骆驼正悠哉悠哉地在水潭边端详着自己的影子。

"我亲爱的朋友,"沙漠之王说,"这世界刚刚诞生,我却听说你什么活儿也不想干?"

骆驼"哼"了一声。

于是沙漠之王坐下来。他双手托腮,准备施展魔法。骆驼依旧在一旁欣赏着自己在水中的倒影。

"从星期一早晨开始,因为你的无所事事,那三种动物已经多干了很多活儿,"沙漠之王说。他继续双手托腮,准备施展魔法。

骆驼又"哼"了一声。

"如果我是你,我不会'哼'第二声。"沙漠之王说,"你'哼'的次数太多了,我希望你去干活儿。"

骆驼又"哼"了一声。但它马上看到曾使它十分骄傲的背部膨胀起来,鼓出了一个摇晃的大包。

"看见了吗?"沙漠之王问道,"这就是你'哼'出来的'峰'。今天是星期四;工作从星期一开始,而你至今还没干过活儿。现在该开始了。"

骆驼问:"我背上有'峰',怎么干活儿啊?"

"这是特意安排的。"沙漠之王说,"因为你错过了三天时间,现在你可以靠驼峰里的给养,不吃不喝地干三天活儿。别说我没为你做什么。离开沙漠去找那三种动物吧,规矩点儿,好好表现。对你自己'哼'一声吧!"

于是骆驼对自己"哼"了一声,去找另外三种动物。从那一天起直到现在,骆驼背上总是驮着那个驼峰(我们管它叫"峰"而不叫"哼",是不想伤害骆驼的感情)。但它永远也没有追回在世界诞生时错过的那三天时间,而且至今也没学会该怎么好好表现。

Just So Stories

This is the picture of the Djinn making the beginnings of the Magic that brought the Humph to the Camel. First he **drew a line**① **in the air**② with his finger, and it became **solid**③; and then he made a cloud, and then he made an egg—you can see them both **at the bottom of**④ the picture—and then there was a magic **pumpkin**⑤ that **turned into**⑥ a big white **flame**⑦. Then the Djinn took his magic fan and **fanned**⑧ that flame till the flame turned into a magic **by itself**⑨. It was a good Magic and a very kind Magic really, though it had to give the Camel a Humph because the Camel was lazy. The Djinn **in charge of**⑩ All Deserts was one of the nicest of the Djinns, so he would never do anything really unkind.

沙漠之王正施展魔法，让骆驼的背上长出驼峰。他先用手指在空中划了一道，空中出现了一条实线。接着他又变出一朵云彩，变出一个鸡蛋——这些你在插图的下部都可以看到。不一会儿，一只神奇的南瓜变成了一团巨大的白色火焰。然后沙漠之王拿出魔扇对着火焰扇起来。他扇啊扇啊，最后火焰变成了一股有魔法的力量。其实这个魔术并无恶意，只是因为骆驼太懒了，沙漠之王不得已才给它安上驼峰。沙漠之王是最善良的神灵之一，他从未做过任何不友善的事情。

① draw a line 画一条线
② in the air 在空中
③ solid /ˈsɒlɪd/ a. 结实的
④ at the bottom of 在…底部
⑤ pumpkin /ˈpʌmpkɪn/ n. 南瓜
⑥ turn into 变成
⑦ flame /fleɪm/ n. 火焰
⑧ fan v. 煽，煽动
⑨ by itself 单独地，独自地
⑩ in charge of 负责，主管

Just So Stories

Here is the picture of the Djinn in charge of All Deserts **guiding**① the Magic with his magic fan. The Camel is eating a **twig**② of **acacia**③, and he has just finished saying "humph" once too often (the Djinn told him he would), and so the Humph is coming. The long **towelly**④-thing **growing out**⑤ of the thing like an onion is the Magic, and you can see the Humph on its shoulder. The Humph fits on the flat part of the Camel's back. The Camel is too busy looking at his own beautiful self in the pool of water to know what is going to happen to him.

Underneath⑥ the truly picture is a picture of the World-so-new-and-all. There are two smoky **volcanoes**⑦ in it, some other mountains and some stones and a lake and a black island and a twisty river and a lot of other things, **as well as**⑧ a **Noah's Ark**⑨. I couldn't draw all the deserts that the Djinn was in charge of, so I only drew one, but it is a most **deserty**⑩ desert.

图中描绘的是沙漠之王用魔扇施展魔法的情景。骆驼嘴里正嚼着一根刺槐树枝，它刚刚又不厌其烦地"哼"了一声（虽然沙漠之王警告过他）于是驼峰就出现了。从洋葱状物体上升腾起一簇毛巾样的东西，那就是带有魔法的力量，它正载着驼峰向骆驼飘近。驼峰恰好落在骆驼的平背上。这时它正恋恋不舍地欣赏着自己在水中的倒影，丝毫没有想到一件大事要发生在自己身上。

此图下面还有一幅画，勾勒出世界刚刚出现时的情形。图中有两座火山正在喷发，还有其他山脉、一堆石头、一个湖泊、一个黑色的岛屿、一条弯曲的小河……还有很多别的东西，比如诺亚方舟。我无法画出沙漠之王管辖下的所有沙漠，所以只画了一个，但这可是世界上最荒凉的沙漠。

① guide /gaɪd/ v. 指导，支配
② twig /twɪg/ n. 小枝
③ acacia /əˈkeɪʃə/ n. 洋槐

④ towelly /ˈtaʊəlɪ/ a. 毛巾状的
⑤ grow out of 从…长出来

⑥ underneath /ˌʌndəˈniːθ/ ad. 在下面
⑦ volcano /vɒlˈkeɪnəʊ/ n. 火山
⑧ as well as 也
⑨ Noah's Ark 诺亚方舟

⑩ deserty 荒凉的

Just So Stories

The Camel's hump is an ugly **lump**①
Which well you may see at the Zoo;
But uglier yet is the hump we get
From having too little to do.

Kiddies and grown-ups too-oo-oo,
 If we haven't enough to do-oo-oo,
We get the hump—
Cameelious hump—
The hump that is black and blue!

We climb out of bed with a **frouzly**② head
And a **snarly**③-yarly voice.
We **shiver**④ and **scowl**⑤ and we **grunt**⑥ and we **growl**⑦
At our bath and our boots and our toys;

And there ought to be a corner for me
(And I know there is one for you)
When we get the hump—
Cameelious hump—
The hump that is black and blue!

The cure for this ill is not to sit still,
Or frowst with a book by the fire;
But to take a large **hoe**⑧ and a **shovel**⑨ also,
And dig till you gently **perspire**⑩;

And then, you will find that the sun and the wind.
And the Djinn of the Garden too,

① lump /lʌmp/ n. 块状，瘤

我们在动物园里看到过骆驼，
那驼峰可真丑陋；
但如果因为懒惰我们也长出了驼峰，
那才更丑。

孩子和大人们，
如果我们没有事做，
会像骆驼一样，
长出难看的驼峰。

② frouzy /ˈfrauzɪ/ a. 不整洁的
③ snarly /ˈsnɑːlɪ/ a. 善于嚣叫的
④ shiver /ˈʃɪvə/ vt. 颤动
⑤ scowl /skaul/ v. 皱眉头
⑥ grunt /grʌnt/ vi.（表示烦恼、反对、疲劳、轻蔑等）发哼声
⑦ growl /graul/ v. 怒吠，咆哮

我们从床上爬起来，
头脑昏昏沉沉，
暴躁地叫嚷着。
对着浴池、对着鞋子、对着玩具，
我们战栗、皱眉、咕哝、咆哮。

当我们长出驼峰，
长出难看的驼峰时，
应该有个属于我的角落。
（你的角落想必已经找到）

⑧ hoe /həu/ n. 锄头
⑨ shovel /ˈʃʌvl/ n. 铲
⑩ perspire /pəsˈpaɪə/ v. 出汗，流汗

想治这个病可不能静坐，
也不能闷坐在火炉旁边读书，
该拿一把大锄头和一只铁锹
干活儿干到额头微微出汗。

这时你会感觉到阳光和微风，
背上那可怕难看的驼峰，
已被花园之神移走。

Have lifted the hump—
The horrible hump—
The hump that is black and blue!

I get it as well as you-oo-oo—
If I haven't enough to do-oo-oo—
We all get hump—
Cameelious hump—
Kiddies and grown-ups too!

我们都一样，
游手好闲会长出驼峰，
大人小孩都是如此！

How the Rhinoceros Got His Skin

Once upon a time, on an **uninhabited**① island on the shores of the **Red Sea**②, there lived a Parsee from whose hat the rays of the sun were reflected in more-than-oriental **splendour**③. And the Parsee lived by the Red Sea with nothing but his hat and his knife and a cooking-**stove**④ of the kind that you must particularly never touch. And one day he took flour and water and **currants**⑤ and plums and sugar and things, and made himself one cake which was two feet across and three feet thick. It was indeed a Superior Comestible (*that's* magic) and he put it on the stove because *he* was allowed to cook on that stove, and he baked it and he baked it till it was all done brown and smelt most **sentimental**⑥. But just as he was going to eat it there came down to the beach from the Altogether Uninhabited Interior one Rhinoceros with a horn on his nose, two piggy eyes, and few **manners**⑦. In those days the Rhinoceros's skin fitted him quite tight. There were no **wrinkles**⑧ in it anywhere. He looked exactly like a Noah's Ark Rhinoceros, but of course much bigger. All the same, he had no manners then, and he has no manners now, and he never will have any manners. He said, 'How!' and the Parsee left that cake and climbed to the top of a palm tree with nothing on but his hat, from which the rays of the sun were always reflected in more-than-oriental splendour. And the Rhinoceros

犀牛皮的故事

① uninhabited
/ˌʌnɪnˈhæbɪtɪd/ a. 无人居住的
② Red Sea 红海
③ splendour /ˈsplendə/ n. 光彩,显赫
④ stove /stəʊv/ n. 炉子
⑤ currant /ˈkʌrənt/ n. 无核葡萄干

⑥ sentimental
/ˌsentɪˈmentl/ a. 感伤性的

⑦ manners /ˈmænəz/ n. 礼貌
⑧ wrinkle /ˈrɪŋkl/ n. 皱纹

从前，红海海岸边有一个荒凉的孤岛，岛上住着一位帕西人。①他戴着一顶帽子，阳光照在上面折射出绚丽多彩的光芒。帕西人住在红海边上，除了一顶帽子、一把刀子和一个做饭用的炉子（这炉子你可不能碰）以外，就什么也没有了。一天，他用面粉、水、葡萄干、砂糖和其他调料，给自己做了一只大蛋糕。这蛋糕直径足有两英尺，有三英尺厚，是个美味的"巨无霸"（真是棒极了）。他把蛋糕放在炉子上（他可以使用这个炉子）烘烤。他烤啊烤啊，直到蛋糕变成褐色，散发出诱人的香气。他正准备一饱口福的时候，一只犀牛从荒凉的内地走到海岸上来。犀牛鼻子上长着角，一双贪婪的眼睛转来转去，一点礼貌也没有。那时，犀牛身上的皮肤绷得紧紧的，没有一丝皱纹，看上去像笨重的交通工具，只是体积大多了。无论过去、现在还是将来，它都是那么没有礼貌。它嚷嚷了一声，"哇——"，帕西人吓得丢下蛋糕，爬上了一棵高高的棕榈

① 帕西人是公元 8 世纪为逃避穆斯林迫害而自波斯移居印度的琐罗亚德教徒的后裔。译注。

· 031 ·

Just So Stories

upset① the oil-stove with his nose, and the cake rolled on the sand, and he **spiked**② that cake on the horn of his nose, and he ate it, and he went away, waving his tail to the **desolate**③ and exclusively uninhabited interior which **abuts**④ on the islands of Mazanderan, Socotra, and Promontories of the Larger Equinox. Then the Parsee came down from his palm-tree and put the stove on its legs and recited the following *Sloka*, which, as you have not heard, I will now proceed to relate:—

Them that takes cakes
Which the Parsee-man bakes
Makes **dreadful**⑤ mistakes.

And there was a great deal more in that than you would think.

Because, five weeks later, there was a heat wave in the Red Sea, and everybody **took off**⑥ all the clothes they had. The Parsee took off his hat; but the Rhinoceros took off his skin and carried it over his shoulder as he came down to the beach to bathe. In those days it **buttoned**⑦ underneath with three buttons and looked like a **waterproof**⑧. He said nothing whatever about the Parsee's cake, because he had eaten it all; and he never had any manners, then, since, or **henceforward**⑨. He **waddled**⑩ straight into the water and blew bubbles through his nose, leaving his skin on the beach.

Presently the Parsee came by and found the skin, and he smiled one smile that ran all round his face two times. Then he danced three times round the skin and rubbed his hands. Then he went to his camp and filled his hat with cake-**crumbs**⑪, for the Parsee never ate anything but cake, and never swept out his camp. He took that skin and he rubbed that skin just as full of old, dry, **stale**⑫, tickly cake-crumbs and some burned

①upset /ʌp'set/ v. 颠覆，推翻
②spike /spaɪk/ v. 用尖物刺穿
③desolate /'desəlɪt/ a. 荒凉的
④abut /ə'bʌt/ v. 邻接，毗连
⑤dreadful /'dredful/ a. 可怕的
⑥take off 脱下
⑦button /'bʌtn/ v. 扣住
⑧waterproof /'wɔ:təpru:f/ n. 防水材料
⑨henceforward /hents'fɔ:wəd/ ad. 今后
⑩waddle /'wɒdl/ v. 蹒跚而行
⑪crumb /krʌm/ n. 碎屑，面包心
⑫stale /steɪl/ a. 不新鲜的，陈腐的

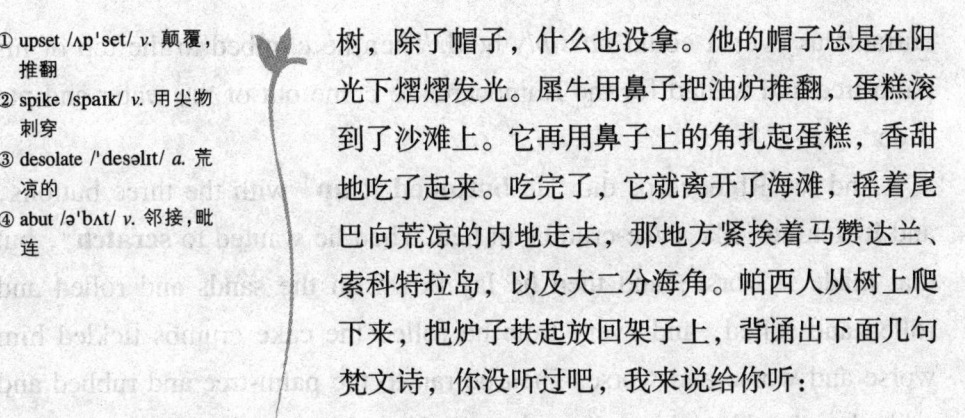

树，除了帽子，什么也没拿。他的帽子总是在阳光下熠熠发光。犀牛用鼻子把油炉推翻，蛋糕滚到了沙滩上。它再用鼻子上的角扎起蛋糕，香甜地吃了起来。吃完了，它就离开了海滩，摇着尾巴向荒凉的内地走去，那地方紧挨着马赞达兰、索科特拉岛，以及大二分海角。帕西人从树上爬下来，把炉子扶起放回架子上，背诵出下面几句梵文诗，你没听过吧，我来说给你听：

谁吃了帕西人的蛋糕，
谁就犯了可怕的错误。

这两句话包含的意思可比你想到的要深刻得多。

原因是这样的：五个星期后，红海上刮起一股热浪，大家热得脱下了身上所有的衣裳。帕西人摘下了帽子，犀牛脱掉了皮衣。它把衣服搭在肩膀上，走到海滩去洗澡。那时，犀牛的皮衣上有三个扣子扣在下面，看上去像一件防水服。关于蛋糕的事，犀牛从未提起过，因为它把蛋糕全都吃了，因为它一点礼貌也没有——现在也没有，将来也不会有。它一路摇摇摆摆，把皮衣扔在海滩上，径直走进水里，用鼻子吹起泡泡来。

这时帕西人走过来，看到犀牛留在沙滩上的皮肤，他笑了笑，满心欢喜。他又围着犀牛皮跳了三圈舞，然后搓搓手。他走进帐篷，往帽子里装满了蛋糕渣儿。帕西人除了蛋糕什么也不吃，而且从不打扫自己的帐篷。他拿起犀牛皮，用又干又硬又粗又刺的蛋糕渣儿尽可能起劲地搓着、

Just So Stories

currants as ever it could *possibly* hold. Then he climbed to the top of his palm-tree and waited for the Rhinoceros to come out of the water and put it on.

And the Rhinoceros did. He **buttoned it up**① with the three buttons, and it **tickled**② like cake-crumbs in bed. Then he wanted to **scratch**③, but that made it worse; and then he lay down on the sands and rolled and rolled and rolled, and every time he rolled the cake crumbs tickled him worse and worse and worse. Then he ran to the palm-tree and rubbed and rubbed and rubbed himself against it. He rubbed so much and so hard that he rubbed his skin into a great **fold**④ over his shoulders, and another fold underneath, where the buttons used to be (but he rubbed the buttons off), and he rubbed some more folds over his legs. And it **spoiled**⑤ his temper, but it didn't make the least difference to the cake-crumbs. They were inside his skin and they tickled. So he went home, very angry indeed and **horribly**⑥ **scratchy**⑦; and from that day to this every **rhinoceros**⑧ has great folds in his skin and a very bad **temper**⑨, all on account of the cake-crumbs inside.

But the Parsee came down from his palm-tree, wearing his hat, from which the rays of the sun were reflected in more-than-oriental splendour, **packed up**⑩ his cooking-stove, and went away **in the direction**⑪ of Orotavo, Amygdala, the **Upland**⑫ **Meadows**⑬ of Anantarivo, and the **Marshes**⑭ of Sonaput.

① button up 扣好
② tickle /'tɪkl/ v. 胳肢,发痒
③ scratch /skrætʃ/ v. 搔痒,抓
④ fold /fəuld/ n. 折层,折痕
⑤ spoil /spɔɪl/ v. 宠坏,破坏
⑥ horribly /'hɔrəblɪ/ ad. 可怕地
⑦ scratchy /'skrætʃɪ/ a. 发痒的
⑧ rhinocero 朝天犀牛
⑨ temper /'tempə/ n. 脾气
⑩ pack up vt. 打包
⑪ in the direction of 超…方向
⑫ upland /'ʌplənd/ n. 高地,山地
⑬ meadow /'medəu/ n. 草地,牧场
⑭ marsh /mɑ:ʃ/ n. 沼泽,湿地

蹭着。干完这一切,他又爬上那棵棕榈树,等犀牛从水里出来穿上它的皮衣服。

犀牛穿上皮衣,扣上了三颗扣子。它感觉痒痒的,好像躺在铺满面包渣儿的床上。它开始抓挠,但越挠越痒。它躺在沙滩上滚来滚去,越滚越觉得痒。它又跑到棕榈树下,在树干上蹭啊蹭啊。它蹭得太用力了,肩部和扣子部位(扣子已被它蹭掉了)的皮肤出现了两条大褶痕,腿上也磨出了皱纹。它一肚子火,但一点办法也没有。蛋糕渣儿刺进了它的皮肤,痒得厉害。犀牛怒气冲天地向家里走去,浑身伤痕累累。从那一天起到现在,每只犀牛身上都有深深的褶痕,它们脾气暴躁,这全都是蛋糕渣儿惹的祸。

帕西人从棕榈树上出溜下来,戴上帽子,绚丽多彩的阳光从帽子上反射出来。他收拾好做饭的炉子,朝奥罗达沃、阿梅哥达拉方向走去,那边有阿嫩达里沃山地草原和索纳布特沼泽。

This is the picture of the Parsee beginning to eat his cake on the Uninhabited Island in the Red Sea on a very hot day; and of the Rhinoceros **coming down from**① the altogether uninhabited interior, which, as you can **truthfully**② see, is all **rocky**③. The Rhinoceros's skin is quite **smooth**④, and the three buttons that button it up are underneath, so you can't see them. The **squiggly**⑤ things on the Parsee's hat are the rays of the sun reflected in more-than oriental splendour, because if I had drawn real rays they would have **filled up**⑥ all the picture. The cake has currants in it; and the wheel-thing lying on the sand in front **belonged to**⑦ one of Pharaoh's **chariots**⑧ when he tried to cross the Red Sea. The Parsee found it, and kept it to play with. The Parsee's name was Pestonjee Bomonjee, and the Rhinoceros was called Strorks, because he **breathed**⑨ through his mouth **instead of**⑩ his nose. I wouldn't ask anything about the cooking-stove if I were you.

这幅画描绘的是在红海上的一个荒岛上。一天，天气很热。帕西人正要吃蛋糕，犀牛从荒凉的内地走来（你可以看到那里都是石头）。犀牛的皮肤很光滑，扣着三颗扣子。扣子在下面，所以你看不见。帕西人帽子上的曲线是反射的太阳光，非常绚丽。如果我如实地描绘下来，这些光线会占据整个画面。你可以看到蛋糕上的葡萄干；沙滩上那个轮子是法老试图穿越红海时从战车上掉下来的，帕西人偶然发现了它，便作为玩具保留了下来。帕西人名为帕斯特杰·本蒙杰，犀牛名叫斯托克斯，它用嘴（而不是鼻子）呼吸。如果我是你，我可不会问有关炉子的事情。

远古传奇

① come down from 从…下来
② truthfully /ˈtruːθfəli/ ad. 说真话的,如实地
③ rocky /ˈrɒki/ a. 岩石的,多石的
④ smooth /smuːð/ a. 平稳的,流畅的
⑤ squiggly a. 弯弯曲曲的
⑥ fill up 充满
⑦ belong to 属于
⑧ chariot /ˈtʃæriət/ n. 二轮战车
⑨ breathe /briːð/ v. 呼吸
⑩ instead of /ɪnˈsted/ 代替,而不是…

Just So Stories

This is the Parsee Pestonjee Bomonjee sitting in his palm tree and watching the Rhinoceros Strorks bathing near the beach of the altogether uninhabited island after Strorks had taken off his skin. The Parsee has put the cake-crumbs into the skin, and he is smiling to think how they will tickle Strorks when Strorks **puts it**[①] on again. The skin is just under the rocks below the palm-tree in a cool place; that is why you can't see it. The Parsee is wearing a new more-than-**oriental**[②] splendour hat of the **sort**[③] that Parsees wear; and he has a knife **in his hand**[④] to cut his name on palm trees. The black things on the islands out **at sea**[⑤] are **bits**[⑥] of ships that got wrecked going down the Red Sea; but all the **passengers**[⑦] were **saved**[⑧] and went home.

The black thing in the water **close to**[⑨] the shore is not a **wreck**[⑩] at all. It is Strorks the Rhinoceros bathing without his skin. He was just as black underneath his skin as he was outside. I wouldn't ask anything about the cooking stove if I were you.

这幅画描绘的是帕西人帕斯特杰·本蒙杰坐在棕榈树上，正看着犀牛斯托克斯脱下皮衣，在荒岛海滩附近洗澡。帕西人已经把蛋糕渣儿揉进了犀牛皮。他正微笑着想象斯托克斯穿上自己的皮肤后会是多么搔痒难忍。犀牛皮放在树下石头底下的阴凉处，所以你看不到它。帕西人戴着一顶新帽子，手里握着一把刀，要在树干上刻下自己的名字。他的帽子比其他帕西人的更富有东方韵味。远处海面上的黑色物体是沉入红海的船只，庆幸的是所有的旅客都获救了，并安全地回到了家中。离海岸很近的地方还有一团黑色的东西，那不是沉船，而是犀牛斯托克斯脱了皮衣后在洗澡。你看它虽然脱了皮衣，看上去却还是一样黝黑。如果我是你，我可不会问有关炉子的事情。

① put on 穿上

② oriental /ɔ(ː)rɪˈentl/ a. 东方人的
③ sort /sɔːt/ n. 种类
④ in one's hand 在…手里
⑤ at sea 在海上
⑥ bit /bɪt/ n. 小块
⑦ passenger /ˈpæsɪndʒə/ n. 乘客,旅客
⑧ save /seɪv/ v. 解救
⑨ close to 靠近
⑩ wreck /rek/ n. 残骸

This uninhabited island
Is off **Cape**① Gardafui,
By the Beaches of Socotra
And the Pink **Arabian**② Sea:
But it's hot—too hot from **Suez**③
For the **likes**④ of you and me
Ever to go
In a P. and O. And **call on**⑤ the Cake-Parsee!

① cape /keɪp/ n. 岬，海角
② arabian /əˈreɪbɪən/ a. 阿拉伯(人)的
③ suez /ˈsju(ː)ɪz/ n. 苏伊士
④ likes /laɪk/ n. 同样的人或物
⑤ call on vt. 号召（约请，访问）

这个荒岛，
远离卡迪那角，
周围是斯科达海岸，
和粉红色的阿拉伯海；

但这里太热，对你我来说——从苏伊士
我们来这里，
拜访那位烤蛋糕的帕西人！

How the Leopard Got His Spots

In the days when everybody started fair, Best Beloved, the **Leopard**① lived in a place called the High Veldt. Member it wasn't the Low Veldt, or the Bush Veldt, or the Sour Veldt, but the sclusively bare, hot, shiny High Veldt, where there was sand and sandy-coloured rock and sclusively **tufts**② of sandy-yellowish grass. The Giraffe and the Zebra and the Eland and the Koodoo and the Hartebeest lived there; and they were sclusively sandy-yellow-brownish all over; but the Leopard, he was a greyish-yellowish **catty-shaped**③ kind of beast, and he matched the sclusively yellowish-greyish-brownish colour of the High Veldt to one hair. This was very bad for the **Giraffe**④ and the **Zebra**⑤ and the rest of them; for he would lie down by a sclusively yellowish-greyish-brownish stone or clump of grass, and when the Giraffe or the Zebra or the Eland or the Koodoo or the Bush-Buck or the Bonte-Buck came by he would surprise them out of their **jumpsome**⑥ lives. He would indeed! And, also, there was an Ethiopian with bows and arrows (a 'sclusively greyish-brownish-yellowish man he was then), who lived on the High Veldt with the Leopard; and the two used to hunt together—the **Ethiopian**⑦ with his bows and arrows, and the Leopard sclusively with his teeth and claws—till the Giraffe and the Eland and the Koodoo and

花豹身上的斑点是怎么长出来的

① leopard /ˈlepəd/ n. 豹

② tuft /tʌft/ n. 一绺

③ catty-shaped 猫状的

④ giraffe /dʒɪˈrɑːf/ n. 长颈鹿

⑤ zebra /ˈziːbrə, ˈzebrə/ n. 斑马

⑥ jumpsome a. 经常跳跃的

⑦ ethiopian /ˌiːθɪˈəʊpjən, -pɪən/ 埃塞俄比亚人

人们刚开始打猎的时候，豹子住在一个叫高原的地方。记住，这个地方不叫低原，不叫灌木原，也不叫贫原。这里非常荒凉、炎热，日照强烈的高原。地上只有沙土和沙土色的岩石，长着一簇簇沙黄色的草丛。长颈鹿、斑马、卷角羚、大羚、狷羚等动物就生活在这里。这些动物全身的皮毛都是浅黄色，只有豹子不同。它外形像猫，皮毛呈淡灰褐色，这与周围灰褐色的环境非常吻合。这下子长颈鹿、斑马和其他动物可就遭了殃。因为豹子可以躺在灰褐色的岩石或草丛旁，等它们走过来，豹子就一下子跳起来，把它们吓得四处逃散。豹子真是这样做的！而且在这里与豹子住在一起的还有一个埃塞俄比亚人（那时他的皮肤是褐色的），他们合起伙来捕捉动物。所不同的是埃塞俄比亚人使用的武器是弓箭，豹子用的是自己的牙齿和爪子。他们把长颈鹿、羚羊等一群动物堵截得无处可逃。它们真的走投无路了！

很长一段时间以后（那时候各种生物总是活得很长），这些动物逐渐学会了如何逃避豹

· 043 ·

the Quagga and all **the rest of**① them didn't know which way to jump, Best Beloved. They didn't indeed!

After a long time—things lived for ever so long in those days—they learned to **avoid**② anything that looked like a Leopard or an Ethiopian; and **bit by bit**③—the Giraffe began it, because his legs were the longest—they went away from the High Veldt. They **scuttled**④ for days and days till they came to a great forest, sclusively full of trees and bushes and **stripy**⑤, **speckly**⑥, **patchy**⑦-blatchy shadows, and there they hid; and after another long time, what with standing half **in the shade**⑧ and half out of it, and what with the slippery-slidy shadows of the trees falling on them, the Giraffe grew **blotchy**⑨, and the Zebra grew stripy, and the Eland and the Koodoo grew darker, with little wavy grey lines on their backs like bark on a tree trunk; and so, though you could hear them and smell them, you could very seldom see them, and then only when you knew **precisely**⑩ where to look. They had a beautiful time in the sclusively speckly-spickly shadows of the forest, while the Leopard and the Ethiopian ran about over the sclusively greyish-yellowish-reddish High Veldt outside, wondering where all their breakfasts and their dinners and their teas had gone. At last they were so hungry that they ate rats and **beetles**⑪ and rock-rabbits, the Leopard and the Ethiopian, and then they had the Big Tummy-ache, both together; and then they met Baviaan—the dog-headed, barking Baboon, who is quite the wisest animal in all South Africa.

Said Leopard to **Baviaan**⑫ (and it was a very hot day), 'Where has all the game gone?'

And Baviaan **winked**⑬. He knew.

Said the Ethiopian to Baviaan, 'Can you tell me the present **habitat**⑭ of the **aboriginal**⑮ **Fauna**⑯?' (That meant just the same thing, but the Ethiopian always used long words. He was a grown-up.)

远古传奇

① the rest of 剩下的

② avoid /əˈvɔɪd/ v. 避免
③ bit by bit 一点点地，渐渐地
④ scuttle /ˈskʌtl/ vt 急匆匆地奔跑
⑤ stripy /ˈstraɪpɪ/ a. 条纹状的，有条纹的
⑥ speckly a. 有斑点的
⑦ patchy /ˈpætʃɪ/ a. 斑驳的
⑧ in the shade 在树荫下
⑨ blotchy a. 到处有污点的

⑩ precisely /prɪˈsaɪslɪ/ ad. 精确地

⑪ beetle /ˈbiːtl/ n. 甲虫

⑫ baviaan 狒狒
⑬ wink /wɪŋk/ v. 眨眼
⑭ habitat /ˈhæbɪtæt/ n. （动植物的）产地，栖息地
⑮ aboriginal /ˌæbəˈrɪdʒənəl/ a. 原始的，土著的
⑯ fauna /ˈfɔːnə/ n. 动物群

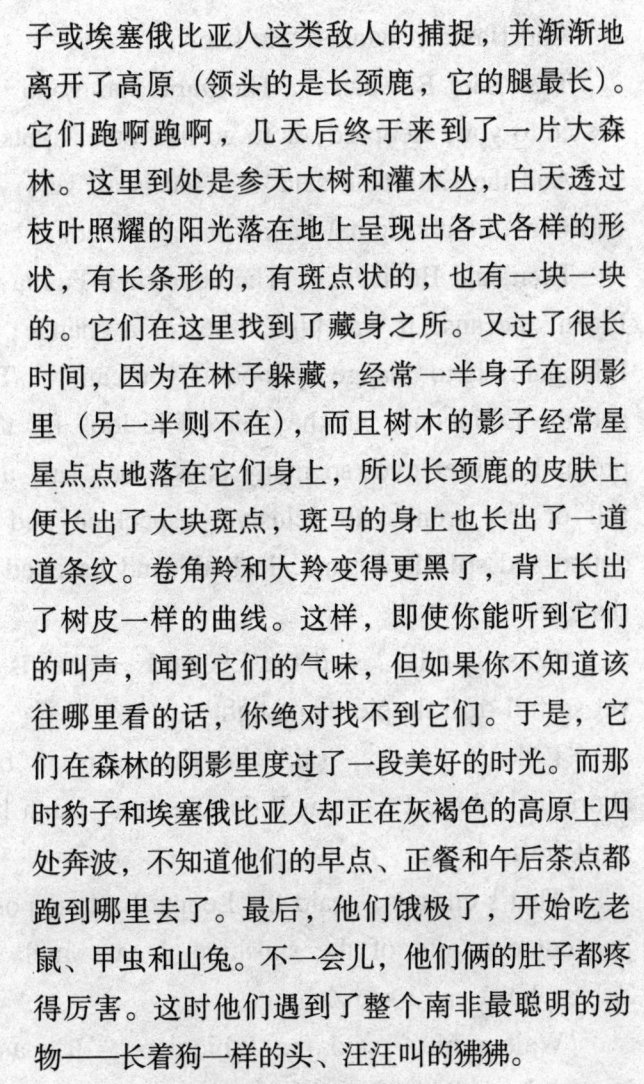

子或埃塞俄比亚人这类敌人的捕捉，并渐渐地离开了高原（领头的是长颈鹿，它的腿最长）。它们跑啊跑啊，几天后终于来到了一片大森林。这里到处是参天大树和灌木丛，白天透过枝叶照耀的阳光落在地上呈现出各式各样的形状，有长条形的，有斑点状的，也有一块一块的。它们在这里找到了藏身之所。又过了很长时间，因为在林子躲藏，经常一半身子在阴影里（另一半则不在），而且树木的影子经常星星点点地落在它们身上，所以长颈鹿的皮肤上便长出了大块斑点，斑马的身上也长出了一道道条纹。卷角羚和大羚变得更黑了，背上长出了树皮一样的曲线。这样，即使你能听到它们的叫声，闻到它们的气味，但如果你不知道该往哪里看的话，你绝对找不到它们。于是，它们在森林的阴影里度过了一段美好的时光。而那时豹子和埃塞俄比亚人却正在灰褐色的高原上四处奔波，不知道他们的早点、正餐和午后茶点都跑到哪里去了。最后，他们饿极了，开始吃老鼠、甲虫和山兔。不一会儿，他们俩的肚子都疼得厉害。这时他们遇到了整个南非最聪明的动物——长着狗一样的头、汪汪叫的狒狒。

豹子对狒狒说（当时天气很热）："猎物都到哪里去了？"

狒狒眨眨眼，它知道答案。

埃塞俄比亚人对狒狒说："你能告诉我那些本地的动物现在的栖息地在哪里吗？"（其实他和豹子问的是同一件事，但埃塞俄比亚人说话时常常使用长句子，他是个大人）。

· 045 ·

And Baviaan winked. He knew.

Then said Baviaan, 'The game has gone into other spots; and my advice to you, Leopard, is to go into other spots as soon as you can.'

And the Ethiopian said, 'That is all very fine, but I wish to know **whither**① the aboriginal Fauna has migrated.'

Then said Baviaan, 'The aboriginal Fauna has joined the aboriginal **Flora**② because it was high time for a change; and my advice to you, Ethiopian, is to change as soon as you can.' That puzzled the Leopard and the Ethiopian, but they set off to look for the aboriginal Flora, and presently, after ever so many days, they saw a great, high, tall forest full of tree trunks all sclusively speckled and sprottied and spotted, dotted and **splashed**③ and **slashed**④ and **hatched**⑤ and crosshatched with shadows.

'What is this,' said the Leopard, 'that is so sclusively dark, and yet so full of little pieces of light?'

'I don't know', said the Ethiopian, 'but it ought to be the aboriginal Flora. I can smell Giraffe, and I can hear Giraffe, but I can't see Giraffe.'

'That's curious,' said the Leopard. 'I suppose it is because we have just come in out of the sunshine. I can smell Zebra, and I can hear Zebra, but I can't see Zebra.'

'Wait a bit,' said the Ethiopian. 'It's a long time since we've hunted them. Perhaps we've forgotten what they were like.'

'**Fiddle**⑥!' said the Leopard. 'I remember them perfectly on the High Veldt, especially their **marrow**⑦-bones. Giraffe is about seventeen feet high, of a sclusively **fulvous**⑧ golden-yellow from head to heel; and Zebra is about four and a half feet high, of a sclusively grey-fawn colour from head to heel.'

'Umm,' said the Ethiopian, looking into the speckly-spickly

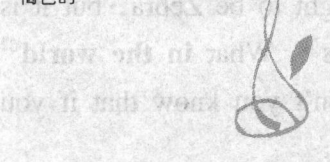

① whither /(h)wɪðə/ conj. &ad.（古体）（无论）去哪里
② flora /ˈflɔːrə/ n. 植物，群落
③ splash /splæʃ/ v. 成斑驳状
④ slash /slæʃ/ vt. 开叉
⑤ hatch /hætʃ/ v. 成阴影

⑥ fiddle /ˈfɪdl/ 瞎搞，胡乱弄
⑦ marrow /ˈmærəʊ/ n. 骨髓
⑧ fulvous /ˈfʌlvəs/ a. 黄褐色的

狒狒眨眨眼，它知道答案。

狒狒说："猎物们到了另外一个地方。豹子，我给你一个忠告，尽快换个'点'吧。"

埃塞俄比亚人说："这不错，但我希望知道那些本地的动物们移居到了哪里。"

狒狒回答道："到了需要改变的时候，本地的动物与本地植物结合在一起。埃塞俄比亚人，我对你的忠告是尽快改变自己。"

豹子和埃塞俄比亚人面面相觑，百思不得其解。但他们还是外出寻找本地的植物。许多天后，他们看到了一片茂密的树林，树干上布满了各种形状的阴影，斑点状的、线状的、交叉状的……

"这是什么，"豹子问，"这里这么黑，到处却又闪着亮点？"

"我也不知道，"埃塞俄比亚人回答道，"但这恐怕就是本地的植物了。我能闻到长颈鹿的味道，也听到了它的声音，却看不到它。"

"这太奇怪了，"豹子说，"我想也许是由于我们刚从亮处走进来的缘故。我能闻到斑马的味道，也能听见它的声音，却看不到它。"

"等一下，"埃塞俄比亚人说，"我们已经有很长时间没有捕猎了，也许我们忘记了它们的模样。"

"胡说！"豹子嚷道，"我清清楚楚地记得它们在高原上的样子，特别是它们的髓骨。长颈鹿大概有17英尺高，从头到脚都是金黄色。斑马大概有四英尺半高，从头到脚都是浅黄褐色。"

"唔，"埃塞俄比亚人打量着森林里的阴影，"它们在暗处应该很显眼，就像鱼肉熏制厂里熟透了的香蕉。"

shadows of the aboriginal Flora-forest. 'Then they ought to **show up**① in this dark place like ripe bananas in a smokehouse.'

But they didn't. The Leopard and the Ethiopian hunted all day; and though they could smell them and hear them, they never saw one of them.

'For goodness sake,' said the Leopard at tea-time, 'let us wait till it gets dark. This daylight hunting is a perfect **scandal**②.'

So they waited till dark, and then the Leopard heard something breathing **sniffily**③ in the **starlight**④ that fell all stripy through the branches, and he jumped at the noise, and it smelt like Zebra, and it felt like Zebra, and when he knocked it down it kicked like Zebra, but he couldn't see it. So he said, 'Be quiet, O you person without any form. I am going to sit on your head till morning, because there is something about you that I don't understand.'

Presently he heard a **grunt**⑤ and a crash and a **scramble**⑥, and the Ethiopian called out, 'I've caught a thing that I can't see. It smells like Giraffe, and it kicks like Giraffe, but it hasn't any form.'

'Don't you trust it,' said the Leopard. 'Sit on its head till the moming—same as me. They haven't any form—any of them.'

So they sat down on them hard till bright morning-time, and then Leopard said, ' What have you at your end of the table, Brother?'

The Ethiopian scratched his head and said, 'It ought to be sclusively a rich fulvous orange-**tawny**⑦ from head to **heel**⑧, and it ought to be Giraffe; but it is covered all over with chestnut **blotches**⑨. What have you at your end of the table, Brother?'

And the Leopard scratched his head and said, 'It ought to be sclusively a **delicate**⑩ greyish-fawn, and it ought to be Zebra; but it is covered all over with black and purple **stripes**⑪. What **in the world**⑫ have you been doing to yourself, Zebra? Don't you know that if you

① show up 出现

② scandal /'skændl/ n. 丑闻

③ sniffy /'snɪfi/ a. 嗤之以鼻的,自命不凡的

④ starlight /'stɑːlaɪt/ n. 星光

⑤ grunt /grʌnt/ n. 呼噜声 vi. (猪等)作呼噜声

⑥ scramble /'skræmbl/ v. 攀缘,搅炒,混杂一起

⑦ tawny /'tɔːnɪ/ a. 黄褐色的,茶色

⑧ heel /hiːl/ n. 脚后跟

⑨ blotch /blɒtʃ/ n. 斑点

⑩ delicate /'delɪkɪt/ a. 细致优雅的,微妙的,美味的

⑪ stripe /straɪp/ n. 条纹

⑫ in the world 究竟,到底

然而动物们并没有这么明显地出现在他们面前。豹子和埃塞俄比亚人找了一天,尽管他们都能闻到动物的气味,听到动物的声音,却连一只动物也没看到。

下午茶的时间到了。"上帝啊,"豹子叹息道,"我们等到天黑以后再说吧。白天打猎真是个天大的笑话。"

于是他们等到天黑。星光从枝叶中透过来,地上落满了长长的影子。豹子听到轻微的喘息声,便朝着声音的方向猛扑过去。这只动物闻起来像斑马,摸上去像斑马,被扑倒在地挣扎时也像斑马,但豹子却看不到它。于是它大喝一声:"老实点,怎么连个正经形状也没有。你身上有些东西我搞不懂,所以我要坐在你的脑袋上直到天亮。"

这时它听到一个轻微的声音,紧接着耳边便是一阵碰撞和混乱声。埃塞俄比亚人喊道:"我抓住了一样东西,但我看不见。它闻起来像长颈鹿,踢起来像长颈鹿,但却没有形状。"

"可别轻信它,"豹子说,"和我一样,你坐在它头上直到天亮。这两个动物都没有形状。"

于是他们就这样坐着,直到天大亮。豹子说:"哥们儿,你那里是个什么东西?"

埃塞俄比亚人挠挠脑袋,说:"这家伙应该从头到脚都是黄褐色,应该是只长颈鹿,但它身上却长满了栗子状的斑点。你那里怎么样,哥们儿?"

豹子挠挠头,说:"这家伙应该浑身灰褐色,应该是只斑马,但身上却长满了黑紫色的条纹。斑马,你到底对自己做了些什么?你难道不知道如果在高原上十英里之外我就能把你认出

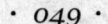

were on the High Veldt I could see you ten miles off? You haven't any form.'

'Yes,' said the Zebra, 'but this isn't the High Veldt. Can't you see?'

'I can now,' said the Leopard. 'But I couldn't all yesterday. How is it done?'

'Let us up,' said the Zebra, 'and we will show you.'

They let the Zebra and the Giraffe **get up**①; and Zebra moved away to some little thorn-bushes where the sunlight fell all stripy, and Giraffe **moved off**② to some **tallish**③ trees where the shadows fell all blotchy.

'Now watch,' said the Zebra and the Giraffe. ' This is the way it's done. One—two—three! And where's your breakfast?'

Leopard stared, and Ethiopian stared, but all they could see were stripy shadows and blotched shadows in the forest, but never a sign of Zebra and Giraffe. They had just walked off and hidden themselves in the shadowy forest.

'Hi! Hi!' said the Ethiopian. 'That's a trick worth learning. Take a lesson by it, Leopard. You show up in this dark place like a bar of soap in a coal-**scuttle**④.'

'Ho! Ho!' said the Leopard. 'Would it surprise you very much to know that you show up in this dark place like a **mustard**⑤-plaster on a **sack**⑥ of coals?'

'Well, **calling names**⑦ won't catch dinner,' said the Ethiopian. 'The long and the little of it is that we don't match our **backgrounds**⑧. I'm going to take Baviaan's advice. He told me I ought to change; and as I've nothing to change except my skin I'm going to change that.'

'What to?' said the Leopard, **tremendously**⑨ excited.

'To a nice working blackish-brownish colour, with a little purple in

来？没个正形。"

"是的，"斑马答道，"但现在不是在高原上，难道你看不见？"

"我现在能看见了，"豹子说，"但昨天不行。这是怎么回事？"

"让我们站起来，"斑马说，"然后就告诉你们。"

他们让斑马和长颈鹿站立起来。斑马走到荆棘丛下，那里太阳光一条条地照射下来；长颈鹿则来到高一些的树下，树影斑斑点点地落在它的身上。

"现在你们看到了，"斑马和长颈鹿说，"就是这么回事。一——二——三，你们的早餐哪儿去了？"

豹子四处张望，埃塞俄比亚人也左右环顾。但他们能看到的只是树林里一条条、一块块的阴影，却再也找不到斑马和长颈鹿的一丝踪迹。这两种动物已经逃跑了，藏在幽暗的森林里。

"嗨，嗨！"埃塞俄比亚人说，"我们上当了。接受这个教训吧，豹子先生。在黑暗里你看起来就像煤筐里的一条肥皂。"

"哈！哈！"豹子回敬道，"难道你不知道你自己就像煤斗里的芥末酱吗？"

"唉，互相指责填不饱肚子，"埃塞俄比亚人说，"关键的一点是我们与这里的背景颜色不融合。我要接受狒狒的忠告。它告诉我应该改变。除了皮肤之外我没什么可变的。我现在就开始更换肤色。"

"变成什么样？"豹子兴奋地问道。

"变成黑褐色，再加点紫色和黄灰色。这种

① get up 起床
② move off 离开
③ tallish /ˈtɔːlɪʃ/ a. 身材较高的
④ scuttle /ˈskʌtl/ v. 急促地跑
⑤ mustard /ˈmʌstəd/ n. 芥末, 芥菜
⑥ sack /sæk/ n. 袋子
⑦ call names 骂人
⑧ background /ˈbækɡraʊnd/ n. 背景
⑨ tremendously /trɪˈmendəslɪ/ ad. 惊人地

it, and touches of **slaty**①-blue. It will be the very thing for hiding in hollows and behind trees.'

So he changed his skin then and there, and the Leopard was more excited than ever; he had never seen a man change his skin before.

'But what about me?' he said, when the Ethiopian had worked his last little finger into his fine new black skin.

'You take Baviaan's advice too. He told you to go into spots.'

'So I did,' said the Leopard. 'I went into other spots as fast as I could. I went into this spot with you, and a lot of good it has done me.'

'Oh,' said the Ethiopian, 'Baviaan didn't mean spots in South Africa. He meant spots on your skin.'

'What's the use of that?' said the Leopard.

'Think of Giraffe,' said the Ethiopian. 'Or if you prefer stripes, think of Zebra. They find their spots and stripes give them perfect **satisfaction**②.'

'Umm,' said the Leopard. 'I wouldn't look like Zebra—not for ever so.'

'Well, **make up your mind**③,' said the Ethiopian, 'because I'd hate to go hunting without you, but I must if you **insist on**④ looking like a sun-flower against a **tarred**⑤ fence.'

'I'll take spots, then,' said the Leopard; 'but don't make them too vulgar-big. I wouldn't look like Giraffe—not for ever so.'

'I'll make them with the tips of my fingers,' said the Ethiopian. 'There's plenty of black left on my skin still. Stand over!'

Then the Ethiopian put his five fingers close together (there was plenty of black left on his new skin still) and pressed them all over the Leopard, and wherever the five fingers touched they left five little black marks, all close together. You can see them on any Leopard's skin you like, Best Beloved. Sometimes the fingers slipped and the marks got a

① slaty /ˈsleɪtɪ/ a. 石板一样的

② satisfaction /ˌsætɪsˈfækʃən/ n. 满意

③ make up one's mind 下定决心
④ insist on 坚持做某事
⑤ tarred /tɑːd/ a. 涂了焦油的

颜色能管用。特别是隐藏在洞穴或树后，再好不过了。"

于是他就站在那里更换了自己的肤色。豹子从未像此刻这么兴奋过，这之前它可从没看见过人更换自己的肤色。

正当埃塞俄比亚人把最后一个小手指上的皮肤变成黑色时，豹子焦急地问："我该怎么办？"

"你也该听从狒狒的忠告。它让你换个'点'。"

"可我是这样做的呀。我拼命跑到了别的地点，并和你一起来到这儿。这对我来说也不错。"

"哎呀，"埃塞俄比亚人说，"狒狒指的不是这个。'点'不是南非的什么地点，它指的是你身上的点。"

"那有什么用？"豹子问。

"想想长颈鹿，"埃塞俄比亚人答道，"但如果你喜欢条纹的话，再想想斑马。它们对自己身上的斑点和条纹再满意不过了。"

"唔，"豹子说，"我可不想长得像只斑马，不想永远那样。"

"拜托清醒清醒吧，"埃塞俄比亚人说，"我愿意和你一起打猎，但如果你偏要长得像黑色篱笆上的一只向日葵的话，我也只能割爱了。"

"那我就选择斑点吧，"豹子说，"但斑点不能太大。我可不想看上去像只长颈鹿——不想永远那样。"

"我可以用手指尖帮你，"埃塞俄比亚人说，"我皮肤上还有很多黑色。站过来！"

于是埃塞俄比亚人五指紧紧并拢（他的皮肤上还留有很多黑色），按在豹子身上，手指碰到

· 053 ·

little **blurred**①; but if you look closely at any Leopard now you will see that there are always five spots—off five fat black finger-tips.

'Now you are a beauty!' said the Ethiopian. 'You can lie out on the bare ground and look like a heap of **pebbles**②. You can lie out on the naked rocks and look like a piece of **pudding**③-stone. You can lie out on a **leafy**④ branch and look like sunshine **sifting**⑤ through the leaves; and you can lie right across the centre of a path and look like nothing **in particular**⑥. Think of that and **purr**⑦!'

'But if I'm all this,' said the Leopard, 'why didn't you go spotty too?'

'Oh, plain black's best,' said the Ethiopian. 'Now come along and we'll see if we can't **get even with**⑧ Mr. One-Two-Three-Where's-your-Breakfast!'

So they went away and lived happily ever afterward, Best Beloved. That is all.

Oh, now and then you will hear grown-ups say, 'Can the Ethiopian change his skin or the Leopard his spots?' I don't think even grown-ups would keep on saying such a silly thing if the Leopard and the Ethiopian hadn't done it once—do you? But they will never do it again, Best Beloved. They are quite **contented**⑨ as they are.

① blurred /blə:d/ v. 使……变模糊(弄脏)

② pebble /'pebl/ n. 鹅卵石
③ pudding /'pudɪŋ/ n. 布丁
④ leafy /'li:fɪ/ a. 叶茂盛的
⑤ sift /sɪft/ v. 筛撒
⑥ in particular 特别是,尤其是
⑦ purr /pə:/ v. 得意地呜呜叫

⑧ get even with vt. 报复

⑨ contented /kən'tentɪd/ a. 满足的,心安的

的地方留下了五个密密的小黑点。这黑点在任何一只豹子身上都能看到。有时手指不小心滑了一下,印记有点模糊;但如果贴得近,在任何一只豹子身上你总能看到五个点——从胖胖的五个黑手指尖上按下的五个点。

"啊,现在你可是个美人了,"埃塞俄比亚人说,"你可以躺在地上,看上去就像一堆鹅卵石;也可以躺在裸露的岩石上,看上去像一块布丁岩,还可以卧在树叶茂盛的枝杈上,看上去就像渗落在树叶间的阳光;甚至可以躺在大路中央,看上去没什么特别之处。想想看,偷着乐去吧!"

"如果真有这么好,"豹子问道,"为什么你自己不长斑点?"

"啊,单纯的黑色是最好的,"埃塞俄比亚人回答道,"现在让我们看看能不能与那些家伙打个平手。看它们还喊不喊:'一——二——三,你们的早餐哪儿去了?'"

于是他们离开了,从此过着幸福的生活。故事到此结束了。

唔,也许你经常听大人们说:"埃塞俄比亚人能更换他们的肤色,花豹能改变它身上的斑点么?"我想,如果花豹和埃塞俄比亚人没这样做过的话,大人们也就不会把这句话挂在嘴边了——你呢?但现在他们不想再这样做了。他们对自己现在拥有的一切非常满意。

Just So Stories

This is Wise Baviaan, the dog-headed Baboon, Who is Quite the Wisest Animal in All South Africa. I have drawn him from a statue that I **made up**① out of my own head, and I have written his name on his belt and on his shoulder and on the thing he is sitting on. I have written it in what is not called **Coptic**② and **Hieroglyphic**③ and **Cuneiformic**④ and **Bengalic**⑤ and **Burmic**⑥ and **Hebric**⑦, all because he is so wise. He is not beautiful, but he is very wise; and I should like to paint him with **paint-box**⑧ colours, but I am not allowed. The **umbrellaish**⑨ thing about his head is his Conventional **Mane**⑩.

这就是长着狗一样脑袋的聪明的狒狒，它是整个南非最聪明的动物。我是按照头脑里的一幅雕像把它描绘下来的，并在它身上的绶带、肩膀和坐台上写下了它的名字。我用的不是科普特语，不是象形文字，不是楔形文字，不是孟加拉语，也不是缅甸语或希伯莱语，原因是它太聪明了。它不漂亮，但它非常聪明。我想用颜料盒里的颜料给它涂上颜色，但没有得到允许。它头上伞状的东西是传统意义上的鬃鬣。

① make up 编造
② coptic /ˈkɔptɪk/ n. 埃及古语
③ hieroglyphic n. 象形文字
④ cuneiformic n. 楔形文字
⑤ bengalic n. 孟加拉语
⑥ burmic 缅甸语
⑦ hebric 希伯来语
⑧ paint-box 颜料盒
⑨ umbrellaish 伞状的
⑩ mane /meɪn/ n. （马等的）鬃毛

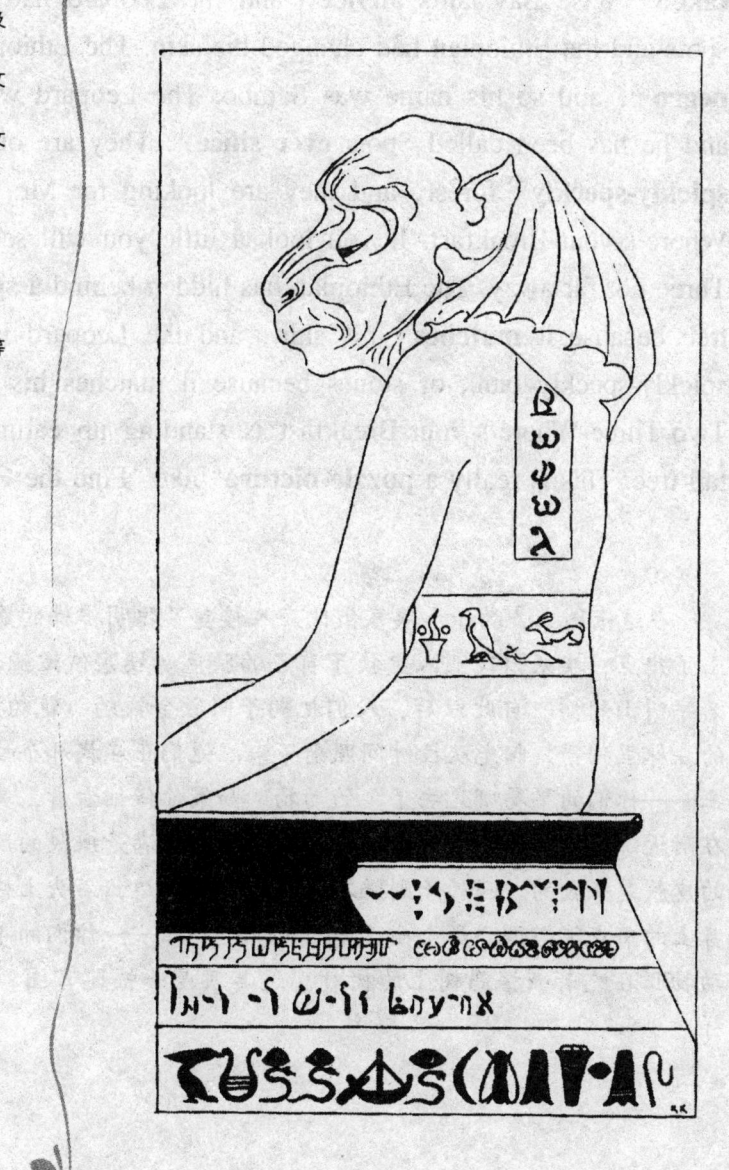

Just So Stories

  This is the picture of the Leopard and the Ethiopian after they had **taken**① Wise Baviaan's **advice**② and the Leopard had gone into other spots and the Ethiopian had changed his skin. The Ethiopian was really a **negro**③, and so his name was Sambo. The Leopard was called Spots, and he has been called Spots **ever since**④. They are out hunting in the **spickly-speckly**⑤ forest, and they are looking for Mr. One-Two-Three-Where's-your-Breakfast. If you look a little you will see Mr. One-Two-Three not far away. The Ethiopian has hidden behind a **splotchy-blotchy**⑥ tree because it **matches**⑦ his skin, and the Leopard is lying beside a spickly-speckly bank of stones because it matches his spots. Mr. One-Two-Three-Where's-your-Breakfast is standing up eating leaves from a tall tree. This is really a **puzzle-picture**⑧ like 'Find the Cat.'

  在这张图上，豹子和埃塞俄比亚人接受了聪明狒狒的建议，豹子身上涂上了斑点，埃塞俄比亚人更换了自己的肤色。埃塞俄比亚人是真正的黑人，名字叫山姆博。自此以后，人们把豹子叫做金钱豹（花豹）。他们正在浓密的森林里狩猎，阳光从枝叶间照射下来。他们正在找那个喊"一——二——三——你们的早餐哪儿去了"的动物。如果你仔细看看，其实要找的动物就在附近。埃塞俄比亚人藏在一棵树后，树干上满是斑驳的阴影，这恰好与他的皮肤是一致的。而豹子则躺在一块大石头旁边，石头上树影斑斑，这与它身上的斑点很搭调。那个喊"一——二——三——你们的早餐哪儿去了"的动物正在吃着一棵高树上的树叶。这其实是一幅迷宫图（像"找猫"图一样）。

远古传奇

① take /teɪk/ v. 接受
② advice /ədˈvaɪs/ n. 忠告,劝告
③ negro /ˈniːɡrəʊ/ n. 黑人
④ ever since 从那以后
⑤ spickly-speckly 斑点状的
⑥ splotchy-blotchy /ˈsplɒtʃɪ/ /ˈblɒtʃɪ/ a. 有斑点的
⑦ match /mætʃ/ v. 相配
⑧ puzzle-picture n 谜图

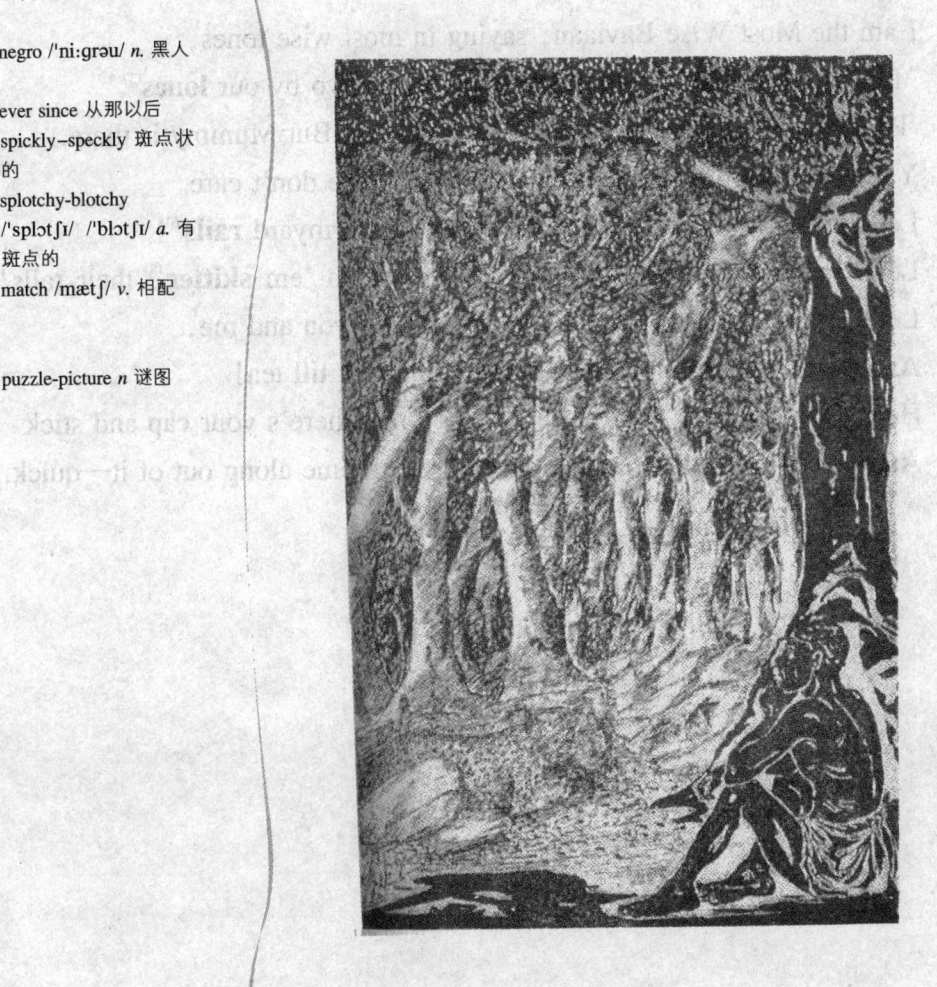

· 059 ·

I am the Most Wise Baviaan, saying in most wise tones,
'Let us **melt**① into the **landscape**②—just us two by our **lones**③.'
People have come—in a **carriage**④—calling. But Mummy is there.
Yes, I can go if you take me—Nurse says she don't care.
Let's go up to the **pig-sties**⑤ and sit on the farmyard **rails**⑥!
Let's say things to the **bunnies**⑦, and watch 'em **skitter**⑧ their tails!
Let's—oh, anything, daddy, so long as it's you and me,
And going truly **exploring**⑨, and not being in till tea!
Here's your **boots**⑩ (I've brought 'em), and here's your cap and stick
And here's your **pipe**⑪ and **tobacco**⑫. Oh, come along out of it—quick.

① melt *v.* 熔化,溶解
② landscape /ˈlændskeɪp/ *n.* 风景,山水
③ lone 只有,孤单的
④ carriage /ˈkærɪdʒ/ *n.* 四轮马车
⑤ pig-sties 猪圈
⑥ rail /reɪl/ *n.* 栏杆,铁轨
⑦ bunny /ˈbʌnɪ/ *n.* 小兔子
⑧ skitter /ˈskɪtə/ *v.* 飞掠而过
⑨ explore /ɪksˈplɔː/ *v.* 探险,探究
⑩ boot /buːt/ *n.* 靴子
⑪ pipe /paɪp/ *n.* 管,烟斗
⑫ tobacco /təˈbækəʊ/ *n.* 烟草

我是最聪明的狒狒,
用最聪明的声调说——
"与周围融为一体只有你我两个。"
人们坐着车子来,
大声叫喊。但妈妈在那儿。

是的,如果你带我,我就跟你走,
——保姆说她并不在意。
我们可以爬到猪圈上或坐在农场的围栏上!
我们跟兔子说话,看它们轻轻摇着尾巴!
我们——喔,爸爸,
只要我和你在一起,干什么都可以,
让我们真正去冒险,
直到下午茶时间才回到家里!
给你靴子(我拿来的),
给你帽子和手杖,
给你烟斗与荷包,
走出家门,
——快,快,快。

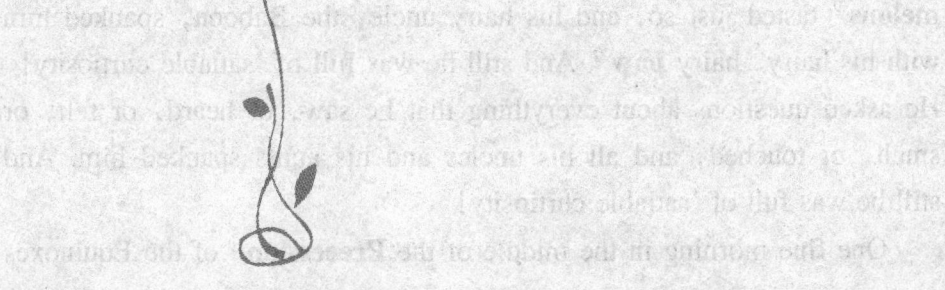

The Elephant's Child

In the High and Far-Off Times the Elephant, O Best Beloved, had no **trunk**①. He had only a blackish, **bulgy**② nose, as big as a boot, that he could **wriggle**③ about from side to side; but he couldn't pick up things with it. But there was one Elephant—a new Elephant—an Elephant's Child—who was full of 'satiable **curtiosity**④, and that means he asked ever so many questions. And he lived in Africa, and he filled all Africa with his 'satiable curtiosities. He asked his tall aunt, the **Ostrich**⑤, why her tail-feathers grew just so, and his tall aunt the Ostrich **spanked**⑥ him with her hard, hard claw. He asked his tall uncle, the Giraffe, what made his skin spotty, and his tall uncle, the Giraffe, spanked him with his hard, hard **hoof**⑦. And still he was full of 'satiable curtiosity! He asked his broad aunt, the **Hippopotamus**⑧, why her eyes were red, and his broad aunt, the Hippopotamus, spanked him with her broad, broad hoof; and he asked his hairy uncle, the Baboon, why **melons**⑨ tasted just so, and his hairy uncle, the Baboon, spanked him with his hairy, hairy **paw**⑩. And still he was full of 'satiable curtiosity! He asked questions about everything that he saw, or heard, or felt, or smelt, or touched, and all his uncles and his aunts spanked him. And still he was full of 'satiable curtiosity!

One fine morning in the middle of the **Precession**⑪ of the Equinoxes

大象的孩子

① trunk /trʌŋk/ n. 象鼻
② bulgy /'bʌldʒɪ/ a. 膨胀的,凸出的
③ wriggle /'rɪgl/ v. 蠕动,蜿蜒前进
④ curiosity /ˌkjʊərɪ'ɒsɪtɪ/ n. 好奇,好奇心
⑤ ostrich /'ɒstrɪtʃ/ n. 驼鸟
⑥ spank /spæŋk/ vt. 拍击
⑦ hoof /huːf/ n. 蹄
⑧ Hippopotamus /ˌhɪpə'pɒtəməs/ n. 河马
⑨ melon /'melən/ n. 甜瓜
⑩ paw /pɔː/ n. 手掌,手爪
⑪ precession /prɪ'seʃən/ n. 先行

　　很久很久以前,大象没有长长的象鼻,只有一个黑色突起的鼻子,有一只皮靴那么大,可以从一侧扭到另一侧,但不能用鼻子捡东西。但有一只大象——确切地说,是大象的孩子,一个新宝宝——对任何事情都非常好奇,问题多得不得了。它住在非洲,对非洲的一切都感到新鲜。它问高个子鸵鸟婶婶为什么长着那样的羽毛尾巴,结果被高个子鸵鸟婶婶用硬硬的爪子扇了屁股。它问高个子长颈鹿叔叔身上的斑点是怎么长出来的,结果被高个子长颈鹿叔叔用厚厚的蹄子踢了屁股。但它的好奇心还是那么强!它又问胖胖的海马姑姑为什么总是瞪着一对红色的眼睛,结果屁股上又被胖胖的海马姑姑用宽大的蹄子重重地踹了一脚。它还去问长毛狒狒舅舅为什么甜瓜的味道是这样的,结果被长毛狒狒舅舅用毛茸茸的爪子挠了屁股。但它依旧那么好奇!它只要看到、听到、闻到、摸到什么东西就要问问题,结果被所有的叔叔、婶婶、舅舅、姑姑打了屁股。但它仍然对一切充满了好奇!

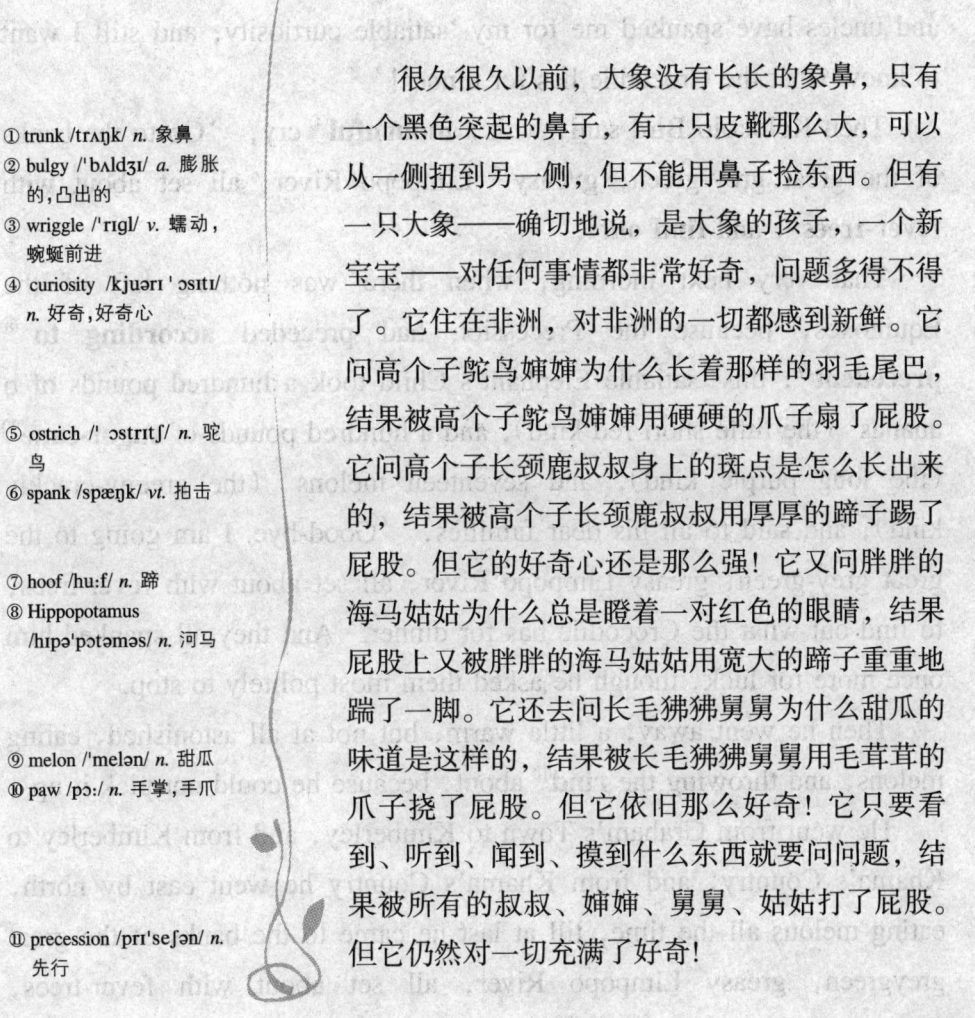

· 063 ·

this 'satiable Elephant's Child asked a new fine question that he had never asked before. He asked, 'What does the **Crocodile**① have for dinner?' Then everybody said, 'Hush!' in a loud and **dreadful** ②tone, and they spanked him immediately and directly, without stopping, for a long time.

By and by, when that was finished, he came upon Kolokolo Bird sitting in the middle of a wait-a-bit **thorn-bush** ③, and he said, 'My father has spanked me, and my mother has spanked me; all my aunts and uncles have spanked me for my 'satiable curtiosity; and still I want to know what the Crocodile has for dinner!'

Then Kolokolo Bird said, with a **mournful**④ cry, 'Go to the banks of the great grey-green, **greasy**⑤ Limpopo River, all set about with **fever-trees**⑥, and **find out**⑦.'

That very next morning, when there was nothing left of the Equinoxes, because the Precession had preceded **according to** ⑧ **precedent**⑨, this 'satiable Elephant's Child took a hundred pounds of b ananas (the little short red kind), and a hundred pounds of **sugar-cane**⑩ (the long purple kind), and seventeen melons (the greeny-crackly kind), and said to all his dear families, 'Good-bye. I am going to the great grey-green, greasy Limpopo River, all set about with fever-trees, to find out what the Crocodile has for dinner.' And they all spanked him once more for luck, though he asked them most politely to stop.

Then he went away, a little warm, but not at all astonished, eating melons, and throwing the **rind**⑪ about, because he could not pick it up.

He went from Graham's Town to Kimberley, and from Kimberley to Khama's Country, and from Khama's Country he went east by north, eating melons all the time, till at last he came to the banks of the great greygreen, greasy Limpopo River, all set about with fever-trees,

① crocodile /ˈkrɔkədaɪl/ n. 鳄鱼
② dreadful /ˈdredful/ a. 可怕的

③ thorn-bush 荆棘丛
④ mournful /ˈmɔ:nful/ a. 悲恸的,悲哀的
⑤ greasy /ˈgri:sɪ, ˈgri:zɪ/ a. 油腻的,滑溜溜的
⑥ fever-tree 蓝桉树
⑦ find out 查出,发现

⑧ according to 根据
⑨ precedent /prɪˈsi:dənt/ a. 在前的,在先的 n. 先例,前例
⑩ sugar-cane 甘蔗

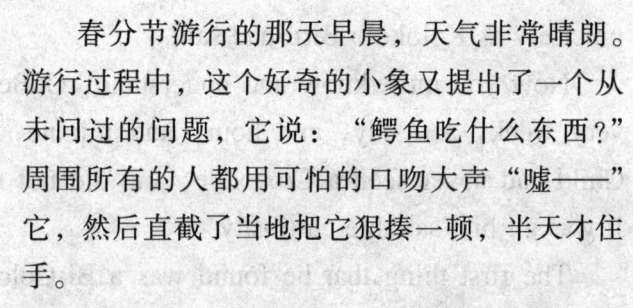

⑪ rind /raɪnd/ n. 皮,壳,外表

春分节游行的那天早晨,天气非常晴朗。游行过程中,这个好奇的小象又提出了一个从未问过的问题,它说:"鳄鱼吃什么东西?"周围所有的人都用可怕的口吻大声"嘘——"它,然后直截了当地把它狠揍一顿,半天才住手。

游行结束后,它看到一只落在荆棘枝上的咕噜咕噜鸟,于是走上前去,对它说:"因为我好奇心太强,所以爸爸打了我的屁股,妈妈打了我的屁股,所有的叔叔、婶婶、舅舅、姑姑都打了我的屁股。但我还是想知道鳄鱼吃的是什么东西!"

咕噜咕噜鸟喉咙里咕噜了一声,说:"到那条灰绿色、滑腻腻的丽姆波波大河去,那里有一片蓝桉树,去找吧。"

第二天早晨,与往常一样,游行结束了。小象拿了100磅香蕉(又红又短的那种)、100磅甘蔗(又紫又长的那种)和17个甜瓜(又绿又脆的那种),对亲爱的家人说:"再见,我要到那条灰绿色的丽姆波波大河去,那里有蓝桉树,我要找到鳄鱼吃的东西。"尽管小象彬彬有礼地请它们住手,但为了图个吉利,它们还是又打了它一顿。

然后小象就出发了,它有点生气,但丝毫不感到惊讶。它一路上吃着甜瓜,把瓜皮扔得满地都是。因为它用鼻子捡不起来。

它从格莱汉姆城走到金柏利,从金柏利走到喀玛城,又从喀玛城一直往东北方向走,一路上吃着甜瓜,最后来到了灰绿色的、滑腻腻的丽姆

Just So Stories

precisely as Kolokolo Bird had said.

Now you must know and understand, O Best Beloved, that till that very week, and day, and hour, and minute, this 'satiable Elephant's Child had never seen a Crocodile, and did not know what one was like. It was all his 'satiable curtiosity.

The first thing that he found was a Bi-Coloured-Python-Rock-Snake **curled**① round a rock.

''scuse me,' said the Elephant's Child most politely, 'but have you seen such a thing as a Crocodile in these **promiscuous**② parts?'

'Have I seen a Crocodile?' said the Bi-Coloured-Python-Rock-Snake, in a voice of dreadful **scorn**③. 'What will you ask me next?'

''scuse me,' said the Elephant's Child, 'but could you kindly tell me what he has for dinner?'

Then the Bi-Coloured-Python-Rock-Snake **uncoiled**④ himself very quickly from the rock, and spanked the Elephant's Child with his **scalesome**⑤, **flailsome**⑥ tail.

'That is odd,' said the Elephant's Child, 'because my father and my mother, and my uncle and my aunt, **not to mention**⑦ my other aunt, the Hippopotamus, and my other uncle, the Baboon, have all spanked me for my 'satiable curtiosity—and I **suppose**⑧ this is the same thing.'

So he said good-bye very politely to the Bi-Coloured-Python-Rock-Snake, and helped to **coil** him **up**⑨ on the rock again, and went on, a little warm, but not at all astonished, eating melons, and throwing the rind about, because he could not pick it up, till he trod on what he thought was a log of wood **at the very edge of**⑩ the great grey-green, greasy Limpopo River, all set about with fever-trees.

But it was really the Crocodile, O Best Beloved, and the Crocodile winked one eye—like this!

① curled /kə:ld/ 卷曲的

② promiscuous /prə'mɪskjuəs/ a. 杂乱的,混杂的

③ scorn /skɔ:n/ v. 轻蔑

④ uncoil /ˌʌn'kɔɪl/ v. 解,解开

⑤ scalesome 长满鳞片的
⑥ flailsome 形如鞭子一样的

⑦ not to mention 更别提

⑧ suppose /sə'pəuz/ v. 推想,假设

⑨ coil up 卷起来,缠起来

⑩ at the very edge of 在…的边缘

波波大河岸边。正像咕噜咕噜鸟所说的那样,这里长着很多蓝桉树。

亲爱的读者,你可一定要明白,直到那一周、那一天、那一时、那一刻,这只好奇的小象还从未亲眼见过鳄鱼,不知道鳄鱼长得什么模样。它只是好奇心太强了。

在这里,它看到的第一样东西就是一条缠绕在巨石上的双色大蟒蛇。

"劳驾,"小象很有礼貌地问道,"您在这个乱七八糟的地方见到过鳄鱼没有?"

"我见过鳄鱼没有?"双色大蟒蛇轻蔑地说道,"你下一个问题是什么?"

"劳驾,"小象问,"您能告诉我它吃些什么东西吗?"

大蟒蛇迅速把身体伸直,从岩石上下来,然后用它那长满鳞片、像鞭子一样的尾巴抽打着小象的屁股。

"好奇怪,"小象说,"因为我的好奇心太强,我的爸爸、妈妈、叔叔、婶婶,还有那个海马姑姑,那个狒狒舅舅,都打我的屁股——这没什么好奇怪的,都一样。"

小象很有礼貌地与双色大蟒蛇道别,并帮助它把身体重新缠绕在巨石上。然后小象又出发了,有点生气,但并不惊讶,一路上吃着甜瓜,把瓜皮扔得到处都是,因为它捡不起来。它走啊走啊,最后碰到一样东西,它以为是长满蓝桉树的丽姆波波河边上的圆木。

· 067 ·

'Savse me,' said the Elephant's Child most politely, 'but do you happen to have seen a Crocodile in these promiscuous parts?'

Then the Crocodile winked the other eye, and **lifted**① half his tail out of the mud; and the Elephant's Child **stepped back**② most politely, because he did not wish to be spanked again.

'Come hither, Little One,' said the Crocodile. 'Why do you ask such things?'

"Savse me," said the Elephant's Child most politely, 'but my father has spanked me, my mother has spanked me, not to mention my tall aunt, the Ostrich, and my tall uncle, the Giraffe, who can kick ever so hard, as well as my broad aunt, the Hippopotamus, and my hairy uncle, the Baboon, and including the Bi-Coloured-Python-Rock-Snake, with the scah some, flailsome tail, just up the bank, who spanks harder than any them; and so, if it's quite all the same to you, I don't want to be spanked any more.'

'Come hither, Little One,' said the Crocodile, 'for I am the Crocodile,' and he wept **crocodile-tears**③ to show it was quite true.

Then the Elephant's Child grew all **breathless**④, and panted, and **kneel down**⑤ on the bank and said, 'You are the very person I have been lookin for all these long days. Will you please tell me what you have for dinner?'

'Come hither, Little One,' said the Crocodile, 'and I'll **whisper**⑥.'

Then the Elephant's Child put his head down close to the Crocodile'**musky**⑦, **tusky**⑧ mouth, and the Crocodile caught him by his little nose which up to that very week, day, hour, and minute, had been no bigger than a boot, though much more useful.

'I think,' said the Crocodile—and he said it between his teeth, like this—'I think today I will begin with Elephant's Child!'

At this, O Best Beloved, the Elephant's Child was much **annoyed**⑨,

远古传奇

① lift /lɪft/ v. 升高，举起
② step back 退回去

③ crocodile-tear 鳄鱼的眼泪，假慈悲的泪
④ breathless /ˈbreθlɪs/ a. 喘不过气来的
⑤ kneel down 跪下来

⑥ whisper /ˈ(h)wɪspə/ v. 耳语，密谈
⑦ musky /ˈmʌski/ a. 麝香气味的
⑧ tusky /ˈtʌski/ a. 有獠牙的

⑨ annoyed /əˈnɔɪd/ adj. 烦闷的

其实那不是圆木，而是一条鳄鱼。啊，亲爱的读者，鳄鱼眨着一只眼——就像这样！

"打扰一下，"小象非常有礼貌地问，"您在这个乱七八糟的地方是否碰巧见过鳄鱼？"

鳄鱼又眨着另一只眼，把半截尾巴从淤泥中翘起来。小象很有礼貌地后退了一步，因为它可不想再被打屁股了。

"过来，小家伙，"鳄鱼说，"你为什么问这个问题？"

"对不起，"小象很有礼貌地回答道，"我爸爸打我的屁股，妈妈打我的屁股，更别提高个子鸵鸟婶婶、踢我踢得生疼的高个子长颈鹿叔叔了，还有那个胖胖的海马姑姑和长毛狒狒舅舅。连河上游那个双色大蟒蛇也用它那长满鳞片的、鞭子一样的尾巴打我的屁股，打得比谁都狠。所以，如果你和它们一样，我可不想再被打了。"

"过来，小家伙，"鳄鱼说，"我就是鳄鱼，"然后它流了几滴鳄鱼的眼泪证明自己的话。

小象几乎停止了呼吸。它的心怦怦跳着，跪倒在岸边说："这些日子我一直在找你。你能告诉我你吃什么东西吗？"

"过来，小家伙，"鳄鱼说，"我悄悄告诉你。"

于是小象就把头靠近鳄鱼长着像狗鱼一样的獠牙的大嘴，突然，鳄鱼一下子咬住了它的鼻

· 069 ·

and he said, speaking through his nose, like this, 'Led go! You are hurtig me!'

Then the Bi-Coloured-Python-Rock-Snake **scuffled**① down from the bank and said, 'My young friend, if you do not now, immediately and **instantly**②, pull as hard as ever you can, it is my opinion that your **acquaintance**③ in the large-pattern leather ulster' (and by this he meant the Crocodile), 'will **jerk**④ you into yonder **limpid**⑤ stream before you can say Jack Robinson.'

This is the way Bi-Coloured-Python-Rock-Snake always talked.

Then the Elephant's Child sat back on his little **haunches**⑥, and pulled, and pulled, and pulled, and his nose began to **stretch**⑦. And the Crocodile **floundered**⑧ into the water, making it all **creamy**⑨ with great sweeps of his tail, and he pulled, and pulled, and pulled.

And the Elephant's Child's nose kept on stretching; and the Elephant's Child spread all his little four legs and pulled, and pulled, and pulled, and his nose kept on stretching; and the Crocodile **threshed**⑩ his tail like an **oar**⑪, and he pulled, and pulled, and pulled, and at each pull the Elephant's Child's nose grew longer and longer—and it hurt him hijjus!

Then the Elephant's Child felt his legs **slipping**⑫, and he said through his nose, which was now nearly five feet long, 'This is too **butch**⑬ for be!'

Then the Bi-Coloured-Python-Rock-Snake came down from the bank, and **knotted**⑭ himself in a double-clove-hitch round the Elephant's Child's hind legs, and said, '**Rash**⑮ and inexperienced traveller, we will now seriously **devote ourselves to**⑯ a little high **tension**⑰, because if we do not, it is my impression that yonder self-propelling man-of-war with the **armour**⑱-plated upper deck' (and by this, O Best Beloved, he meant the Crocodile), 'will **permanently**⑲ **vitiate**⑳ your future career.'

① scuffle /'skʌfl/ v. 混战
② instantly /'ɪnstəntlɪ/ ad. 立即地
③ acquaintance /ə'kweɪntəns/ n. 熟人，相识
④ jerk /dʒɜːk/ v. 急推，急动
⑤ limpid /'lɪmpɪd/ a. 清澈的
⑥ haunch /hɔːntʃ/ n. ，腰部
⑦ stretch /stretʃ/ v. 伸展，张开
⑧ flounder /'flaʊndə/ v. 挣扎，折腾
⑨ creamy /'kriːmɪ/ a. 含乳脂的

⑩ thresh /θreʃ/ 反复的打击
⑪ oar /ɔː; /eɪ/ n. 桨，橹

⑫ slipping /'slɪpɪŋ/ a. 渐渐松弛的

⑬ butch 男性化的
⑭ knotted /'nɒtɪd/ a. 有节的，
⑮ rash /ræʃ/ a. 轻率的，匆忙
⑯ devote oneselves to 投：身于
⑰ tension /'tenʃən/ n. 紧张
⑱ armour n. 甲胄，铁甲
⑲ permanently /'pɜːməntlɪ/ ad. 永久地
⑳ vitiate /'vɪʃɪeɪt/ v. 伤，损害

子。在那一周、那一天、那一时、那一刻之前，这鼻子虽然还管用，但长得还没有一只皮靴大。

"我想，"鳄鱼从牙缝里挤出几个字，"我想今天开始吃大象的孩子。"

听了这话，小象很生气，它带着鼻音（就像这样）说："放呆（开）我！我很冻（痛）——！"

这时双色大蟒蛇从岸边滑了过来，说："亲爱的小朋友，如果你现在不赶快使出吃奶的劲儿往外拽鼻子，那么在你喊出杰克·罗伯逊之前，对面的那个大号皮外套（它指的是鳄鱼）就会把你拖进远处清澈的小溪里。"

双色大蟒蛇说起话来老是这样。

小象用自己的屁股坐起来，拔啊拔啊，拔啊拔啊，鼻子被抻长了。而鳄鱼跳进水里，尾巴把水搅得浑浑的。它也在拔啊拔啊。

小象的鼻子不断地被拉长；它伸出四只小短腿使劲地从鳄鱼嘴里拽出鼻子，结果鼻子越来越长；而鳄鱼的尾巴像船桨一样猛烈地摆动着，它也拼命地拉着。每拉一下，小象的鼻子就被抻长一截——它疼极了！

小象脚下一滑，鼻子被抻得差不多有五英尺长。它拖着长长的鼻音说："我臭（受）不了了！"

这时双色大蟒蛇又从岸上滑过来，用自己的身体在小象的后腿上打了一个双重丁香结，对小象说："你这个小旅行家太鲁莽，没有经验。我们现在必须集中精力，全力以赴，否则你的未来

That is the way all Bi-Coloured-Python-Rock Snakes always talk.

So he pulled, and the Elephant's Child pulled, and the Crocodile pulled; but the Elephant's Child and the Bi-Coloured-Python-Rock-Snake pulled hardest; and at last the Crocodile let go of the Elephant's Child's nose with a **plop**① that you could hear all up and down the Limpopo.

Then the Elephant's Child sat down most hard and sudden; but first he was careful to say 'Thank you' to the Bi-Coloured-Python-Rock-Snake; and next he was kind to his poor pulled nose, and **wrapped** it all **up**② in cool banana leaves, and hung it in the great grey-green, greasy Limpopo to cool.

'What are you doing that for?' said the Bi-Coloured-Python-Rock-Snake.

'Scuse me,' said the Elephant's Child, 'but my nose is badly **out of shape**③, and I am waiting for it to **shrink**④.'

'Then you will have to wait a long time,' said the Bi-Coloured-Python-Rock-Snake. 'Some people do not know what is good for them.'

The Elephant's Child sat there for three days waiting for his nose to shrink. But it never grew any. shorter, and, besides, it made him **squint**⑤. For, O Best Beloved, you will see and understand that the Crocodile had pulled it out into a really truly trunk same as all Elephants have today.

At the end of the third day a fly came and **stung**⑥ him on the shoulder, and before he knew what he was doing he **lifted up**⑦ his trunk and hit that fly dead with the end of it.

''Vantage number one!' said the Bi-Coloured-Python-Rock-Snake. 'You couldn't have done that with a mere-**smear**⑧ nose. Try and eat a little now.'

① plop /plɒp/ n. 掉下的声音

② wrap up 裹起来

③ out of shape 处于不良的状况
④ shrink /ʃrɪŋk/ v. 收缩，退缩

⑤ squint /skwɪnt/ v. 使变斜视眼

⑥ sting /stɪŋ/ v. 刺
⑦ lift up 举起

⑧ smear /smɪə/ n. 油迹，污点

就会葬送在那条上层是装甲钢甲板的军舰（它指的是鳄鱼）手里。"

这就是大蟒蛇惯常的说话方式。

于是大蟒蛇拉，小象拉，鳄鱼也拉，小象和大蟒蛇最用力，最后鳄鱼扑通一声松开了小象的鼻子——你都能听到丽姆波波河波浪上下翻滚的声音。

小象一屁股坐在地上。但它先是有礼貌地向双色大蟒蛇表示感谢，然后心疼起自己被拉长的鼻子。它用冰凉的香蕉叶把鼻子包起来，然后悬在灰绿色、滑腻腻的丽姆波波河上让鼻子冷却下来。

"你这是干什么？"双色大蟒蛇问道。

"对不起，"小象说，"我的鼻子被拽得走形了。我在等它缩回去。"

"那你可得等很长时间，"双色大蟒蛇说，"有些人就是不知好歹。"

小象在那里坐了三天，等着鼻子缩回去像原来一样。但鼻子什么变化也没有，而且小象还把眼睛拽斜了。亲爱的读者，是鳄鱼把小象的鼻子拉成了现在这个样子，长成了真正的象鼻。

第三天晚上，一只苍蝇飞过来，叮在小象的肩膀上。小象连想都没有想，便挥起鼻子，用鼻子尖儿打死了苍蝇。

"优势之一！"双色大蟒蛇说，"你原来的那个小鼻子可做不到这一点。现在试着吃点东西。"

Just So Stories

Before he thought what he was doing the Elephant's Child put out his trunk and **plucked**① a large **bundle**② of grass, dusted it clean against his forelegs, and **stuffed**③ it into his mouth.

'Vantage number two!' said the Bi-Coloured-Python-Rock-Snake. 'You couldn't have done that with a mere-smear nose. Don't you think the sun is very hot here?'

'It is,' said the Elephant's Child, and before he thought what he was doing he **schlooped**④ up a schloop of mud from the banks of the great grey-green, greasy Limpopo, and **slapped**⑤ it on his head, where it made a cool schloopy-sloshy mud-cap all trickly behind his ears.

' Vantage number three! ' said the Bi-Coloured-Python-Rock-Snake. 'You couldn't have done that with a mere-smear nose. Now how do you feel about being spanked again?'

'Scuse me,' said the Elephant's Child, 'but I should not like it at all.'

'How would you like to spank somebody?' said the Bi-Coloured-Python-Rock-Snake.

'I should like it very much indeed,' said the Elephant's Child.

'Well,' said the Bi-Coloured-Python-Rock-Snake, 'you will find that new nose of yours very useful to spank people with.'

'Thank you,' said the Elephant's Child, ' I'll remember that; and now I think I'll go home to all my dear families and try.'

So the Elephant's Child went home across Africa **frisking**⑥ and **whisking**⑦ his trunk. When he wanted fruit to eat he pulled fruit down from a tree, instead of waiting for it to fall as he used to do. When he wanted grass he plucked grass up from the ground, instead of going on his knees as he used to do. When the flies bit him he **broke off**⑧ the branch of a tree and used it as a fly-whisk; and he made himself a new, cool, **slushy-squshy**⑨ mud-cap whenever the sun was hot. When he felt lonely walking through Africa he sang to himself down his trunk, and

① pluck /plʌk/ v. 摘,猛拉
② bundle /ˈbʌndl/ n. 捆,束
③ stuff /stʌf/ v. 塞满,填充
④ schloop 唱
⑤ slap /slæp/ v. 拍击

⑥ frisk /frɪsk/ v. &n. 蹦跳
⑦ whisk /(h)wɪsk/ n. 扫帚,毛掸子,
⑧ break off 折断

⑨ slushy-squshy 泥泞的

小象连想都没想，就用鼻子拔起一堆草，用前腿顶着，掸去尘土，然后塞进嘴里。

"优势之二！"双色大蟒蛇说，"你原来那个小鼻子可做不到这一点。你不觉得这儿的阳光很毒吗？"

"是的，"小象回答道。它想都没想就用鼻子从河岸上舀起一捧湿土拍在自己的头上，给自己在耳后戴上了一顶凉爽的泥帽。

"优势之三！"双色大蟒蛇说，"你原来那个小鼻子可做不到这一点。现在你对自己被打屁股作何感想？"

"对不起，"小象说，"我不喜欢被打。"

"想打别人吗？"双色大蟒蛇问。

"再想不过了，"小象回答道。

"那么，"双色大蟒蛇说，"你会发现新鼻子可是个打人的好帮手。"

"谢谢您，"小象说，"我会记住的。我想我该回家了，到家后再试试。"

于是小象就穿过非洲大陆，摆动着鼻子踏上归途。它想吃水果的时候就用鼻子直接到树上去摘，不用像以前那样等着果子掉下来；想吃草的时候，就用鼻子把草拔起来，不用像以前那样还得跪下来；如果有苍蝇来叮咬，就用鼻子折下一根树枝来回驱赶苍蝇；太阳晒的时候，就给自己戴上一顶凉爽的新泥帽。独自在非洲行走的时候，如果感到孤独，它就给自己唱歌，声音向下通过鼻子传出去，比几个乐队的演奏还要响。为了验证双色大蟒蛇的话，小

the noise was louder than several **brass**① bands. He went **especially**② out of his way to find a broad Hippopotamus (she was no **relation**③ of his), and he spanked her very hard, to **make**④ sure that the Bi-Coloured-Python-Rock-Snake had spoken the truth about his new trunk. The rest of the time he picked up the melon rinds that he had dropped on his way to the Limpopo—for he was a Tidy Pachyderm.

One dark evening he came back to all his dear families, and he coiled up his trunk and said, 'How do you do?' They were very glad to see him, and immediately said, 'Come here and be spanked for your 'satiable curtiosity.'

'Pooh,' said the Elephant's Child. 'I don't think you peoples know anything about spanking; but I do, and I'll show you.'

Then he **uncurled**⑤ his trunk and knocked two of his dear brothers head over heels.

'O Bananas!' said they, 'where did you learn that **trick**⑥, and what have you done to your nose?'

'I got a new one from the Crocodile on the banks of the great grey-green, greasy Limpopo River,' said the Elephant's Child. 'I asked him what he had for dinner, and he gave me this to keep.'

'It looks very ugly,' said his hairy uncle, the Baboon.

'It does,' said the Elephant's Child. 'But it's very useful,' and he picked up his hairy uncle, the Baboon, by one hairy leg, and **hove**⑦ him into a **hornets'**⑧ nest.

Then that bad Elephant's Child spanked all his dear families for a long time, till they were very warm and greatly **astonished**⑨. He pulled out his tall Ostrich aunt's **tail-feathers**⑩; and he caught his tall uncle, the Giraffe, by the **hind-leg**⑪, and dragged him through a thorn-bush; and he **shouted**⑫ at his **broad**⑬ aunt, the Hippopotamus, and blew **bubbles**⑭ into her ear when she was sleeping in the water after meals;

① brass /brɑːs/ n. 黄铜
② especially /ɪsˈpeʃəlɪ/ ad. 特别，尤其
③ relation /rɪˈleɪʃən/ n. 关系，亲戚
④ make sure 确保

⑤ uncurl /ˈʌnˈkəːl/ vt. 弄直
⑥ trick /trɪk/ n. 诡计，欺诈 v. 戏弄，欺骗

⑦ hove /həʊv/ v. 举起
⑧ hornet /ˈhɔːnɪt/ n. 大黄蜂类，难缠的人物
⑨ astonish /əˈstɒnɪʃ/ v. 使...惊讶
⑩ tail-feather 尾巴羽毛
⑪ hind-leg 后腿
⑫ shout /ʃaʊt/ v. 呼喊
⑬ broad /brɔːd/ a. 宽广的
⑭ bubble /ˈbʌbl/ n. 泡沫

象还特意找到一头胖海马（这头海马可不是小象的亲戚），狠狠地打了它的屁股。余下的时间，小象都用来捡那些来时扔在地上的瓜皮了——它可是个爱清洁的厚皮动物。

小象终于在一个漆黑的夜晚回到了家里。它卷起鼻子说："你们都好吗？"大家见到它很高兴，立即说："你的好奇心让你走到这儿来挨打。"

"噗——"，小象说，"你们这些人不知道什么是打屁股，可是我知道。我让你们开开眼。"

然后它伸直鼻子，把两个哥哥打了个倒栽葱。

"天哪，"大家惊叹道，"你在哪儿学的这本事？你鼻子怎么了？"

"我从灰绿色、滑腻腻的丽姆波波河的鳄鱼那里得到了一个新鼻子，"小象说，"我问它吃什么，结果它给了我这个。"

"看上去可真丑，"长毛狒狒舅舅说。

"是的，"小象答道，"但非常有用。"然后它就抓起长毛狒狒舅舅的一只毛茸茸的胳膊，把它卷起来塞进了马蜂窝。

在以后很长一段时间里，这个坏小子把家里的人打了个遍，家人被打得满腔怒火，惊骇万分。它拔掉了鸵鸟婶婶尾巴上的羽毛，抓住长颈鹿的后腿，把这个高个子叔叔拖进了一片荆棘林。小象还对着胖海马姑姑大喊大叫，趁它饭后睡觉时把石头扔进它的耳朵里——但它不允许任

but he never let any one **touch**① Kolokolo Bird.

At last② things grew so exciting that his dear families **went off**③ one by one **in a hurry**④ to the banks of the great grey-green, greasy Limpopo River, all set about with fever-trees, to borrow new noses from the Crocodile. When they came back nobody spanked anybody any more; and ever since that day, O Best Beloved, all the Elephants you will ever see besides all those that you won't, have trunks precisely like the trunk of the 'satiable Elephant's Child.

① touch /tʌtʃ/ v. 接触
② at last 最终
③ go off 离开
④ in a hurry 急匆匆的

何人碰那只咕噜咕噜鸟。

　　到后来，这个大家庭可就热闹了——它们一个一个急匆匆地赶到灰绿色、滑腻腻、长着一片蓝桉树的丽姆波波河，向鳄鱼要长长的象鼻子。回来以后，它们谁也不打谁了。从那一天开始，亲爱的读者，你看到的大象都像那个好奇的小象一样，甩着一只长长的鼻子。

Just So Stories

This is the Elephant's Child having his nose pulled by the Crocodile. He is much surprised and astonished and hurt, and he is talking through his nose and saying, 'Led go①! You are hurtig me!' He is pulling very hard, and so is the Crocodile; but the BiColoured-Python-Rock-Snake is hurrying through the water to help the Elphant's Child. All that black **stuff**② is the banks of the great gray-green, greasy Limpopo River (but I am not allowed to paint these pictures), and the bottly-tree with the twisty roots and the eight leaves is one of the fever trees that grow there.

Underneath③ the truly picture are **shadows**④ of African animals walking into an African **ark**⑤. There are two lions, two ostriches, two oxen, two camels, two sheep, and two other things that look like **rats**⑥, but I think they are rock-rabbits. They don't mean anything. I put them in because I thought they looked **pretty**⑦. They would look very fine if I were allowed to paint them.

小象的鼻子被鳄鱼抻长了。它又惊又疼,拖着长长的鼻音说:"放呆(开)我,我很冻(痛)——!"它使劲地拉,鳄鱼也使劲地拉。双色大蟒蛇正飞快地越过水流去帮助大象的孩子。图中的黑色部分就是灰绿色、滑腻腻的丽姆波波河(我可不能给它涂上颜色)。那棵长着八片叶子、根部盘绕的瓶状树就是生长在那里的蓝桉树。

下面是一幅影子图,描绘了非洲动物走进非洲方舟的情景。其中有两头狮子、两只鸵鸟、两头牛、两头骆驼、两只羊和另外两只看起来像老鼠似的东西,但我想那应该是野兔。这些动物没有什么特别的意义。我之所以把这幅画放在这里,是因为它很美。如果我能涂上颜色,这画看起来就更漂亮了。

远古传奇

① let go 放开

② stuff /stʌf/ n. 材料，东西

③ underneath /ˌʌndəˈniːθ/ ad. 在下面
④ shadow /ˈʃædəʊ/ n. 影像
⑤ ark /ɑːk/ n. 方舟
⑥ rat /ræt/ n. 鼠
⑦ pretty /ˈprɪtɪ/ a. 漂亮的

· 081 ·

Just So Stories

This is just a picture of the Elephant's Child going to **pull**① bananas **off** a **banana-tree**② after he had got his fine new long trunk. I don't think it is a very nice picture; but I couldn't make it any better, because elephants and bananas are hard to draw. The **streaky**③ things behind the Elephant's Child mean **squoggy**④ **marshy**⑤ country somewhere in africa. The Elephant's Child made most of his mud-cakes out of the mud that he found there. I think it would look better if you painted the banana-tree green and the Elephant's Child red.

这幅画描绘的是大象的孩子得到新鼻子后，用鼻子从香蕉树上采摘香蕉的情景。这画画得不太好，但没办法，因为大象和香蕉实在太难画了。小象后面条纹状的部分是非洲某处的沼泽地。小象的泥巴蛋糕大部分都是在那里做的。我想，如果把香蕉树涂上绿色，把小象涂成红色，那看上去就棒极了。

① pull off 从…拔下来，拉出来
② banana-tree 香蕉树
③ streaky /'stri:kɪ/ a. 有条纹的，有斑点的
④ squoggy 泥一般的
⑤ marshy /'mɑ:ʃɪ/ a. 沼泽般的

I keep six honest **serving-men**①:
(They taught me all I knew)
Their names are What and Why and When
And How and Where and Who.
I **send**② them over land and sea,
I send them east and west;
But after they have worked for me,
I give them all a **rest**③.
I let them rest **from** nine **till**④ five.
For I am busy then, as well as breakfast, lunch, and tea,
For they are **hungry**⑤ men:
But different **folk**⑥ have different **views**⑦:
I know a person small—
She keeps ten **million**⑧ serving-men,
Who get no rest at all She sends 'em **abroad**⑨ on her own **affairs**⑩,
From the second she opens her eyes—
One million Hows, two million Wheres,
And seven million Whys!

远古传奇

① serving-man 侍者

② send /send/ v. 送给,传
③ rest n. 休息
④ from...till 从…到…

⑤ hungry /ˈhʌŋgrɪ/ a. 饥饿的
⑥ folk /fəuk/ n. 人们
⑦ view /vjuː/ n. 见解
⑧ million /ˈmɪljən/ n. 百万
⑨ abroad /əˈbrɔːd/ ad. 到国外
⑩ affair /əˈfeə/ n. 事件,事情

我有六个忠实的仆人;
(我的知识都是它们教会的)
它们的名字分别是"什么"、"为什么"、"何时"
"怎么"、"哪里"和"谁"。
我派它们到陆地和海洋,
我派它们到东方和西方;
但等到工作结束后,
我就让它们休息一下
我让它们从九点休息到五点,
因为那时我很忙,
还要吃早饭,午饭并喝茶,
因为它们总是感到饥饿。
但不同的人有不同看法:
我认识一个小孩——
她有1000万个仆人,
整天不得休息。
从她一睁开眼,
就按自己的需要,
把仆人统统派到国外。
——100万个"怎么回事",
200万个"在哪里",
700万个"为什么"!

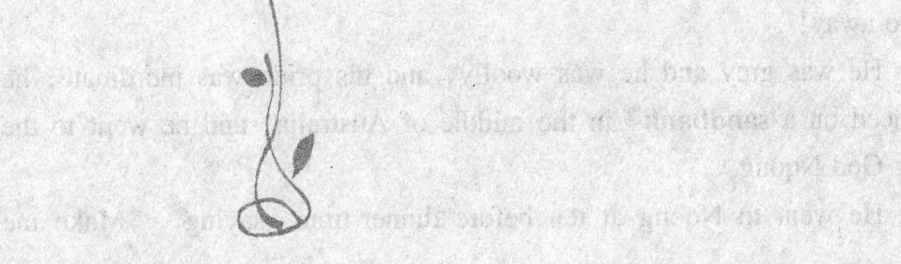

· 085 ·

The Sing-Song of Old Man Kangaroo

Not always was the Kangaroo as now we do **behold**① him, but a Different Animal with four short legs. He was grey and he was **woolly**②, and his pride was **inordinate**③; he danced on an **outcrop**④ in the middle of Australia, and he went to the Little God Nqa.

He went to Nqa at six before breakfast, saying, 'Make me different from all other animals by five this afternoon.'

Up jumped Nqa from his seat on the sand-tim and shouted, 'Go away!'

He was grey and he was woolly, and his pride was inordinate; he danced on a **rock-ledge**⑤ in the middle of Australia, and he went to the Middle God Nquing.

He went to Nquing at eight after breakfast, saying, ' Make me different from all other animals; make me, also, **wonderfully**⑥ popular by five this afternoon.'

Up jumped Nquing from his **burrow**⑦ in the **spinifex**⑧ and shouted, 'Go away!'

He was grey and he was woolly, and his pride was inordinate; he danced on a **sandbank**⑨ in the middle of Australia, and he went to the Big God Nqong.

He went to Nqong at ten before dinner-time, saying, 'Make me

一只老雄袋鼠的兄长乏味的故事

① behold /bɪˈhəʊld/ v. 看，注视
② woolly /ˈwʊlɪ/ a. 蓬乱的
③ inordinate /ɪnˈɔːdɪnɪt/ a. 过度的，非常的
④ outcrop /ˈaʊtkrɒp/ v. 露出

⑤ rock-ledge 石矿层

⑥ wonderfully /ˈwʌndəfəlɪ/ ad. 惊人地，极佳地
⑦ burrow /ˈbʌrəʊ/ v. 挖洞
⑧ spinifex /ˈspɪnɪfeks/ n. /植/ 三齿稃

⑨ sandbank /ˈsændbæŋk/ n. 沙洲，沙丘

很久很久以前，袋鼠可不是现在这个样子。那时它长着灰色的长毛，四条小短腿，整日趾高气扬。它在澳大利亚中部露出地表的岩石上又蹦又跳，然后去找小神灵恩卡。

早饭前六点钟的时候它找到恩卡，对恩卡说："在今天下午五点钟之前，把我变得和其他动物不一样！"

恩卡一下子从他沙土公寓的椅子上跳起来，对它吼道："滚！"

袋鼠毛茸茸的，整日趾高气扬。它在澳大利亚中部突起的岩石上又蹦又跳，然后去找大神灵恩奎。

早饭后八点钟它找到恩奎，对恩奎说："在今天下午五点钟之前，让我变得与众不同，而且极受欢迎！"

恩奎一下子从三齿稃洞穴里跳起来，对它吼道："滚！"

袋鼠毛茸茸的，整日趾高气扬。它在澳大利亚中部的沙洲上又蹦又跳，然后去找老精灵恩琼。

different from all other animals; make me popular and wonderfully run after by five this afternoon.'

Up jumped Nqong from his bath in the **salt-pan**① and shouted, 'Yes, I will!'

Nqong called Dingo—Yellow-Dog Dingo—always hungry, dusty in the sunshine, and showed him Kangaroo. Nqong said, 'Dingo! Wake up, Din-go! Do you see that gentleman dancing on an **ashpit**②? He wants to be popular and very truly run after. Dingo, make him so!'

Up jumped Dingo—Yellow-Dog Dingo—and said, 'What, that cat-rab-bit?'

Off ran Dingo—Yellow-Dog Dingo—always hungry, **grinning**③ like a **coalscuttle**④,—ran after Kangaroo.

Off went the proud Kangaroo on his four little legs like a **bunny**⑤.

This, O Beloved of mine, ends the first part of the tale!

He ran through the desert; he ran through the mountains; he ran through the salt-pans; he ran through the **reed**⑥-beds; he ran through the blue **gums**⑦; he ran through the spinifex; he ran till his front legs ached.

He had to!

Still ran Dingo—Yellow-Dog Dingo—always hungry, grinning like a **rattrap**⑧, never getting nearer, never getting farther,—ran after Kangaroo.

He had to!

Still ran Kangaroo—Old Man Kangaroo. He ran through the ti-trees; he ran through the **mulga**⑨; he ran through the long grass; he ran through the short grass; he ran through the **Tropics**⑩ of **Capricorn**⑪ and **Cancer**⑫; he ran till his **hind**⑬ legs ached.

He had to!

Still ran Dingo—Yellow-Dog Dingo—hungrier and hungrier, grinning

远古传奇

① salt-pan 盐田，盐场

② ashpit 灰坑

③ grin /grɪn/ v. 露齿而笑
④ coal-scuttle 煤斗
⑤ bunny /'bʌnɪ/ n. 小兔子

⑥ reed /riːd/ n. 芦苇
⑦ gum /gʌm/ n. 树胶，橡皮

⑧ rattrap /'ræt træp/ n. 捕鼠机

⑨ mulga 树林
⑩ tropics /'trɒpɪks/ n. 热带
⑪ capricorn /'kæprɪkɔːn/ n. 摩羯宫，
⑫ cancer /'kænsə/ n. 巨蟹座
⑬ hind /haɪnd/ a. 后部的

正餐前十点钟它找到恩琼，对恩琼说："今天下午五点钟之前把我变得与众不同，大受欢迎，而且大家都要追随我！"

恩琼一下子从盐田的浴盆里跳出来，对它大声吼道："好吧，我会的！"

恩琼召来了一只黄色的野狗。这只狗总是饥肠辘辘，在阳光下满身尘土。恩琼把它领到袋鼠面前，说："狗！醒一醒！狗！看到那位在灰坑里跳舞的绅士了吗？它想受人爱戴并被人追随。狗！让它如愿吧！"

这只黄色的野狗一跃而起，问道："什么，是那只长得像猫的兔子吗？"

野狗总是饥肠辘辘，咧嘴一笑时像个煤斗。它"嗖——"地一声蹿了出去，开始猛追袋鼠。

那只骄傲的袋鼠也"嗖——"地一声蹿了出去，它的四只小短腿跑起来像只小兔子。

啊，亲爱的读者，这是故事的第一部分。

它穿过沙漠和高山，穿过盐田和芦苇地，又穿过一片片桉树林和三齿稃，跑得前腿发疼。

但袋鼠别无选择！

那只永远饥肠辘辘的野狗，咧嘴一笑时像个鼠夹子。它与袋鼠保持着一段不远不近的距离，不停地追逐着袋鼠。

袋鼠别无选择！

袋鼠还在跑——这只老雄袋鼠穿过铁树林、相思树林，穿过高高低低的草原，穿过南北回归线。它跑啊跑啊，后腿开始疼痛。

但它别无选择！

身后那只黄色的野狗还不远不近地追着。它

· 089 ·

like a horse-collar, never getting nearer, never getting farther; and they came to the Wollgong River.

Now, there wasn't any bridge, and there wasn't any **ferry-boat**①, and Kangaroo didn't know how to get over; so he stood on his legs and hopped.

He had to!

He hopped through the Flinders; he hopped through the Cinders; he hopped through the deserts in the middle of Australia. He hopped like a Kangaroo.

First he hopped one yard; then he hopped three yards; then he hopped five yards; his legs growing stronger; his legs growing longer. He hadn't any time for rest or **refreshment**②, and he wanted them very much.

Still ran Dingo—Yellow-Dog Dingo—very much **bewildered**③, very much hungry, and **wondering**④ what in the world or out of it made Old Man Kangaroo hop.

For he hopped like a **cricket**⑤; like a pea in a **saucepan**⑥; or a new rubber ball on a **nursery**⑦ floor.

He had to!

He **tucked up**⑧ his front legs; he hopped on his hind legs; he **stuck out**⑨ his tail for a balance-weight behind him; and he hopped through the Darling Downs.

He had to!

Still ran Dingo—Tired-Dog Dingo—hungrier and hungrier, very much bewildered, and wondering when in the world or out of it would Old Man Kangaroo stop.

Then came Nqong from his bath in the salt-pans, and said, 'It's five o'clock.'

Down sat Dingo—Poor Dog Dingo—always hungry, **dusky**⑩ in the sunshine; hung out his tongue and howled.

① ferry-boat *n.* 渡船

② refreshment /rɪˈfreʃmənt/ *n.* 提神之事物

③ bewildered /bɪˈwɪldəd/ *a.* 困惑的

④ wonder /ˈwʌndə/ *v.* 惊奇,想知道

⑤ cricket /ˈkrɪkɪt/ *n.* 蟋蟀

⑥ saucepan /ˈsɔːspən; (us) -pæn/ *n.* 长柄而有盖子的深锅子

⑦ nursery 托儿所

⑧ tuck up 折起

⑨ stick out 突出,伸出

⑩ dusky /ˈdʌskɪ/ *a.* 微黑的

似乎越来越饿,咧嘴一笑时像一只马颈圈。它们来到了乌鲁岗河边。

河上没有桥,河边也没有渡船。袋鼠不知道怎么才能过河,于是它直起身子开始齐足跳。

它别无选择!

它就这样跳过了碎石路,跳过了煤渣路,跳过了澳大利亚中部沙漠。它跳得像现在的袋鼠一样。

起初它能跳一码远,然后能跳三码远,然后能跳到五码远。它的后腿越来越长,越来越壮。尽管它极想停下来休息或吃点东西,可它没时间。

那只黄色的野狗还在奔跑——它很迷惑,而且饥肠辘辘,不理解这只老袋鼠为什么能够跳着跑。

这只雄袋鼠跳起来像只蟋蟀,又像平底锅上的一粒豌豆,还像托儿所地板上落下的一只新皮球。

但袋鼠别无选择!

它把前腿蜷缩起来,用后腿跳跃,并伸出尾巴保持平衡。就这样,它又跳跃着穿过了达灵温带草原。

但袋鼠别无选择!

那只野狗已经筋疲力尽,但还在跑着。它越跑越饿,而且越来越困惑,不明白是什么力量让袋鼠跳跃起来。

这时恩琼从盐田浴池里走出来,说:"五点钟了。"

那只可怜的饥肠辘辘的野狗,扑通一声坐在了地上。它在阳光下满身灰尘,伸出舌头开始嚎叫。

· 091 ·

Down sat Kangaroo—Old Man Kangaroo—stuck out lis tail like a milking-stool behind him, and said, 'Thank goodness that's finished!'

Then said Nqong, who is always a gentleman, 'Why aren't you **grateful**① to Yellow-Dog Dingo? Why, don't you thank him for all he has done for you?'

Then said Kangaroo—Tired Old Kangaroo—'He's **chased**② me out of the homes of my childhood; he's chased me out of my **regular**③ meal-times; he's **altered**④ my shape so I'll never get it back; and he's played Old Scratch with my legs.'

Then said Nqong, 'Perhaps I'm mistaken, but didn't you ask me to make you different from all other animals, as well as to make you very truly sought after? And now it is five o'clock.'

'Yes,' said Kangaroo. 'I wish that I hadn't. I thought you would do it by **charms**⑤ and **incantations**⑥, but this is a **practical joke**⑦.'

'Joke!' said Nqong from his bath in the blue gums. 'Say that again and I'll **whistle**⑧ up Dingo and run your hind legs off.'

'No,' said the Kangaroo. 'I must **apologise**⑨. Legs are legs, and you needn't alter 'em so far as I am **concerned**⑩. I only **meant to**⑪ explain to Your **Lordliness**⑫ that I've had nothing to eat since morning, and I'm very empty indeed.'

'Yes,' said Dingo—Yellow-Dog Dingo, —'I am just in the same situation. I've made him different from all other animals; but what may I have for my tea?'

Then said Nqong from his bath in the salt-pan, 'Come and ask me about it tomorrow, because I'm going to wash.'

So they were left in the middle of Australia, Old Man Kangaroo and Yel-low-Dog Dingo, and each said, 'That's your **fault**⑬.'

远古传奇

① grateful /'greɪtful/ a. 感激的,感谢的

② chase /tʃeɪs/ v. 追捕,追逐

③ regular /'regjulə/ a. 有规律的

④ alter /'ɔ:ltə/ v. 改变

⑤ charm /tʃɑ:m/ n. 魔力

⑥ incantations /ɪnkæn'teɪʃən/ n. 诀语,咒语

⑦ a practical joke /'præktɪkəl 'dʒəuk/ n. 恶作剧

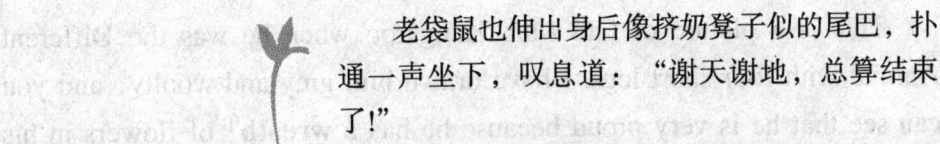

⑧ whistle /(h)wɪsl/ v. 吹口哨 n. 口哨

⑨ apologise /ə'pɒlədʒaɪz/ v. 道歉

⑩ concerned /kən'sɜ:nd/ v. 与...有关

⑪ mean to 打算

⑫ lordliness n. 贵族式,

⑬ fault /fɔ:lt/ n. 过失

老袋鼠也伸出身后像挤奶凳子似的尾巴,扑通一声坐下,叹息道:"谢天谢地,总算结束了!"

恩琼一向彬彬有礼,很有风度。他说:"你为什么不感谢野狗呢?为什么不谢谢它为你所做的一切呢?"

筋疲力尽的袋鼠说:"它追着我离开了童年的故土,我正常的就餐时间被它破坏了,而且它改变了我的形象,我再也变不回原来的模样了,还对我的腿施了魔法。"

恩琼说:"也许是我犯了个错误,但你难道没有让我把你变得与众不同,让人追随?现在已经是五点钟了。"

"是的,"袋鼠说,"我希望我没那样做过。我想你能用魔法和咒语实现我的愿望。结果却搞成了一场恶作剧。"

"恶作剧!"泡在桉树林浴池里的恩琼说道,"如果你再说一遍,我会吹声口哨,让野狗追得你后腿掉下来。"

"不,"袋鼠说,"我道歉。腿还是腿,你不要再变了。我只想向阁下解释我从早上起来还没吃一点儿东西,现在简直是饥饿难耐。"

"是的,"黄色的野狗说,"我也一样。是我让它变得与众不同的,可我的下午茶点又在哪儿呢?"

恩琼躺在盐田的浴池里说:"明天上午再来问我这个问题。现在我要洗澡了。"

于是袋鼠和野狗离开了澳大利亚中部,边走边互相指责着:"都是你的错。"

· 093 ·

This is a picture of Old Man Kangaroo when he was the Different Animal with four short legs. I have drawn him grey and woolly, and you can see that he is very proud because he has a **wreath**① of flowers in his hair. He is dancing on an outcrop（that means a **ledge**② of rock）in the middle of **Australia**③ at six o'clock before breakfast. You can see that it is six o'clock, because the sun is just **getting up**④. The thing with the ears and the open mouth is Little God Nqa. Nqa is very much **surprised**⑤, because he has never seen a **Kangaroo**⑥ dance like that before. Little God Nqa is just saying, '**Go away**⑦,' but the Kangaroo is so busy dancing that he has not heard him yet.

The Kangaroo hasn't any real name **except**⑧ Boomer. He **lost**⑨ it because he was so proud.

图上是很久以前老袋鼠的模样。它那时与现在的袋鼠不一样，长着四条小短腿。它身上的毛又灰又长，头上戴着一顶花环，非常骄傲。早饭前六点钟，它在澳大利亚中部突出的岩石上又蹦又跳。你能看出当时是早上六点，因为太阳刚刚升起。对面那个长着耳朵、嘴巴张得大大的人就是小精灵恩卡。恩卡很惊讶，因为这以前他从未看到过袋鼠这样跳舞。小精灵恩卡正对袋鼠说："滚！"但袋鼠跳得正欢，它没有听到。

除了"老雄袋鼠"外，它没有别的名字。这是因为它太骄傲了。

远古传奇

① wreath /ri:θ/ n. 花环,花圈
② ledge /ledʒ/ n. 突出之部份,矿层
③ Australia /ɔ'streiliə/ n. 澳大利亚
④ get up 起床
⑤ surprised /sə'praizd/ a. 感到惊讶的
⑥ Kangaroo /kæŋgə'ru:/ n. 袋鼠
⑦ go away vt. 离开(走掉)
⑧ except /ɪk'sept/ prep. 除了...之外
⑨ lose /lu:z/ v. 遗失

This is the picture of Old Man Kangaroo at five in the afternoon, when he had got his beautiful hind legs just as the Big God Nqong had promised. You can see that it is five o'clock, because Big God Nqong's pet tame clock says so. That is Nqong, in his bath, saying "go away". Old Man Kangaroo is being rude to Yellow Dog Dingo. Yellow Dog Dingo has been trying to catch Kangaroo all across Australia. You can see the marks of Kangaroo's big new feet running ever so far back over the bare hills. Yellow Dog Dingo is drawn black, because I am not allowed to paint these pictures with real colours out of the paint-box; and besides, Yellow Dog Dingo got dreadfully black and dusty after running through the Flinders and the Cinders.

I don't know the names of the flowers growing round Nqong's bath. The two little squatty things out in the desert are the other two gods that Old Man Kangaroo spoke to early in the morning. That thing with the letters on it is Old Man Kangaroo's pouch. He had to have a pouch just as he had to have legs.

| Just So Stories

This is the picture of Old Man Kangaroo at five in the afternoon, when he had got his beautiful hind legs just as Big God Nqong had **promised**①. You can see that it is five o'clock, because Big God Nqong's **pet tame**② clock says so. That is Nqong, in his bath, **sticking** his feet **out**③. Old Man Kangaroo is being **rude**④ to Yellow-Dog Dingo. Yellow-Dog Dingo has been trying to catch kangaroo all across Australia. You can see the marks of Kangaroo's big new feet tuning ever so far back over the **bare**⑤ hills. Yellow-Dog Dingo is drawn black, because I am not allowed to paint these pictures with real colours out of the paint-box; and **besides**⑥, Yellow-Dog Dingo got dreadfully black and dusty after running through the **Flinders**⑦ and the **Cinders**⑧.

I don't know the names of the flowers growing round Nqong's bath. The two little **squatty**⑨ things out in the desert are the other two gods that Old Man Kangaroo spoke to early in the morning. That thing with the letters on it is Old Man Kangaroo's **pouch**⑩. He had to have a pouch just as he had to have legs.

下午五点钟，正像老精灵恩琼允诺得那样，老袋鼠长出了漂亮的后腿。你可以看出这是下午五点钟，因为老精灵的宠物钟的指针正指向五点。恩琼正在洗澡，两只脚丫伸在外面。老袋鼠对野狗很粗鲁。这只黄色的野狗试图抓住袋鼠，追着它穿越了整个澳大利亚。你可以看到袋鼠新后爪印遍布它们身后光秃秃的小山。黄色的野狗被涂成了黑色，因为我不能用色彩盒里的真实颜色为它上色。而且，这只野狗追随着袋鼠穿越了碎石路和煤渣路，它变得漆黑无比，且满身灰尘。

恩琼的浴池边上长着一些花，我不知道花的名字。沙漠里那两个矮胖的人是另外两个精灵，袋鼠上午和他们讲过话。袋鼠身上写着字母的东西是它的肚囊。它不得不长这个肚囊，就像它不得不长那样的腿一样。

① promise /ˈprɒmɪs/ n. 诺言, 约定
② pet name 昵称, 爱称
③ stick out 突出
④ rude /ruːd/ a. 粗鲁的
⑤ bare /bɛə/ a. 赤裸的, 荒凉的
⑥ besides /bɪˈsaɪdz/ prep. 除…之外
⑦ flinders /ˈflɪndəz/ n. 破片
⑧ cinder /ˈsɪndə/ n. 煤渣, 灰烬
⑨ squatty /ˈskwɒtɪ/ a. 矮胖的
⑩ pouch /paʊtʃ/ n. 小袋, 小包

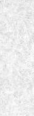

This is the **mouth-filling**① song
Of the **race**② that was run by a Boomer,
Run in a single **burst**③—only event of its kind—
Started by big God Nqong from Warrigaborrigarooma,
Old Man Kangaroo first; Yellow-Dog Dingo behind.
Kangaroo **bounded**④ away,
His back-legs working like **pistons**⑤—
Bounded from morning till dark
Twenty-five feet to a bound.
Yellow-Dog Dingo lay
Like a yellow cloud **in the distance**⑥—
Much too busy to bark.
My! But they covered the ground!
Nobody knows where they went,
Or followed the track that they flew in,
For that **Continent**⑦
Hadn't been given a name.
They ran thirty degrees,
From Torres Straits to the Leeuwin
(Look at the Atlas, please),
And they ran back as they came.
S'posing you could trot
From Adelaide to the Pacific,
For an afternoon's run—
Half what these gentlemen did—
You would feel rather hot,
But your legs would develop **terrific**⑧—
Yes, my **importunate**⑨ son,
You'd be a **Marvellous**⑩ Kid!

① mouth-filling a. 说大话的,很长的
② race /reɪs/ n. 赛跑
③ burst /bəːst/ v. 爆裂,突发
④ bound /baʊnd/ v. 跳跃
⑤ piston /ˈpɪstən/ n. 活塞
⑥ in the distance 在远处
⑦ continent /ˈkɒntɪnənt/ n. 大陆,洲
⑧ terrific /təˈrɪfɪk/ a. 极好的,非常的
⑨ importunate /ɪmˈpɔːtjunɪt/ a. 缠扰不休的
⑩ marvellous /ˈmɑːvɪləs/ a. 惊奇的

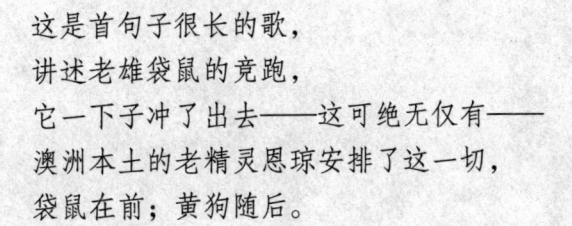

这是首句子很长的歌,
讲述老雄袋鼠的竞跑,
它一下子冲了出去——这可绝无仅有——
澳洲本土的老精灵恩琼安排了这一切,
袋鼠在前;黄狗随后。

袋鼠一路跳跃,
它的后腿像活塞,
从早晨跳到天黑,
一步25英尺。

远处跟着一只野狗,
像一片黄色的云彩,
忙着跑步,没空叫唤,
天哪!它们穿过了整个大地!
没有人知道它们跑向哪里,
或跟随它们的足迹,
从不知名的大陆,
它们跑了30度,
从托里斯海峡到卢因角,
(拜托你看看地图)
它们又跑了回来。

假设你能从阿德莱德跑到太平洋沿岸,
跑整整一个下午——
——只跑两位绅士路程的一半,
你会觉得炎热难耐,
但双腿会有美妙的发展,
是的,我纠缠不休的孩子,
你会变得了不起!

The Beginning of the Armadillos

This, O Best Beloved, is another story of the High and Far-Off Times. In the very middle of those times was a Stickly-Prickly **Hedgehog**[①], and he lived on the banks of the **turbid**[②] **Amazon**[③], eating **shelly**[④] **snails**[⑤] and things. And he had a friend, a Slow-Solid **Tortoise**[⑥], who lived on the banks of the turbid Amazon, eating green **lettuces**[⑦] and things. And so that was all right, Best Beloved. Do you see?

But also, and at the same time, in those High and Far-Off Times, there was a **Painted Jaguar**[⑧], and he lived on the banks of the turbid Amazon too; and he ate everything that he could catch. When he could not catch deer or monkeys he would eat frogs and beetles; and when he could not catch frogs and beetles he went to his Mother Jaguar, and she told him how to eat hedgehogs and tortoises.

She said to him ever so many times, **graciously**[⑨] waving her tail, 'My son, when you find a Hedgehog you must drop him into the water and then he will uncoil, and when you catch a Tortoise you must **scoop**[⑩] him out of his shell with your paw.' And so that was all right, Best Beloved.

One beautiful night on the banks of the turbid Amazon, Painted Jaguar found Stickly-Prickly Hedgehog, and Slow-Solid Tortoise sitting

犰狳的起源

① hedgehog /'hedʒhɔg/ n. 刺猬
② turbid /'tə:bɪd/ a. 混浊的
③ Amazon /'æməzən/ n. 亚马逊河
④ shelly /'ʃelɪ/ a. 多壳的
⑤ snail /sneɪl/ n. 蜗牛
⑥ tortoise /'tɔ:təs/ n. 龟
⑦ lettuce /'letɪs/ n. 莴苣
⑧ jaguar /'dʒægwɑ:/ n. 美洲虎

⑨ graciously /'greɪʃəslɪ/ ad. 仁慈地
⑩ scoop /sku:p/ v. 汲取，舀取

亲爱的读者，这又是一个发生在很久很久以前的故事。那时，在河水浑浊的亚马逊河岸，住着一只浑身是刺的刺猬，它以吃蜗牛和其他东西为生。它有一个朋友，是一只慢慢吞吞、稳稳当当的乌龟，也住在河水浑浊的亚马逊河岸，以吃绿莴苣和其他东西为生。就这样，亲爱的读者，明白吗？

也是在很久很久以前，河水浑浊的亚马逊河岸还住着一只美洲豹。它身上长着美丽的花纹，每日抓到什么就吃什么。抓不到鹿或猴子的时候，它就吃青蛙和甲虫；抓不到青蛙或甲虫的时候，它就去找妈妈。它妈妈便开始教它如何吃刺猬和乌龟。

豹妈妈优雅地摆动着尾巴，一遍又一遍地教它："我的儿子，如果抓到一只刺猬，你一定要把它扔进水里，这样它才会把身体平展开；抓到乌龟的时候，要用爪子把它从硬壳里挖出来。"就这样，亲爱的读者。

一个美好的夜晚，在亚马逊河岸，长满刺的刺猬和慢吞吞的乌龟正坐在一棵倒塌的树下，这

under the trunk of a fallen tree. They could not run away, and so Stickly-Prickly curled himself up into a ball, because he was a Hedgehog, and Slow-Solid Tortoise drew in his head and feet into his shell as far as they would go, because he was a Tortoise; and so *that* was all right, Best Beloved. Do you see?

'Now **attend**① to me,' said Painted Jaguar, 'because this is very important. My mother said that when I meet a Hedgehog I am to drop him into the water and then he will uncoil, and when I meet a Tortoise I am to scoop him out of his shell with my paw. Now which of you is Hedgehog and which is Tortoise? because, to save my **spots**②, I can't tell.'

'Are you sure of what your Mummy told you?' said Stickly-Prickly Hedgehog. 'Are you quite sure? Perhaps she said that when you uncoil a Tortoise you must shell him out of the water with a scoop, and when you paw a Hedgehog you must drop him on the shell.'

'Are you sure of what your Mummy told you?' said Slow-and-Solid Tortoise. 'Are you quite sure? Perhaps she said that when you water a Hedgehog you must drop him into your paw, and when you meet a Tortoise you must shell him till he uncoils.'

'I don't think it was at all like that,' said Painted Jaguar, but he felt a little **puzzled**③; 'but, please, say it again more **distinctly**④.'

'When you scoop water with your paw you uncoil it with a Hedgehog,' said Stickly-Prickly. 'Remember that, because it's important.'

'But,' said the Tortoise, 'when you paw your meat you drop it into a Tortoise with a scoop. Why can't you understand?'

'You are making my spots **ache**⑤,' said Painted Jaguar; 'and besides, I don't want your **advice**⑥ at all. I only wanted to know which of you is Hedgehog and which is Tortoise.'

远古传奇

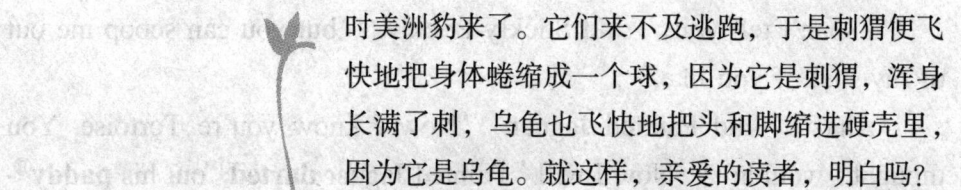

时美洲豹来了。它们来不及逃跑，于是刺猬便飞快地把身体蜷缩成一个球，因为它是刺猬，浑身长满了刺，乌龟也飞快地把头和脚缩进硬壳里，因为它是乌龟。就这样，亲爱的读者，明白吗？

"现在听我的，"美洲豹说，"这很重要。我妈妈说遇到刺猬的时候，就把它丢进水里，这样它的身体就平展开了；遇到乌龟的时候，我就用爪子把它从硬壳里挖出来，那么，你们哪一个是刺猬，哪一个是乌龟？我分辨不出来。你们告诉我，省省我的力气。"

"你能肯定你妈妈是那样说的吗？"浑身是刺的刺猬说，"你十分肯定吗？也许它说的是如果要取出乌龟肉，你得把它从水里捞出来，用勺子去掉它的壳；抓着刺猬的时候，必须从外表入手杀死它。"

"你能肯定你妈妈是那样说的吗？"慢慢吞吞、稳稳当当的乌龟说，"你十分肯定吗？也许它说的是你给刺猬灌水时必须把它扔进你的爪子里；遇到乌龟的时候，必须剥它的壳直到它把头脚全伸出来。"

"我想它不是这样说的，"美洲豹有点迷茫，"但是，请再清清楚楚地讲一遍。"

"用爪子舀水的时候你该用刺猬将水展平，"刺猬说，"记住，这可挺重要的。"

"但是，"乌龟说，"如果你要找吃的，要用勺子挖乌龟的肉。你怎么不懂？"

"我简直烦透了，"美洲豹说，"而且我也根本不需要你们的劝告。我只想知道你们中的哪一个是刺猬，哪一个是乌龟。"

① attend /əˈtend/ v. 专心，留意听
② spot /spɒt/ n. 斑点
③ puzzle /ˈpʌzl/ n. 难题，迷惑
④ distinctly /dɪˈstɪŋktlɪ/ ad. 显然地
⑤ ache /eɪk/ n. 痛 v. 痛
⑥ advice /ədˈvaɪs/ n. 忠告,劝告

· 103 ·

Just So Stories

'I shan't tell you,' said Stickly-Prickly. 'but you can scoop me out of my shell if you like.'

'Aha!' said Painted Jaguar. 'Now I know you're Tortoise. You thought I wouldn't! Now I will.' Painted Jaguar **darted**[1] out his **paddy**[2]-paw just as Stickly-Prickly **curled** himself **up**[3], and of course Jaguar's paddy-paw was just filled with **prickles**[4]. Worse than that, he knocked Stickly-Prickly away and away into the woods and the bushes, where it was too dark to find him. Then he put his paddy-paw into his mouth, and of course the prickles hurt him worse than ever. As soon as he could speak he said, 'Now I know he isn't Tortoise at all. But '—and then he **scratched**[5] his head with his un prickly paw—'how do I know that this other is Tortoise?'

'But I am Tortoise,' said Slow-and-Solid. 'Your mother was quite right. She said that you were to scoop me out of my shell with your paw. Begin.'

'You didn't say she said that a minute ago', said Painted Jaguar, sucking the prickles out of his paddy-paw. 'You said she said something quite different.'

'Well, **suppose**[6] you say that I said that she said something quite different, I don't see that it **makes any difference**[7]; because if she said what you said I said she said, it's just the same as if I said what she said she said. **On the other hand**[8], if you think she said that you were to uncoil me with a scoop, instead of pawing me into drops with a shell, I can't help that, can I?'

'But you said you wanted to be scooped out of your shell with my paw,' said Painted Jaguar.

'If you'll think again you'll find that I didn't say anything of the kind. I said that your mother said that you were to scoop me out of my shell,' said Slow-and-Solid.

① dart /dɑːt/ v. 投射，疾走
② paddy /ˈpædɪ/ n. 稻田
③ curl up 蜷曲，卷起
④ prickle /ˈprɪkl/ v. 刺痛

⑤ scratch /skrætʃ/ v. 搔痒，抓

⑥ suppose /səˈpəʊz/ v. 假设
⑦ make any difference 产生什么区别
⑧ on the other hand 另一方面

"我不会告诉你的，"刺猬说，"但如果你愿意，可以把我从硬壳里挖出来。"

"啊，"美洲豹喊道，"现在我知道你是乌龟了。你以为我不知道！现在我要行动了。"它立刻把肉乎乎的爪子伸向刺猬。这时刺猬把身体蜷缩起来，这样美洲豹的爪子上边扎满了刺。更糟糕的是，它把刺猬一直打到了树林和灌木丛中，那里光线太暗了，再也找不到刺猬。然后，美洲豹把爪子伸进嘴里，这样它就被刺得更疼了。它刚能开口讲话，就说："现在我知道它根本不是乌龟。但是——"它用没被刺到的那只爪子挠挠头，"我怎么知道另外一个是乌龟呢？"

"但我的确是乌龟啊，"乌龟说，"你妈妈说得对。它说你应该用爪子把我从硬壳里挖出来。来吧。"

"一分钟前你还不这样说，"美洲豹一边用嘴巴把爪子上的刺拔出来，一边说，"你说它说的完全是两码事。"

"好吧，如果你说我说它说的完全是两码事，我可认为没有什么区别。因为它说你说我说它说的话，就像我说它说它说的话一样。另一方面，如果你认为它说应该把我用勺子挖出来，而不是用爪子把我弄成带壳的小碎块儿，我也无能为力，对不对？"

"但你说过愿意让我用爪子把你从硬壳中挖出来呀，"美洲豹说。

"如果你再想想，你会发现我从来没这么说过。我说你妈妈告诉你应该把我从硬壳里挖出来。"乌龟说。

'What will happen if I do?' said the Jaguar most **sniffily**① and most **cautious**②.

' I don't know, because I'ye never been scooped out of my shell before; but I tell you **truly**③, if you want to see me swim away you've only got to drop me into the water.'

'I don't **believe**④ it,' said Painted Jaguar. 'You've **mixed up**⑤ all the things my mother told me to do with the things that you asked me whether I was sure that she didn't say, till I don't know whether I'm on my head or my painted tail; and now you come and tell me something I can understand, and it makes me more **mixy**⑥ than before. My mother told me that I was to drop one of you two into the water, and as you seem so **anxious**⑦ to be dropped I think you don't want to be dropped. So jump into the turbid Amazon and be quick about it.'

'I **warn**⑧ you that your Mummy won't be pleased. Don't tell her I didn't tell you,' said Slow-Solid.

'If you say another word about what my mother said—' the Jaguar answered, but he had not finished the sentence before Slow-and-Solid quietly **dived**⑨ into the turbid Amazon, swam under water for a long way, and came out on the bank where Stickly-Prickly was waiting for him.

'That was a very **narrow escape**⑩,' said Stickly-Prickly. 'I don't like Painted Jaguar. What did you tell him that you were?'

'I told him truthfully that I was a **truthful**⑪ Tortoise, but he wouldn't believe it, and he made me jump into the river to see if I was, and I was, and he is surprised. Now he's gone to tell his Mummy. Listen to him!'

They could hear Painted Jaguar **roaring**⑫ up and down among the trees and the bushes by the side of the turbid Amazon, till his Mummy came.

① sniffily /'snɪfɪlɪ/ ad. 嗤之以鼻的

② cautious /'kɔ:ʃəs/ a. 十分小心的

③ truly /'tru:lɪ/ ad. 真实地,不假

④ believe /bɪ'li:v/ v. 认为,相信

⑤ mix up 混淆

⑥ mixy a. 混淆的,困惑的

⑦ anxious /'æŋkʃəs/ a. 积极的

⑧ warn /wɔ:n/ v. 警告

⑨ dive /daɪv/ v. 跳水

⑩ narrow escape 险些逃离

⑪ truthful /'tru:θful/ a. 符合实际的

⑫ roar /rɔ:/ v. 吼,大声说出

"如果我这样做了,怎么样?"美洲豹傲慢而又极为谨慎地说。

"我不知道,因为我从未被人从硬壳里挖出来过。但我可以坦白地告诉你,如果你想看着我游走的话,把我扔进水里就行了。"

"我不相信,"美洲豹说,"你把我妈妈告诉我的话搅得一塌糊涂。你问我能不能肯定它这样说过,最后把我弄得晕头转向。而现在你又来告诉我一些我能明白的事情,我被弄得更糊涂了。我妈妈让我把你们当中的一个扔进水里,既然你表现得这么积极,这么想被扔进水里,我想你并不希望我把你扔进水里去。那么,跳进亚马逊河里,快!"

"我警告你,这样做你妈妈可不会高兴的。别对它说我没告诉你。"乌龟说。

"如果你再说一句关于我妈妈的话,"美洲豹话还没说完,乌龟已经悄悄地跳进混浊的亚马逊河里。它在河里游了很长一段路,然后上岸来到刺猬等待它的地方。

"真是虎口脱险,"刺猬说,"我不喜欢美洲豹。你是怎么对它说的?"

"我坦白地告诉它我是一只真正的乌龟,但它不相信,而且还让我跳进水里看我讲的是不是实话。结果把它吓了一跳。现在它要把这件事告诉它妈妈。我们去听听它们说些什么!"

它们听到美洲豹在岸边的森林和灌木丛中低呼高喊。最后,它妈妈出来了。

"儿子,儿子!"豹妈妈连声呼唤着,优雅地

· 107 ·

'Son, son!' said his mother ever so many times, graciously waving her tail, 'what have you been doing that you shouldn't have done?'

'I tried to scoop something that said it wanted to be scooped out of its shell with my paw, and my paw is full of prickles,' said Painted Jaguar.

'Son, son!' said his mother ever so many times, graciously waving her tail, 'by the prickles in your paddy-paw I see that that must have been a Hedgehog. You should have dropped him into the water.'

'I did that to the other thing; and he said he was a Tortoise, and I didn't believe him, and it was quite true, and he has dived under the turbid Amazon, and he won't come up again, and I haven't anything at all to eat, and I think we **had better**① find **lodgings**② somewhere else. They are too clever on the turbid Amazon for poor me!'

'Son, son!' said his mother ever so many times, graciously **waving**③ her tail, 'now attend to me and **remember**④ what I say. A Hedgehog curls himself up into a ball and his prickles stick out every which way **at once**⑤. By this you may know the Hedgehog.'

'I don't like this old lady one little bit,' said Stickly-Prickly, under the shadow of a large leaf. 'I **wonder**⑥ what else she knows?'

'A Tortoise can't curl himself up,' Mother Jaguar **went on**⑦, ever so many times, graciously waving her tail. 'He only draws his head and legs into his shell. By this you may know the Tortoise.'

'I don't like this old lady at all—at all,' said Slow-and-Solid Tortoise. 'Even Painted Jaguar can't forget those **directions**⑧. It's a great pity that you can't swim, Stickly-Prickly.'

'Don't talk to me,' said Stickly-Prickly. 'Just think how much better it would be if you could curl up. This is a **mess**⑨! Listen to Painted Jaguar.'

摆动着尾巴，"你做了什么不该做的事情了？"

"一个家伙说它想让我用爪子把它从硬壳里挖出来。我试图这么做，结果爪子上扎满了刺。"美洲豹抱怨说。

"儿子，儿子！"豹妈妈连呼唤着，优雅地摆动着尾巴，"从你胖爪子上的刺看来，我想你一定是遇到了刺猬。你本该把它扔进水里。"

"我把另一个家伙扔进了水里。它说它是乌龟，我不相信。但那是真的。它跳进河里再也不出来了。结果我什么也没有吃到。我想我们最好去别的地方找个住处，在亚马逊河岸，对于可怜的我来说，刺猬和乌龟实在太聪明了！"

"儿子，儿子！"豹妈妈连声呼唤着，优雅地摆动着尾巴，"现在听我的，并记住我的话。刺猬把自己蜷成一个球，而且身上的刺立刻向各个方向竖起来。这样你就能认出哪个是刺猬了。"

"我不太喜欢这个老女人，"刺猬藏在一片大叶子的阴影下，说道，"我想知道它还懂些什么？"

"乌龟的身体可蜷不起来，"豹妈妈继续说，说了好多遍，依然优雅地摆动着尾巴。"它能立刻把头和脚缩进硬壳里去。这样你就能认出哪一个是乌龟了。"

"我一点也不喜欢这个老女人———一点也不，"乌龟说，"即使美洲豹这个笨蛋也忘不了这些教导。刺猬，你不会游泳，这太遗憾了。"

"先别说我，"刺猬回敬道，"好好想想自己。如果你能蜷成一团，那该多好。什么乱七八糟的！听听美洲豹在说些什么？"

① had better 最好做某事
② lodging /ˈlɔdʒɪŋ/ n. 寄宿处
③ wave /weɪv/ v. 摇摆
④ remember /rɪˈmembə/ v. 记得
⑤ at once 立刻，马上
⑥ wonder /ˈwʌndə/ v. 想知道
⑦ go on 继续
⑧ direction /daɪˈrekʃən/ n. 指导
⑨ mess /mes/ n. 乱七八糟

Painted Jaguar was sitting on the banks of the turbid Amazon sucking prickles out of his Paws and saying to himself—

'Can't curl, but can swim—

Slow-Solid, that's him!

Curls up, but can't swim—

Stickly-Prickly, that's him!'

'He'll never forget that this month of Sundays,' said Stickly-Prickly. '**Hold up**[①] my chin, Slow-and-Solid. I'm going to try to learn to swim. It may be **useful**[②].'

'**Excellent**[③]!' said Slow-and-Solid; and he held up Stickly-Prickly's chin, while Stickly-Prickly **kicked**[④] in the waters of the turbid Amazon.

'You'll make a fine swimmer yet,' said Slow-and-Solid. 'Now, if you can **unlace**[⑤] my **back plates**[⑥] a little, I'll see what I can do towards curling up. It may be useful.'

Stickly-Prickly helped to unlace Tortoise's back-plates, so that by twisting and **straining**[⑦] Slow-and-Solid actually managed to curl up a tiddy wee bit.

'Excellent!' said Stickly-Prickly; 'but I shouldn't do any more just now. It's making you black in the face. Kindly lead me into the water once again and I'll practise that **side-stroke**[⑧] which you say is so easy.' And so Stickly-Prickly practised, and Slow-Solid swam **alongside**[⑨].

'Excellent!' said Slow-and-Solid. 'A little more practise will make you a **regular**[⑩] Whale. Now, if I may trouble you to unlace my back and front plates two holes more, I'll try that **fascinating**[⑪] bend that you say is so easy. Won't Painted Jaguar be surprised!'

'Excellent!' said Stickly-Prickly, all wet from the turbid Amazon. 'I declare, I shouldn't know you from one of my own family. Two holes, I think, you said? A little more expression, please, and don't

远古传奇

美洲豹正坐在河水混浊的亚马逊河岸，一边把爪子上的刺拔出来，一边自言自语：

不能团成团儿，但会游泳，
是乌龟！
能团成团儿，但下不了水，
是刺猬！

"它很长时间都不会忘记这些话，"刺猬说，"抬着我的下巴，乌龟。我要试着学游泳。这也许有用。"

"太棒了！"乌龟说。刺猬在水里踢着水，乌龟帮它抬着下巴。

"你会成为一名出色的游泳选手的，"乌龟说，"现在，你把我后背上的甲壳松开一点，我看看是否能把身体蜷起来。这也许有用。"

刺猬帮乌龟把背上的甲壳松了松，乌龟扭动、紧抱起自己的身体，稍稍蜷起了一点。

"太棒了！"刺猬说，"但现在我再也不能这样做了。这样你的脸色会变青的。请让我再下一次水，我想试一下侧泳，你说过侧泳很容易。"

于是刺猬开始练习，乌龟在它旁边与它一起游。

"太棒了！"乌龟说，"再练练你会成为一条真正的鲸鱼。好，我想麻烦你把我背后的甲壳再松开两个眼儿，我再试试弯起身子。你说过这很容易。美洲豹不会觉得惊讶吧！"

"太棒了！"刺猬浑身湿淋淋地说，"你真像我们家族的成员。你说再松两个眼儿？拜托来点儿表情，别嘀嘀咕咕的，美洲豹会听见我们说话

① hold up 举起
② useful /'juːsful/ *a.* 有用的
③ excellent /'eksələnt/ *a.* 极好的，优秀的
④ kick /kɪk/ *v.* 踢
⑤ unlace /ˌʌn'leɪs/ *v.* 解开带子
⑥ back plate 后背
⑦ strain /streɪn/ *v.* 拉紧
⑧ side-stroke 侧泳
⑨ alongside /əˌlɒŋ'saɪd/ *ad.* 在旁边
⑩ regular /'regjulə/ *a.* 正规的
⑪ fascinating /'fæsɪneɪtɪŋ/ *a.* 迷人的

· 111 ·

grunt① quite so much, or Painted Jaguar may hear us. When you've finished, I want to try that long dive which you say is so easy. Won't Painted Jaguar be surprised!'

And so Stickly-Prickly dived, and Slow-and-Solid dived alongside.

'Excellent!' said Slow-and-Solid. 'A little more attention to **holding your breath**② and you will be able to keep house at the bottom of the turbid Amazon. Now I'll try that exercise of wrapping my hind legs round my ears which you say is so **peculiarly**③ **comfortable**④. Won't Painted Jaguar be surprised!'

'Excellent!' said Stickly-Prickly. 'But it's straining your back-plates a little. They are all **overlapping**⑤ now, instead of lying side by side.'

'Oh, that's the result of exercise,' said Slow-and-Solid. 'I've noticed that your prickles seem to be melting into one another, and that you're growing to look rather more like a **pine-cone**⑥, and less like a **chestnut-burr**⑦, than you used to.'

'Am I?' said Stickly-Prickly. 'That comes from my **soaking**⑧ in the water. Oh, won't Painted Jaguar be surprised!'

They went on with their exercises, each helping the other, till morning came; and when the sun was high they rested and dried themselves. Then they saw that they were both of them quite different from what they had been.

'Stiekly-Prickly,' said Tortoise after breakfast, 'I am not what I was yesterday; but I think that I may yet **amuse**⑨ Painted Jaguar.'

'That was the very thing I was thinking just now,' said Stickly-Prickly. 'I think **scales**⑩ are a **tremendous**⑪ **improvement**⑫ on prickles—to say nothing of being able to swim. Oh, won't Painted Jaguar be surprised! Let's go and find him.'

By and by⑬ they found Painted Jaguar, still **nursing**⑭ his paddy-

① grunt /grʌnt/ v. 咕哝

② hold one's breath 屏住呼吸
③ peculiarly /pɪˈkjuːlɪəlɪ/ ad. 古怪地，特有地
④ comfortable /ˈkʌmfətəbl/ a. 舒适的

⑤ overlapping /ˌəʊvəˈlæpɪŋ/ a. 相互重叠的

⑥ pine-cone 松塔
⑦ chestnut-burr 栗子壳

⑧ soak /səʊk/ v. 浸

⑨ amuse /əˈmjuːz/ v. 消遣，娱乐
⑩ scales /skeɪz/ n. 鳞属
⑪ tremendous /trɪˈmendəs/ a. 巨大的
⑫ improvement /ɪmˈpruːvmənt/ n. 改进
⑬ by and by 渐渐的
⑭ nurse /nɜːs/ v. 看护，照顾

的。等你练完了，我还想试试潜水，你说过这挺容易的。美洲豹该不会感到惊讶吧！"

于是刺猬开始潜水，乌龟在一旁与它一起潜水。

"太棒了！"乌龟说，"再集中一点儿精力屏住呼吸的话，你简直就可以住在亚马逊河底。现在我要试着用后腿包住耳朵，你说过这个姿势舒服极了。美洲豹不会感到惊讶吧！"

"太棒了！"刺猬说，"但你把后面的甲壳拉紧了。现在这些甲壳不再一块块平铺在一起，而是互相叠加着。"

"哇，这是锻炼的结果，"乌龟说，"我也注意到你的皮刺开始融为一体。你过去长得像栗子壳，现在看起来却像个松果。"

"是吗？"刺猬问，"那可能是因为在水中浸泡的缘故。哇，美洲豹不会感到惊讶吧！"

它们互相帮助，继续练习着，直到天亮。太阳高高地挂在空中的时候，它们开始休息，把身体晒干。刺猬和乌龟发现自己的模样与往常不一样了。

早饭后，乌龟说："刺猬，我已经不是昨天的我了，但我想这也许会把美洲豹吓一跳。"

"我刚才也是这么想的，"刺猬说，"我觉得与毛刺比较起来，鳞片可是个巨大的进步——更不用提学会游泳了。哇，美洲豹不会感到惊讶吧！我们去找找它。"

不久后它们找到了美洲豹。它还在护理那只昨晚受伤的爪子。美洲豹太惊讶了，它踩着尾巴连连后退了三步。

Just So Stories

paw that had been hurt the night before. He was so astonished that he fell three times backward over his own painted tail without stopping.

'Good morning!' said Stickly-Prickly. 'And how is your dear gracious Mummy this morning?'

'She is. quite well, thank you,' said Painted Jaguar; 'but you must forgive me if I do not at this precise moment **recall**① your name.'

'That's unkind of you,' said Stickly-Prickly, 'seeing that this time yesterday you tried to scoop me out of my shell with your paw.'

'But you hadn't any shell. It was all prickles,' said Painted Jaguar. 'I know it was. Just look at my paw!'

'You told me to drop into the turbid Amazon and be drowned,' said Slow-Solid. 'Why are you so rude and **forgetful**② today?'

'Don't you remember what your mother told you?' said Stickly-Prickly, —

'Can't curl, but can swim—
Stickly-Prickly, that's him!
Curls up, but can't swim—
Slow-Solid, that's him!'

Then they both curled themselves up and rolled round and round Painted Jaguar till his eyes turned truly **cart-wheels**③ in his head.

Then he went to fetch his mother.

'Mother,' he said, 'there are two new animals in the **woods**④ today, and the one that you said couldn't swim, swims, and the one that you said couldn't curl up, curls; and they've gone shares in their prickles, I think, because both of them are **scaly**⑤ all over, instead of one being smooth and the other very prickly; and, besides that, they are rolling round and round in circles, and I don't feel **comfy**⑥.'

'Son, son!' said Mother Jaguar ever so many times, graciously waving her tail, 'a Hedgehog is a Hedgehog, and can't be anything but

远古传奇

"早晨好!"刺猬说,"你那举止优雅的妈妈今天上午还好吧?"

"它很好,谢谢你们,"美洲豹说,"但请你们原谅,我一时想不起你们的名字。"

"这可是你的不对了,"刺猬说,"想想昨晚你还要用爪子把我从硬壳里挖出来呢。"

"但你身上没有硬壳呀,而当时你身上长满了毛刺,"美洲豹说,"我知道那是毛刺,看看我的爪子就行了。"

"你还让我跳进混浊的亚马逊河里淹死,"乌龟说,"你今天怎么这么粗鲁和健忘?"

"难道你忘了你妈妈教你的话了吗?"刺猬开始背诵起来:

不能团成团儿,但会游泳,
是乌龟!
能团成团儿,但下不了水,
是刺猬!

然后它们两个全都把身体团成一团儿,围绕着美洲豹在地上滚来滚去,直到豹子的眼睛瞪得真的像车轮那样大。

然后它把妈妈找来。

"妈妈,"它说,"今天森林里有两只新动物。您说不会游泳的那只动物能游泳,你说不会团成团儿的那只动物能团成一团儿。我想它们大概分享了那些毛刺吧,因为两只动物身上都长满了鳞片,而不像以前那样,一只外表光滑,一只则长满了毛刺。而且,它们还绕着我滚来滚去,

① recall /rɪˈkɔːl/ v. 回想起

② forgetful /fəˈgetful/ a. 健忘的

③ cart-wheel /ˈkɑːtwiːl/ n. 车轮

④ woods /wʊdz/ n. 树林

⑤ scaly /ˈskeɪlɪ/ a. 鳞状的

⑥ comfy /ˈkʌnfɪ/ a. 舒服的

a Hedgehog; and a Tortoise is a Tortoise, and can never be anything else.'

'But it isn't a Hedgehog, and it isn't a Tortoise. It's a little bit of both, and I don't know its **proper**① name.'

'**Nonsense**②!' said Mother Jaguar. 'Everything has its proper name. I should call it "Armadillo" till I found out the real one. And I should **leave it alone**③.'

So Painted Jaguar did as he was told, **especially**④ about leaving them alone; but the curious thing is that from that day to this, O Best Beloved, no one on the banks of the turbid Amazon has ever called Stickly-Prickly and Slow-Solid anything except **Armadillo**⑤. There are Hedgehogs and Tortoises in other places, of course (there are some in my garden); but the real old and clever kind, with their scales lying lippety-lappety one over the other, like pine-cone scales, that lived on the banks of the turbid Amazon in the High and **Far-Off**⑥ Days, are always called Armadillos, because they were so clever.

So that's all right, Best Beloved. Do you **see**⑦?

远古传奇

① proper /ˈprɔpə/ a. 适当的
② nonsense /ˈnɔnsəns/ n. 荒唐
③ leave it alone 别管它了
④ especially /ɪsˈpeʃəlɪ/ ad. 特别,尤其
⑤ Armadillo /ɑːməˈdɪləu/ n. 犰狳
⑥ far-off /ˈfɑːrˈɔf/ a. 遥远的
⑦ see /siː/ v. 看见,明白

我感到很不舒服。"

"儿子,儿子!"豹妈妈连声呼唤着,优雅地摆动着尾巴,"刺猬就是刺猬,它不能是别的动物,只能是刺猬;乌龟就是乌龟,它也不能是别的动物,只能是乌龟。"

"但那既不是刺猬,也不是乌龟。两种动物的特征它都带点儿。我不知道它正确的名字是什么。"

"胡说八道!"豹妈妈说,"每种动物都有它正确的名字。在我找到它正确的名字之前,先叫它'犰狳'。我不想管了。"

于是美洲豹就按照妈妈的话去做了,不再理睬它们。但亲爱的读者,奇怪的是,从那以后,河水混浊的亚马逊河岸上再也没有叫刺猬或乌龟的动物,只有犰狳。当然它们在别的地方还叫刺猬和乌龟(我的花园里就有几只),但那些最初生长在混浊的亚马逊河岸鳞甲叠盖的松果样动物,因为它们实在太聪明了,一直被人们叫做犰狳。

就是这样。亲爱的读者,你明白了吗?

117

Just So Stories

This is an **inciting**① map of the Turbid Amazon. It **hasn't anything to do with**② the story except that there are two Armadillos in it—up by the top. The inciting part are the **adventures**③ that happened to the men who went along the road **marked**④. I meant to draw Armadillos when I began the map, and I meant to draw **manatees**⑤ and **spider**⑥-tailed monkeys and big snakes and lots of Jaguars, but it was more inciting to do the map and the **venturesome**⑦ adventures. You begin at the bottom **left-hand**⑧ corner and follow the little arrows all about, and then you come quite round again to where the **adventuresome**⑨ people went home in a ship called the ***Royal***⑩ ***Tiger***. This is a most adventuresome picture, and all the adventures are told about in writing, so you can be quite sure which is an adventure and which is a tree or a boat.

这是一幅神秘的浑浊的亚马逊河图。除了图上端的两只犰狳外，这幅画与这个故事没有什么联系。最富有吸引力的内容是人们沿着标注的路去探险。开始画这幅画时，我本想画犰狳，画海牛、蛛猴、大蛇和很多只美洲豹，但更刺激的是画出探险的场面。你从图的左下端看起，沿着小箭头，你就会到达探险的人们乘坐一艘名为"皇家虎"的船返回家园的地方。这是一张探险图，所有的探险故事都用文字表述出来，这样，你就能分清哪个是探险历程，哪个是大树或船只。

① inciting /ɪnˈsaɪtɪŋ/ a. 刺激的,煽动的
② have something to do with 与…有关
③ adventure /ədˈventʃə/ n. 冒险,奇遇
④ marked /mɑːkt/ a. 有记号的
⑤ manatee /ˈmænəˈtiː/ n. 海牛
⑥ spider-tail 长蜘蛛尾巴的
⑦ venturesome /ˈventʃəsəm/ a. 冒险的
⑧ left-hand /ˈlefthænd/ a. 左手的
⑨ adventuresome /ədˈventʃəsəm/ a. 爱冒险的
⑩ royal /ˈrɔɪəl/ a. 王室的,皇家的

Just So Stories

This is a picture of the whole story of the Jaguar and the Hedgehog and the Tortoise and the Armadillo all in a heap. It looks rather the same any way you turn it. The Tortoise is in the middle, learning how to **bend**①, and that is why the shelly plates on his back are so **spread**② apart. He is standing on the Hedgehog, who is waiting to learn how to swim. The Hedgehog is a Japanesy Hedgehog, because I couldn't find our own Hedgehogs in the garden when I wanted to draw them. (It was daytime, and they had gone to bed under the **dahlias**③.) **Speckly**④ Jaguar is looking over the edge, with his paddy-paw carefuly **tied up**⑤ by his mother, because he pricked himself scooping the Hedgehog. He is much surprised to see what the Tortoise is doing, and his paw is hurting him. The **snouty**⑥ thing with the little eye that Speckly Jaguar is trying to climb over is the Armadillo that the Tortoise and the Hedgehog are going to **turn into**⑦ when hey have finished bending and swimming. It is all a **magic**⑧ picture, and that is one of the reasons why I haven't drawn the Jaguar's **whiskers**⑨. The other reason was that he was so young that his whiskers had not grown. The Jaguar's **pet name**⑩ with his Mummy was Doffles.

这张图把美洲豹、刺猬、乌龟和犰狳画成了一团儿。无论往哪个方向转，看上去都很相似。乌龟在中间，正在学习如何蜷曲身体，这就是为什么它身上甲壳断裂的原因。它站在刺猬身上；刺猬正在学习游泳。这是只日本刺猬，因为我想画刺猬的时候在花园里找不到模特＜当时是白天，它们在大丽花下睡着了）。长着斑纹的美洲豹正盯着这一团儿看。它想挖出刺猬的时候被毛刺扎了手，现在那只肉爪子已被豹妈妈仔细地包扎好。它看到乌龟做的事时很吃惊，手还在隐隐作痛。美洲豹试图爬过一只长着大鼻子和小眼睛的家伙，它的名字叫犰狳，刺猬和乌龟练完团身和游泳后就变成了这种动物。这张图很神秘，这也是我没有画出美洲豹胡须的一个原因。另一个原因是它年纪太小了，胡子还没长出来。豹妈妈亲昵地叫它"多费莱斯"。

① bend /bend/ v. 弯曲,
② spread /spred/ a. 扩延的

③ dahlias /'deɪljə/ n. /植/ 大丽花属
④ speckly 长斑点的
⑤ tie up 系紧, 系起来

⑥ snouty a. 长着大鼻子的

⑦ turn into 变成
⑧ magic /'mædʒɪk/ a. 有魔力的
⑨ whisker /'hwɪskə/ n. 腮须胡须
⑩ pet name 爱称

I've never **sailed**① the Amazon,
I've never **reached**② **Brazil**③;
But the Don and Magdalena,
They can go there when they will!
Yes, weekly from Southampton,
Great **steamers**④, white and gold,
Go rolling down to **Rio**⑤
(Roll down—roll down to Rio!)
And I'd like to roll to Rio
Some day before I'm old!
I've never seen a Jaguar,
Nor yet an Armadill—
O dilloing in his **armour**⑥,
And I s'pose I never will,
Unless⑦ I go to Rio
These **wonders**⑧ to behold—
Rolldown—**roll down**⑨ to Rio
Roll really down to Rio!
Oh, **I'd love to**⑩ roll to Rio
Some day before I'm old!

① sail /seɪl/ v. 航行
② reach /riːtʃ/ v. 到达
③ Brazil /brəˈzɪl/ n. 巴西

我从未到过亚马逊河，
我从未到过巴西；
但是唐和梅格黛琳娜，
他们却想去就去！

④ steamer /ˈstiːmə/ n. 汽船，轮船
⑤ Rio n. 里约热内卢

是的，每周从南开普顿启程，
伟大的白色和古铜色皮肤的水手，
一路冲向里约热内卢！
我也要去里约热内卢，
在我变老之前的某一天！

⑥ armour n. 甲胄，铁甲

我没见到过美洲豹，
也没见过犰狳，
我永远也不敢，
抚摸它全身的盔甲。

⑦ unless /ənˈles, ʌnˈles/ conj. 除非
⑧ wonders n. 奇观
⑨ roll down 滚下来
⑩ would love to 想要/愿意（做）

除非我到了里约热内卢，
去看看这些奇观，
一路冲向里约热内卢，
我想一路冲向里约热内卢，
在我变老之前的某一天。

How the First Letter was Written

Once upon a most early time was a Nedithic man. He was not a **Jute**① or an **Angle**②, or even a **Dravidian**③, which he might well have been, Best Beloved, but never mind why. He was a **Primitive**④, and he lived **cavily**⑤ in a Cave, and he wore very few clothes, and he couldn't read and he couldn't write and he didn't want to, and except when he was hungry he was quite happy. His name was Tegumai Bopsulai, and that means, 'Man-who-does-not-put-his-foot-forward-in-a-hurry'; but we, O Best Beloved, will call him Tegumai, **for short**⑥. And his wife's name was Teshumai Tewindrow, and that means, 'Lady-who-asks-a-very-many-questions'; but we, O Best Beloved, will call her Teshumai, for short. And this little girl-daughter's name was Taffimai Metallumai, and that means, 'Small-person-without-any-manners-who-ought-to-be-spanked'; but I'm going to call her Taffy. And she was Tegumai Bopsulai's Best Beloved and her own Mummy's Best Beloved, and she was not spanked half as much as was good for her; and they were all three very happy. As soon as Taffy could run about she went everywhere with her Daddy Tegumai, and sometimes they would not come home to the Cave till they were hungry, and then Teshumai Tewindrow would say, 'Where in the world have you two been to, to get so **shocking**⑦

第一封信是怎么写出来的

① Jute /dʒuːt/ n. 朱特人
② Angle /'æŋgl/ n. 盎格鲁人
③ Dravidian /drə'vɪdɪən/ n. 德拉威人
④ primitive /'prɪmɪtɪv/ n. 原始人
⑤ cavily 原始的

⑥ for short 简称, 缩写

　　很久以前新石器时代有一个人，他既不是朱特人、①盎格鲁人、②也不是达罗毗荼人，③虽然他很应该是，但亲爱的读者，别在意这是为什么。他是个生活在山洞里的原始人，基本上不穿衣服，不会读也不会写。除了饥肠辘辘或兴致勃勃的时候，他压根儿也不想读或写。他的名字叫做特奎曼·鲍普苏莱，意思是"不匆匆忙忙向前迈脚的男人"，但亲爱的读者，为简便起见，我们还是叫他特奎曼。他妻子的名字叫特舒曼·特温德鲁，意思是"问很多问题的女人"，但亲爱的读者，为简单起见，我们还是叫她特舒曼。他们有一个小女儿，名字叫特菲曼·梅塔柳迈，意思是"没有礼貌、该打屁股的小孩子"，但我要叫她特菲。她是父母的掌上明珠，尽管打屁股有时对她来说是件好事，但因为爸爸妈妈太爱她

---

① 古代居住在北欧 Jutland 半岛的日耳曼人的一个部落集团的成员；公元5至6世纪时，一部分朱特人入侵英国东南部，在今肯特地区定居。译注。
② 日耳曼部族的一支，5世纪时与朱特人和撒克逊人一起侵入英格兰。译注。
③ 主要分布于印度南部，斯里兰卡北部。译注。

⑦ shocking /'ʃɒkɪŋ/ a. 可怕的

Just So Stories

远古传奇

① beaver /ˈbiːvə/ n. 海狸
② spear /spɪə/ vt 用矛刺
③ carp–fish 鲤鱼
④ accidently /ˈæksɪˈdentlɪ/ ad. 偶然地(附带地)
⑤ jab /dʒæb/ v. 戳,刺,猛击
⑥ kettle /ˈketl/ n. 水壶
⑦ fall into 分成
⑧ drown /draʊn/ v. 淹死
⑨ make the best of 充分利用
⑩ reindeer- sinew /ˈreɪndɪə/ /ˈsɪnjuː/ 鹿腱
⑪ lump /lʌmp/ n. 块状,瘤
⑫ wax /wæks/ n. 蜡,蜡状物
⑬ resin /ˈrezɪn/ n. 树脂,松香
⑭ nuisance /ˈnjuːsns/ n. 讨厌的东西,讨厌的人
⑮ slang /slæŋ/ n. 俚语
⑯ awful /ˈɔːful/ a. 可怕的
⑰ convenience /kənˈviːnjəns/ n. 便利,方便
⑱ tribe /traɪb/ n. 部落

了,她很少挨打。特菲刚会跑,就和爸爸到各个地方去,有时直到肚子饿了的时候才回到洞穴。这时特舒曼·特温德鲁就会说:"你们两个到底到哪儿去了,浑身脏兮兮的!特奎曼,说句实在的,你比我的特菲强不到哪儿去。"

现在请仔细听好!

一天,特奎曼·鲍普苏莱往下游走,穿过河狸聚集的沼泽地来到瓦格河,他想用渔叉抓些鲤鱼做晚餐。特菲也跟着去了。特奎曼的渔叉是用木头做的,叉子头上装着鲨鱼齿。还没捉到一条鱼,特奎曼把渔叉刺向河底,因用力过猛,叉子从中间断开了。这里离家里很远很远(当然他们随身带着装着午饭的小袋子),而且特奎曼也忘了带备用的渔叉。

"这儿的鱼太多了!"特奎曼说,"可修理渔叉需要半天的时间。"

"家里还有你的一把大黑渔叉呢!"特菲说,"我跑回山洞向妈妈要。"

"看看你那胖胖的小腿,这样跑回去太远了,"特奎曼说,"而且你还可能陷进沼泽地里淹死。我们必须变废为宝。"他坐下,取出一个小皮工具包,包里装满了鹿腱和皮条,还有一团团蜂蜡和松香。他开始修理渔叉。特菲也在一旁坐下,把脚趾泡在水里,双手托着下巴颏,使劲地想啊想啊,最后她说:

"听我说,爸爸,你和我不会写字,这真太他妈讨厌了,是不是?不然我们就可以发个信给妈妈要只新渔叉。"

"特菲,"特奎曼说,"我跟你说过多少遍

· 127 ·

Tegumai's language. He stood on the bank and smiled at Taffy, because he had a little girl-daughter of his own at home. Tegumai drew a **hank**① of deer-sinews from his mendy-bag and began to mend his spear.

'Come here,' said Taffy. 'Do you know where my Mummy lives?' And the Stranger-man said 'Um!'—being, as you know, a Tewara.

'Silly!' said Taffy, and she **stamped**② her foot, because she saw a **shoal**③ of very big carp going up the river just when her Daddy couldn't use his spear.

'Don't bother **grown-ups**④,' said Tegumai, so busy with his spear-mend-ing that he did not turn round.

'I aren't,' said Taffy. 'I only want him to do what I want him to do, and he won't understand.'

'Then don't bother me,' said Tegumai, and he went on pulling and straining at the deer-sinews with his mouth full of loose **ends**⑤. The Stranger-man—a **genuine**⑥ Tewara he was—sat down on the grass, and Taffy showed him what her Daddy was doing. The Stranger-man thought, 'This is a very wonderful child. She stamps her foot at me and she **makes faces**⑦. She must be the daughter of that noble **Chief**⑧ who is so great that he won't **take any notice of**⑨ me.' So he smiled more politely than ever.

'Now,' said Taffy, 'I want you to go to my Mummy, because your legs are longer than mine, and you won't fall into the beaver-swamp, and ask for Daddy's other spear—the one with the black **handle**⑩ that hangs over our fireplace.'

The Stranger-man (and he was a Tewara) thought, 'This is a very, very wonderful child. She waves her arms and she shouts at me, but I don't understand a word of what she says. But if I don't do what she

① hank /hæŋk/ n. 一束，一卷

② stamp /stæmp/ v. 顿足
③ shoal /ʃəʊl/ n. 鱼群

④ grown-up 成年人

⑤ ends 东西的末端
⑥ genuine /ˈdʒenjuɪn/ a. 真正的

⑦ make faces 做鬼脸
⑧ chief /tʃiːf/ n. 部落首领
⑨ take notice of 注意到

⑩ handle /ˈhændl/ n. 柄，把手

了，不要说脏字。'他妈的'不是个好词——但你说的也对，如果我们能往家里写信，那可方便多了。"

正在这时，一个陌生人沿着河边走来。他是另外一个叫特瓦拉部落的人，特奎曼的话他一句也听不懂。他站在岸边对特菲微笑，因为他的家里也有这么大的一个小女孩。特奎曼从工具包里拿出一绞鹿腱，开始修理渔叉。

"到这儿来，"特菲说，"你知道我妈妈住在哪儿吗？"那个陌生人"嗯——"了一声；你知道，他是特瓦拉部落的人。

"傻瓜！"特菲说。她跺跺脚，因为她看到一群肥大的鲤鱼游上水面，可这时她爸爸的渔叉却不能用。

"别烦大人，"特奎曼说。他忙着修理渔叉，没有回头看。

"我没烦人，"特菲说，"我只想让他按我说的去做，可是他听都听不懂。"

"那就别烦我，"特奎曼说。他用牙齿把鹿腱又撕又拽，嘴里都是松散的残絮。那个陌生人——一个真正的特瓦拉人——坐在草地上，特菲把爸爸正在干的活儿展示给他看。陌生人心想："这个孩子非常神奇。她冲我跺脚，做鬼脸，她一定是那个贵族首领的女儿。那位贵族首领太伟大了，所以他根本没有注意到我。"他笑得更有礼貌了。

"嗳，"特菲说，"我要你去找我妈妈，因为你的腿比我长，不会掉进沼泽地里。你去拿我爸爸的另一只渔叉——那只挂在火炉上面、带黑色手柄的渔叉。"

那个陌生人（一个特瓦拉人）心想："这个

· 129 ·

wants, I greatly fear that that **haughty**① Chief, Man-who-turns-his-back-on-callers, will be angry.' He got up and twisted a big flat piece of bark off a **birch**②-tree and gave it to Taffy. He did this, Best Beloved, to show that his heart was as white as the birch-bark and that he meant no harm; but Taffy didn't quite understand.

'Oh!' said she. 'Now I see! You want my Mummy's living-**address**③? Of course I can't write, but I can draw pictures if I've anything sharp to **scratch**④ with. Please lend me the shark's tooth off your **necklace**⑤.'

The Stranger-man (and he was a Tewara) didn't say anything, so Taffy put up her little hand and pulled at the beautiful bead and seed and sharktooth necklace round his neck.

The Stranger-man (and he was a Tewara) thought, 'This is a very, very, very wonderful child. The shark's tooth on my necklace is a magic shark's tooth, and I was always told that if anybody touched it without my **leave**⑥ they would immediately **swell**⑦ up or burst, but this child doesn't swell up or burst, and that important Chief, Man-who-attends-strictly-to-his-bus- iness, who has not yet taken any notice of me at all, doesn't seem to be afraid that she will swell up or burst. I had better be more polite.'

So he gave Taffy the shark's tooth, and she lay down flat on her t ummy with her legs in the air, like some people on the **drawing-room**⑧ floor when they want to draw pictures, and she said, 'Now I'll draw you some beautiful pictures! You can look over my shoulder, but you mustn't **joggle**⑨. First I'll draw Daddy **fishing**⑩. It isn't very like him; but Mummy will know, because I've drawn his spear all broken. Well, now I'll draw the other spear that he wants, the black-handled spear. It looks as if it was sticking in Daddy's back, but that's because the shark's

远古传奇

① haughty /ˈhɔːtɪ/ a. 傲慢的

② birch /bəːtʃ/ n. 桦树，桦木

③ address /əˈdres/ n. 住址
④ scratch /skrætʃ/ v. 搔痒，抓
⑤ necklace /ˈneklɪs/ n. 项链

⑥ leave /liːv/ n. 许可
⑦ swell up 膨胀，肿起来

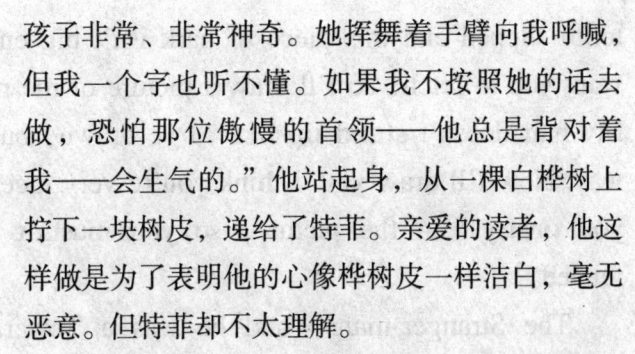

⑧ drawing-room /ˈdrɔːɪŋrʊm/ n. 画室

⑨ joggle /ˈdʒɒgl/ v. 轻摇，摇动
⑩ fishing /ˈfɪʃɪŋ/ n. 钓鱼

孩子非常、非常神奇。她挥舞着手臂向我呼喊，但我一个字也听不懂。如果我不按照她的话去做，恐怕那位傲慢的首领——他总是背对着我——会生气的。"他站起身，从一棵白桦树上拧下一块树皮，递给了特菲。亲爱的读者，他这样做是为了表明他的心像桦树皮一样洁白，毫无恶意。但特菲却不太理解。

"啊，"她说，"现在我明白了！你想要我妈妈的地址？当然了，我不会写字，但如果有个带尖头的东西，我可以画画。请把你项链上的鲨鱼齿借给我用一用。"

陌生人（他是个特瓦拉人）什么也没说，于是特菲就伸出她的小手用力拉扯他脖子上挂的美丽的珠子、贝壳和鲨鱼齿。

陌生人（是个特瓦拉人）心想："这孩子非常、非常、非常神奇。我脖子上的鲨鱼齿非常奇妙，我常听人说，如果没得到我的同意，任何人只要一碰它身体就会膨胀、爆裂。但这孩子既没膨胀也没爆裂，而且那位根本没注意到我的、全神贯注做自己事的大首领看上去也不担心她会膨胀或爆裂。我最好表现得更有礼貌一点儿。"

于是他把鲨鱼齿递给特菲。特菲趴在地上，两只脚丫跷起来，好像那些在画室里想画画的人摆出的姿势。她说："现在我给你画几幅漂亮的画！你可以从我的背后看，但不许来回摆动。我先画爸爸捉鱼。这不太像他，但妈妈会知道的，因为我画出他的渔叉都断裂了。好，现在我要画爸爸需要的另一把渔叉，那把带黑色手柄的。看上去渔叉好像贴在爸爸的后背，但那是因为鲨鱼

· 131 ·

tooth slipped and this piece of bark isn't big enough. That's the spear I want you to fetch; so I'll draw a picture of me myself **splaining**① to you. My hair doesn't **stand up like**② I've drawn, but it's easier to draw that way. Now I'll draw you. I think you're very nice really, but I can't make you **pretty**③ in the picture, so you mustn't be **ffended**④. Are you fended?'

The Stranger-man (and he was a Tewara) smiled. He thought, 'There must be a big battle going to be fought somewhere, and this extraordinary child, who takes my magic shark's tooth but who does not swell up or burst, is telling me to call all the great Chief's tribe to help him. He is a great Chief, or he would have noticed me.'

'Look,' said Taffy, drawing very hard and rather **scratchily**⑥, 'now I've drawn you, and I've put the spear that Daddy wants into your hand, just to **remind**⑦ you that you're to bring it. Now I'll show you how to find my Mummy's living-address. You go along till you come to two trees (those are trees), and then you go over a hill (that's a hill), and then you come into a beaver-swamp all full of beavers. I haven't put in all the beavers, because I can't draw beavers, but I've drawn their heads, and that's all you'll see of them when you cross the swamp. **Mind**⑧ you don't fall in! Then our Cave is just beyond the beaver-swamp. It isn't as high as the hills really, but I can't draw things very small. That's my Mummy outside. She is beautiful. She is the most beautifullest Mummy there ever was, but she won't be 'ffended when she sees I've drawn her so **plain**⑨. She'll be pleased of me because I can draw. Now, **in case**⑩ you forget, I've drawn the spear that Daddy wants outside our Cave. It's **inside**⑪ really, but you show the picture to my Mummy and she'll give it you. I've made her holding up her hands, because I know she'll be so pleased to see you. Isn't it a beautiful picture? And do you quite understand, or shall I 'splain again?'

① splain=explain /ɪksˈpleɪn/ 解释,说明
② stand up 竖起来
③ pretty /ˈprɪtɪ/ a. 漂亮的
④ 'ffended=offended 生气
⑤ extraordinary /ɪksˈtrɔːdnrɪ, ɪksˈtrɔːdɪnərɪ/ a. 非常的,特别的
⑥ scratchily /ˈskrætʃɪlɪ/ 潦草地
⑦ remind /rɪˈmaɪnd/ v. 提醒
⑧ mind /maɪnd/ v. 小心
⑨ plain /pleɪn/ a. 不好看的,普通的
⑩ in case 以防万一
⑪ inside /ˈɪnˈsaɪd/ ad. 在里面

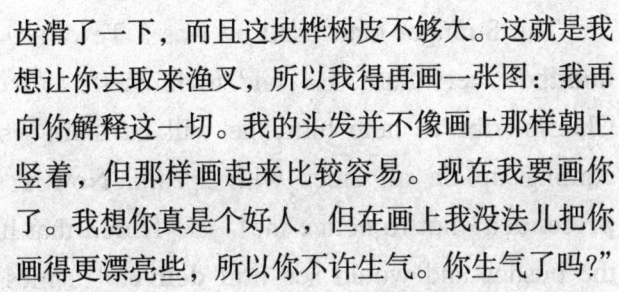

齿滑了一下,而且这块桦树皮不够大。这就是我想让你去取来渔叉,所以我得再画一张图:我再向你解释这一切。我的头发并不像画上那样朝上竖着,但那样画起来比较容易。现在我要画你了。我想你真是个好人,但在画上我没法儿把你画得更漂亮些,所以你不许生气。你生气了吗?"

陌生人(他是个特瓦拉人)笑了,他想:"这儿一定要发生一场大战。这个拿着我的鲨鱼齿却没有膨胀或爆裂的非凡的孩子告诉我去把他们部落所有的人招来帮助他们。他是个伟大的首领,不然的话他就该注意到我了。"

"看,"特菲用力而潦草地画着,"现在我已经画完了你,也已把爸爸想要的渔叉交给你去取,这会儿只想提醒你去把它取来。现在我来告诉你怎样找到我妈妈住的地方。你一直走,直到看见两棵树(这些是树),然后爬过一座小山(那是小山),然后来到一片沼泽地,那里全是河狸。我没有把河狸全都画下来,因为我不会画河狸,但我画出了它们的头,你穿过沼泽地时就会看到。小心不要跌倒!我们的山洞就在沼泽地后面。它其实并不像小山那么高,但我没法儿把东西画小。那是我妈妈站在山洞口。她很美丽,是世界上最美的妈妈。但她看到我把她画得那么普通也不会生气,她会为我高兴的,因为我会画画了。喏,为了不让你忘记,我把爸爸要的渔叉画在了山洞的外边,其实它在山洞里面。你把画给妈妈看,她会把渔叉交给你。画上的妈妈举起双手,因为她看到你很高兴。这画儿美不美?你明白了吗,要不要我再讲一遍?"

The Stranger-man (and he was a Tewara) looked at the picture and **nodded**① very hard. He said to himself, 'If I do not fetch this great Chief's tribe to help him, he will be **slain**② by his **enemies**③ who are coming up on all sides with spears. Now I see why the great Chief **pretended**④ not to notice me! He feared that his enemies were hiding in the bushes and would see him **deliver**⑤ a message to me. Therefore he turned his back, and let the wise and wonderful child draw the terrible picture showing me his **difficulties**⑥. I will away and get help for him from his tribe.' He did not even ask Taffy the road, but **raced off**⑦ into the bushes like the wind, with the birch-bark in his hand, and Taffy sat down most pleased.

Now this is the picture that Taffy had drawn for him!

'What have you been doing, Taffy?' said Tegumai. He had mended his spear and was carefully waving it **to and fro**⑧.

'It's a little arrangement of my own, Daddy dear,' said Taffy. 'If you won't ask me questions, you'll know all about it in a little time, and you'll be surprised. You don't know how surprised you'll be, Daddy! Promise you'll be surprised.'

'Very well,' said Tegumai, and went on fishing.

The Stranger-man—did you know he was a Tewara? —hurried away with the picture and ran for some miles, till quite by accident he found Teshumai Tewindrow at the door of her Cave, talking to some other Neolithic ladies who had come in to a Primitive lunch. Taffy was very like Teshumai, especially about the upper part of the face and the eyes, so the Stranger-man— always a pure Tewara—smiled politely and handed Teshumai the **birch-bark**⑨. He had run hard, so that he **panted**⑩, and his legs were **scratched**⑪ with **brambles**⑫, but he still tried to be polite.

As soon as Teshumai saw the picture she screamed like anything and

① nod /nɒd/ v. 点头
② slain /sleɪn/ slay 的过去分词 被杀死
③ enemy /ˈenɪmɪ/ n. 敌人
④ pretend /prɪˈtend/ v. 假装,伪称
⑤ deliver /dɪˈlɪvə/ v. 递送

⑥ difficulty /ˈdɪfɪkəltɪ/ n. 困难
⑦ race off 跑开

⑧ to and fro a. 往复的

⑨ birch-bark /ˈbɜːtʃ bɑːk/ n. 桦树皮
⑩ pant /pænt/ v. 气喘,气喘吁吁地讲
⑪ scratch /skrætʃ/ v. 划伤
⑫ bramble /ˈbræmbl/ n. 荆棘

陌生人(他是个特瓦拉人)看着这幅画,使劲地点了点头。他心里说:"如果我不去把这位伟大首领部落里的人找来帮助他,他就会被从四面八方冲下来的、手里拿着渔叉的敌人杀死。现在我明白为什么这位伟大的首领假装没有注意到我的原因。他担心藏在灌木丛里的敌人看到他让我带信。所以他转过身去,让这位聪明、神奇的孩子把这些可怕的场面画下来以展示他的困境。我要去找他部落里的人来帮他。"他甚至没有向特菲问路,手里拿着那张桦树皮,风风火火地走进灌木丛中。特菲满意地坐下了。

瞧,这就是特菲给他画的那幅图!

"特菲,你在干什么?"特奎曼问道。他已经修好了渔叉,正小心地前后挥动着。

"亲爱的爸爸,这是我自己安排的。"特菲回答道,"如果你什么都不问,一会儿你就全知道了,而且会大吃一惊。爸爸,你简直想象不到你会多么惊讶!答应我要大吃一惊啊。"

"很好,"特奎曼说,他继续叉鱼。

陌生人——你知道他是个特瓦拉人吗?——手里拿着画匆匆忙忙地跑了几里路,偶然发现特舒曼·特温德鲁正站在山洞口,与其他新石器时代的妇女们边吃着原始的午饭边聊天。特菲与特舒曼长得很像,特别是脸上部和眼睛。于是陌生人(一个真正的特瓦拉人)很有礼貌地笑了笑,把桦树皮递给了特舒曼。他刚才使劲地跑,跑得气喘吁吁,两腿被荆棘划伤了,但他还是表现得彬彬有礼。

特舒曼一看到图画,就大叫一声向陌生人冲

· 135 ·

flew at the Stranger-man. The other Neolithic ladies at once knocked him down and sat on him in a long line of six, while Teshumai pulled his hair. 'It's as plain as the nose on this Stranger-man's face,' she said. 'He has stuck my Tegumai all full of **spears**①, and frightened poor Taffy so that her hair stands all on end; and not content with that, he brings me a **horrid**② picture of how it was done. Look!' She showed the picture to all the Neolithic ladies sitting patiently on the Stranger-man. 'Here is my Tegumai with his arm broken; here is a spear sticking into his back; here is a man with a spear ready to throw; here is another man throwing a spear from a Cave, and here are a whole pack of people' (they were Taffy's beavers really, but they did look rather like people), 'coming up behind Tegumai. Isn't it **shocking**③!'

'Most shocking!' said the Neolithic ladies, and they filled the Stranger-man's hair with mud (at which he was surprised), and they beat upon the Reverberating Tribal Drums, and called together all the **chiefs**④ of the Tribe of Tegumai, with their Hetmans and Dolmans, all Neguses, Woons, and Akhoonds of the organisation, in addition to the Warlocks, Angekoks, Jujumen, Bonzes, and the rest, who decided that before they chopped the Stranger-man's head off he should instantly lead them down to the river and show them where he had hidden poor Taffy.

By this time the Stranger-man (in spite of being a Tewara) was really annoyed. They had filled his hair quite solid with mud; they had rolled him up and down on **knobby**⑤ **pebbles**⑥; they had sat upon him in a long line of six; they had **thumped**⑦ him and **bumped**⑧ him till he could hardly breathe; and though he did not understand their language, he was almost sure that the names the Neolithic ladies called him were not **ladylike**⑨. However, he said nothing till all the Tribe of Tegumai

远古传奇

① spear /spɪə/ n. 鱼叉；
② horrid /ˈhɒrɪd/ adj. 可怕的，毛骨悚然的，极可厌的

③ shocking /ˈʃɒkɪŋ/ adj. 可怕的，过份的

④ chief /tʃiːf/ n. 头目，酋长

⑤ knobby /ˈnɒbɪ/ adj. 凹凸不平的
⑥ pebble /ˈpebl/ n. 小石头
⑦ thump /θʌmp/ v. 重击，捶击
⑧ bump /bʌmp/ v. 碰撞；撞
⑨ ladylike /ˈleɪdɪ laɪk/ adj. 娴淑的，高雅的，如淑女的

过来。其他妇女立即把他打倒在地，六个人排成一排坐在他身上，特舒曼在一旁撕扯着他的头发。"事情明摆着，"她说，"他用渔叉刺得特奎曼浑身是伤，还吓坏了我可怜的特菲，瞧她的头发都竖起来了。这还不够，他还拿了一张画满这可怕图景的画来给我看。"她把图给那些耐心地坐在陌生人身上的妇女们看："看这儿，我的特奎曼胳膊都断了，背上还扎着一只渔叉；这里有个人拿着一把渔叉正要行刺。这儿还有一个男人从山洞里扔出一把渔叉，这儿还有一大群人（其实那是特菲画的河狸，但看起来很像人的模样）从特奎曼身后跑来。这一切难道不可怕吗？"

"太可怕了！"妇女们答道。她们用泥巴糊满了陌生人的头发（这让他很奇怪），然后敲响了部落的回音鼓，把部落里所有的头目、连同赫特曼人、多佛尔人、尼格斯人、渥恩人、阿克洪恩人，还有沃洛克人、恩格库科斯人、朱裘人、布朗兹人等等。他们决定，在脑袋被砍下来之前，这个陌生人应该立即带他们到河边去，告诉他们他把可怜的特菲藏到了哪里。

这时，这个陌生人（尽管他是个特瓦拉人）真的被惹怒了。他的头发被泥巴糊成了硬块，还被他们在凹凸不平的石头上踢得滚来滚去；他们六个人排成一排坐在他身上；他们对他又撞又捶，使他几乎窒息；尽管他听不懂他们的语言，但他也能肯定那些女人们对他出言不逊。但在这个部落所有的人聚集在一起之前，他什么也没

Just So Stories

were **assembled**①, and then he led them back to the bank of the Wagai river, and there they found Taffy making **daisy**②-chains, and Tegumai carefully **spearing**③ small **carp**④ with his mended **spear**⑤.

'Well, you have been quick!' said Taffy. 'But why did you bring so many people? Daddy dear, this is my surprise. Are you surprised, Daddy?'

'Very,' said Tegumai, 'but it has ruined all my fishing for the day. Why, the whole dear, kind, nice, clean, quiet Tribe is here, Taffy.'

And so they were. First of all walked Teshumai Tewindrow and the Neolithic ladies, tightly holding on to the Stranger-man, whose hair was full of mud (although he was a Tewara). Behind them came the Head Chief, the Vice-Chief, the Deputy and Assistant Chiefs (all armed to the upper teeth), the Hetmans and Heads of Hundreds, Platoffs with their Platoons, and Dolmans with their Detachments; Woons, Neguses, and Akhoonds ranking in the rear (still armed to the teeth). Behind them was the Tribe in **hierarchical**⑥ order, from owners of four caves (one for each season), a private **reindeer-run**⑦, and two **salmon-leaps**⑧, to **feudal**⑨ and **prognathous**⑩ Villeins, semi-entitled to half a bearskin of winter nights, seven yards from the fire, and **adscript**⑪ **serfs**⑫, holding the **reversion**⑬ of a scraped **marrow**⑭-bone under **heriot**⑮ (Aren't those beautiful words, Best Beloved?). They were all there, **prancing**⑯ and shouting, and they frightened every fish for twenty miles, and Tegumai thanked them in a **fluid**⑰ **Neolithic**⑱ **oration**⑲.

Then Teshumai Tewindrow ran down and kissed and hugged Taffy very much indeed; but the Dead Chief of the Tribe of Tegumai took Tegumai by the top-knot feathers and shook him severely.

'Explain! Explain! Explain!' cried all the Tribe of Tegumai.

① assemble /əˈsembl/ v. 集会，集合，聚集
② daisy /ˈdeɪzi/ n. 雏菊
③ spear /spɪə/ v. 用渔叉刺，戳
④ carp /kɑːp/ n. 鲤鱼
⑤ spear /spɪə/ n. 矛；鱼叉；
⑥ hierarchical /ˌhaɪəˈrɑːkɪkəl/ adj. 等级排列的；
⑦ reindeer-run /ˈreɪnˌdɪəˌrʌn/ n. 驯鹿饲养场
⑧ salmon-leap /ˈsæmənˌliːp/ n. 大麻哈鱼鱼道
⑨ feudal /ˈfjuːdl/ adj. 封地的
⑩ prognathous /ˈprɒɡnəθəs/ adj. 凸颚的隶民
⑪ adscript /ˈædskrɪpt/ adj. 后记的
⑫ serf /sɜːf/ n. 农奴
⑬ reversion /rɪˈvɜːʃn/ n. 剩下
⑭ marrow /ˈmærəʊ/ n. 髓；骨髓
⑮ heriot /ˈherɪət/ n. 租地继承税；文中指积攒
⑯ prance /prɑːns/ n. 腾跃；欢跃
⑰ fluid /ˈfluːɪd/ adj. 流动的（文中指流利的）
⑱ neolithic /ˌniːəˈlɪθɪk/ adj. 新石器时代的；
⑲ oration /ɔːˈreɪʃn/ n. 致辞 致谢

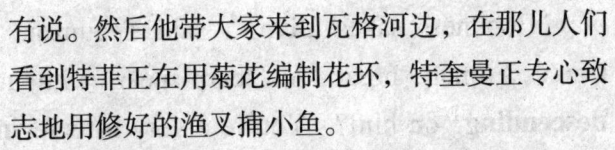

有说。然后他带大家来到瓦格河边，在那儿人们看到特菲正在用菊花编制花环，特奎曼正专心致志地用修好的渔叉捕小鱼。

"啊，你回来得可真快！"特菲说，"但你为什么带这么多的人来？亲爱的爸爸，这就是我给你的惊喜。你感到惊讶了吗，爸爸？"

"非常惊讶，"特奎曼说，"但这把我一天的捕鱼计划全打乱了。特菲，为什么我们这个亲切、善良、友好、清洁、安宁的部落全搬到这里来了？"

的确，所有的人都来了。走在最前面的是特舒曼·特温德鲁和其他几个妇女，她们紧紧抓着那个陌生人。陌生人头发上净是泥巴（尽管他是个特瓦拉人）。跟在她们后面的是总首领、副总首领、副首领和首领助理（全都全副武装）、几百个赫特曼人、几个排的布拉特人、几个多佛尔人小分队，渥恩人、尼格斯人和阿克洪恩人殿后（也是全副武装）。再往后则按照等级排列。从四个山洞（一个季节一个洞穴）的主人，一个私有驯鹿饲养场主人，两条大马哈鱼鱼道的主人，到封地凸颌隶民，他们有时有资格在冬夜睡半张熊皮，离火堆七码远，还有附属于土地的农奴，手里拿着向领主进贡后剩下的可食用的动物髓骨，这些骨头可是辛辛苦苦积攒的（亲爱的读者，这些词汇是不是很美？）。他们都站在那里，跳跃呼喊着，吓跑了20里河滩上的鱼。特奎曼操着流利的新石器时代的语言向他们致谢。

特舒曼·特温德鲁跑过来，使劲地亲吻、拥抱特菲。但是部落的首领却一把抓住特奎曼的头

'Goodness sakes alive!' said Tegumai. 'Let go of my top-knot. Can't a man break his carp-spear without the whole countryside **descending**① on him? You're a very **interfering**② people.'

'I don't believe you've brought my Daddy's black-handled spear after all,' said Taffy. 'And what are you doing to my nice Stranger-man?'

They were thumping him by twos and threes and tens till his eyes turned round and round. He could only **gasp**③ and point at Taffy.

'Where are the bad people who speared you, my darling?' said Teshumai Tewindrow.

'There weren't any,' said Tegumai. 'My only visitor this morning was the poor **fellow**④ that you are trying to **choke**⑤. Aren't you well, or are you ill, O Tribe of Tegumai?'

'He came with a horrible picture,' said the Head Chief, —'a picture that showed you were full of spears.'

'Er-um-Pr'aps I'd better 'splain that I gave him that picture,' said Taffy, but she did not feel quite **comfy**⑥.

'You!' said the Tribe of Tegumai all together. 'Small-person-with-no-manners-who-ought-to-be-spanked! You?'

'Taffy dear, I'm afraid we're in for a little trouble,' said her Daddy, and put his hand round her, so she didn't care.

'Explain! Explain! Explain!' said the Head Chief of the Tribe of Tegumai, and he **hopped**⑦ on one foot.

'I wanted the Stranger-man to **fetch**⑧ Daddy's spear, so I **drawded**⑨ it,' said Taffy. 'There wasn't lots of spears. There was only one spear. I drawded it three times to make sure. I couldn't help it looking as if it stuck into Daddy's head—there wasn't room on the birch-bark; and those things that Mummy called bad people are my **beavers**⑩. I drawded them to show him the way through the **swamp**⑪; and I drawded Mummy at

① descend /dɪˈsend/ v. 降临 下降；
② interfere /ˌɪntə(r)ˈfɪə/ v. 妨碍；抵触；（文中指管闲事）
③ gasp /gɑːsp/ v. 喘气，喘着气说
④ fellow /ˈfeləʊ/ n. 人，同事，朋友（文中指陌生人）
⑤ choke /tʃəʊk/ v. 窒息，（文中指掐死）
⑥ comfy /ˈkʌmfɪ/ adj. 舒服的；轻松的
⑦ hop /hɒp/ v. 跳起（文中指跺）
⑧ fetch /fetʃ/ v. 去拿……给；
⑨ draw /drɔː/ v. 绘制，画；
⑩ beaver /ˈbiːvə/ n. 海狸，河狸；

饰，使劲地摇晃着他。

"说清楚！说清楚！说清楚！"整个部落的人大声呼喊着。

"我的天呐！"特奎曼说，"放开我的头饰。如果一个人折断了渔叉，难道整个部落就都得降临到他身边吗？你们可真爱管闲事。"

"我不相信你们会拿来爸爸那只带黑手柄的渔叉，"特菲说，"你们是怎么对待这善良的陌生人的？"

他被越来越多的人踢踹着，最后他的眼睛来回转着。他只能喘着粗气看着特菲。

"亲爱的，那些打你的坏人在哪里？"特舒曼·特温德鲁问。

"没有人打我，"特奎曼说，"今天上午我唯一的一位客人就是这位你们想掐死的陌生人。您生病了吗？我们的部落到底怎么了吗？"

"他拿来一张可怕的图画，"首领说，"画上的你身上扎满了渔叉！"

"哦——哦——，也许我最好解释一下，那幅画是我给他的，"特菲说，她感到有点儿不自在。

"你！"整个部落的人惊叹道，"没有礼貌、该打屁股的小孩！你？"

"亲爱的特菲，恐怕我们有点儿小麻烦了，"她爸爸说着把手搭在女儿身上，那样她就不害怕一了。

"说清楚！说清楚！说清楚！"部落首领一边跺脚一边喊道。

"我想让陌生人去拿我爸爸的渔叉，所以就画了这幅画，"特菲说，"上面并没有画很多渔

the mouth of the Cave looking pleased because he is a nice Stranger-man, and I think you are just the stupidest people in the world,' said Taffy. 'He is a very nice man. Why have you filled his hair with mud? Wash him!'

Nobody said anything at all for a long time, till the Head Chief laughed; then the Stranger-man (who was at least a Tewara) laughed; then Tegumai laughed till he fell down flat on the **bank**①; then all the Tribe laughed more and worse and louder. The only people who did not laugh were Teshumai Tewindrow and all the Neolithic ladies. They were very polite to all their husbands, and said '**idiot**②!' ever so often.

Then the Head Chief of the Tribe of Tegumai cried and said and sang, 'O Small-person-without-any-manners-who-ought-to-be-spanked, you've hit upon a great **invention**③!'

'I didn't intend to; I only wanted Daddy's black-handled spear,' said Taffy.

'Never mind. It is a great invention, and some day men will call it writing. At present it is only pictures, and, as we have seen today, pictures are not always **properly**④ understood. But a time will come, O Babe of Tegumai, when we shall make letters—all twenty-six of 'em, —and when we shall be able to read as well as to write, and then we shall always say exactly what we mean without any mistakes. Let the Neolithic ladies wash the mud out of the stranger's hair.'

'I shall be glad of that,' said Taffy, 'because, after all, though you've brought every single other spear in the Tribe of Tegumai, you've forgotten my Daddy's black-handled spear.'

Then the Head Chief cried and said and sang, 'Taffy dear, the next time you write a **picture-letter**⑤, you'd better send a man who can talk our language with it, to explain what it means. I don't mind it myself,

叉，其实只有一把。为了明确起见，我一共画了三次。它看起来好像扎进了我爸爸的脑袋——这实在没办法，树皮太小没地方画；而且画上妈妈称为坏人的东西是我画的河狸。我把河狸画出来是为了给他指出穿过沼泽地的路，画妈妈高兴地站在洞门口是因为他是个大好人。我觉得你们这些人才是世界上最最愚蠢的人，"特菲说，"他是个大好人。你们为什么在他的头发上抹上泥巴？给他洗干净！"

很长一段时间没有人开口，最后首领放声大笑，陌生人（特瓦拉人）也笑了，特奎曼笑得倒在岸边，整个部落的人越笑声音越大。唯独特舒曼·特温德鲁和其他妇女没有笑，她们对丈夫们很有礼貌，只是说："白痴！"她们也经常这样说。

然后部落首领拖着长腔大声说道："啊，那个没有礼貌、该打屁股的小孩，你偶然之间做出了一项发明！"

"我本来没想这样做，我只想要爸爸那只带黑手柄的渔叉，"特菲说。

"不要紧，这是一项很伟大的发明，有一天人们会把它叫做写字。现在还只是图画，正像我们今天所看到的，人们不能正确地理解图片的内容。但会有这么一天的，小宝贝，那时我们会创造字母——一共 26 个——我们不仅会写还会读，并且还能准确无误地把事情讲清楚。女人们，你们去把陌生人的头发洗干净吧。"

"那样我会很高兴的，"特菲说，"因为尽管你们几乎把整个部落的渔叉都拿来了，还是忘记了我爸爸那只带黑手柄的渔叉。"

首领又拖着长腔大声说道："亲爱的特菲，

① bank /bæŋk/ n. 田埂；河岸

② idiot /ˈɪdɪət/ n. 白痴，极蠢之人

③ invention /ɪnˈvenʃn/ n. 发明，

④ properly /ˈprɑpə(r)lɪ/ adv. 正确地；

⑤ picture-letter /ˈpɪktʃə(r) ˈletə(r)/ n. 图片信

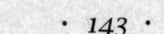

143

because I am a Head Chief, but it's very bad for the rest of the Tribe of Tegumai, and, as you can see, it surprises the stranger.'

Then they **adopted**① the Stranger-man (a **genuine**② Tewara of Tewar) into the Tribe of Tegumai, because he was a **gentleman**③ and did not make a **fuss**④ about the mud that the Neolithic ladies had put into his hair. But from that day to this (and I **suppose**⑤ it is all Taffy's fault), very few little girls have ever liked learning to read or write. Most of them **prefer**⑥ to draw pictures and play about with their Daddies—just like Taffy.

① adopted /əˈdɒptɪd/ adj. 被收养的；被采用的；（文中指邀请）
② genuine /ˈdʒenjʊɪn/ adj. 真正的
③ gentleman /ˈdʒentlmən/ n. 绅士，先生
④ fuss /fʌs/ v. 喋喋不休
⑤ suppose /səˈpəʊz/ v. 推想，猜想
⑥ prefer /prɪˈfɜː/ v. 更喜欢

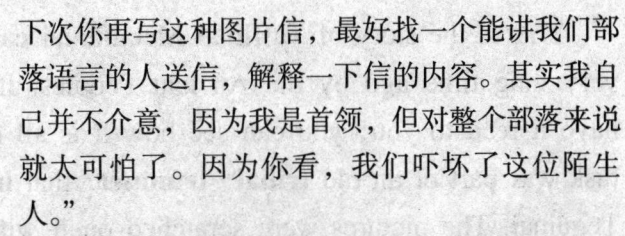

下次你再写这种图片信，最好找一个能讲我们部落语言的人送信，解释一下信的内容。其实我自己并不介意，因为我是首领，但对整个部落来说就太可怕了。因为你看，我们吓坏了这位陌生人。"

然后他们邀请这位陌生人（一个真正的特瓦拉人）加入自己的部落，因为他是个绅士，并没有因为妇女们往他头上抹泥巴就喋喋不休。但从那一天开始直到现在（我想那全是特菲的错），女孩子们都不喜欢读书写字，只喜欢画画，还有和爸爸一起玩——就像特菲一样。

Just So Stories

This is the story of Taffimai Metallumai **carved**① on an old **tusk**② a very long time ago by the Ancient Peoples. If you read my story, or have it read to you, you can see how it is all told out on the tusk. The tusk was part of an old **tribal**③ **trumpet**④ that **belonged**⑤ to the Tribe of Tegumai. The pictures were scratched on it with **a nail**⑥ or something, and then the scratches were filled up with black **wax**⑦, but all the dividing lines and the five little rounds at the bottom were filled with red wax. When it was new there was a sort of **network**⑧ of **beads**⑨ and shells and precious stones at one end of it; but now that has been broken and lost—all except the little bit that you see. The letters round the tusk are **magic**⑩—Runic magic—and if you can read them you will find out something rather new. The tusk is of **ivory**⑪—very yellow and scratched. It is two feet long and two feet round, and weighs eleven **pounds**⑫ nine **ounces**⑬.

很久以前古人把特罪曼·梅塔柳迈的故事雕刻在这根长牙上。如果你读过或听过这个故事，你就会知道在长牙上这个故事是怎么讲的。这根长牙是特奎曼所在部落的号角的一部分。图画是用钉子之类的硬物刻上去的，然后在刻痕上涂上黑蜡。但分界线和底部的五个小圆圈是用红蜡固定的。刚做好的时候，长牙一端还有珠子、贝壳和宝石等一套装饰物，但到了现在都已经断裂或丢失了——除了你看到的那一点儿。长牙上的文字很神奇——带着魔力，如果你能读懂的话，就能发现些很新的东西。这根象牙颜色很黄，划痕累累。它有两英尺长，直径也是两英尺；重量是11磅9盎司。

① carve /kɑːv/ v. 刻，雕刻；
② tusk /tʌsk/ n. 长牙，
③ tribal /ˈtraɪbl/ adj. 部落的；
④ trumpet /ˈtrʌmpɪt/ n. 喇叭，号角
⑤ belong /bɪˈlɒŋ/ v. 属于
⑥ nail /neɪl/ n. 钉子
⑦ wax /wæks/ n. 蜡，蜡状物
⑧ network n. 网眼织物；网状物；（文中指装饰物）
⑨ bead /biːd/ n. 珠子
⑩ magic /ˈmædʒɪk/ n. 魔力，魔法
⑪ ivory /ˈaɪvəri/ n. 象牙
⑫ pound /paʊnd/ n. 磅
⑬ ounce /aʊns/ n. 盎司

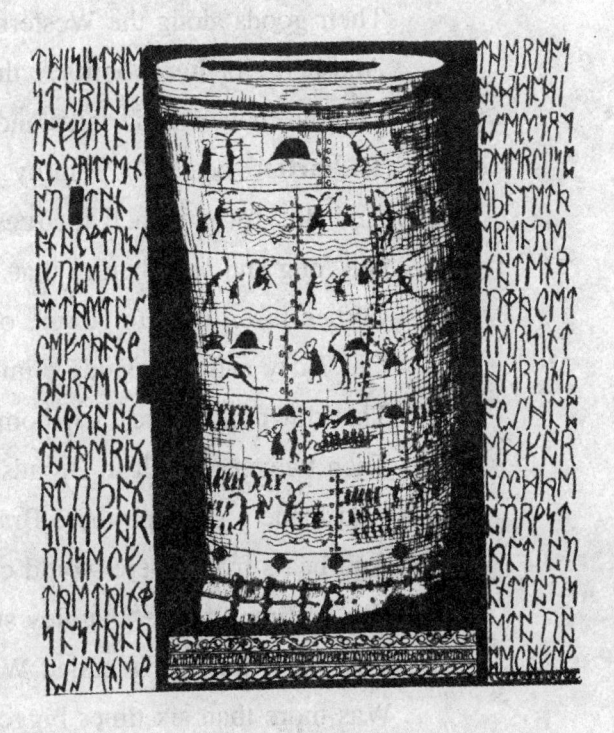

There runs a road by Merrow Down—
A **grassy**① track today it is
An hour out of Guildford town,
Above the river Wey it is.
Here, when they heard the horse-bells ring,
The ancient Britons dressed and rode
To watch the dark **Phoenicians**② bring
Their goods along the Western Road.
And here, or **hereabouts**③, they met
To hold their **racial**④ talks and such—
To **barter**⑤ beads for Whitby jet,
And **tin**⑥ for gay shell **torques**⑦ and such.
But long and long before that time
(When bison used to **roam**⑧ on it)
Did Taffy and her Daddy climb
That down, and had their home on it.
Then **beavers**⑨ built in Broadstonebrook
And made a swamp where Bramley stands
And bears from Shere would come and look
For Taffimai where Shamley stands.
The Wey, that Taffy called Wagai,
Was more than six times bigger then;
And all the Tribe of Tegumai
They cut a noble **figure**⑩ then!

① grassy /'ɡræsɪ/ n. 草

② Phoenician /fɪ'nɪʃɪən/ n. 腓尼基人

③ hereabout /ˌhɪrə'baʊt/ adv. 在这一带

④ racial /'reɪʃl/ adj. ，种族的；种族之间的

⑤ barter /'bɑːtə/ v. 交换

⑥ tin /tɪn/ n. 锡

⑦ torque /tɔrk/ n. 颈圈

⑧ roam /rəʊm/ v. 漫步，在…漫步；

⑨ beaver /'biːvə/ n. 海狸，河狸

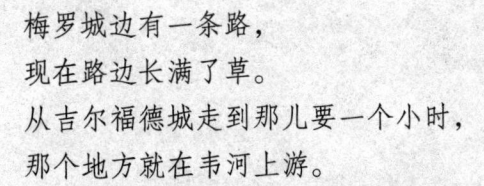

⑩ figure /'fɪɡə/ n. 图形，（文中指人像）

梅罗城边有一条路，
现在路边长满了草。
从吉尔福德城走到那儿要一个小时，
那个地方就在韦河上游。

这里曾经是马铃一响，古代不列颠人便穿好衣服、骑上马，
去看一看黑黑的腓尼基人，
沿着西方的路带来了什么货物。

这里，或者，这一带，他们聚首，
用种族语言谈话，
并用珠子交换怀特比煤矿，
用锡换取漂亮的贝壳颈圈……

但在此之前，很久很久以前
（那时野牛在这里漫步）
特菲和她爸爸是否登上那城镇，
并在那里建立起自己的家？

然后河狸来到了布鲁德斯通溪边，
在布拉姆利站立的地方形成一块沼泽地。
希尔地区的大熊也来看看，
在沙姆利站立的地方寻找特菲曼的影子。

特菲把韦河叫瓦格河，
那时的河要比现在大六倍。
所有特奎曼部落的人，
在那儿雕刻了一个贵族人像！

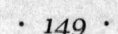

· 149 ·

How the Alphabet was Made

The week after Taffimai Metallumai (we will still call her Taffy, Best **Beloved**①) made that little mistake about her Daddy's spear and the Stranger-man and the picture-letter and all, she went carp-fishing again with her Daddy. Her Mummy wanted her to stay at home and help hang up **hides**② to dry on the **big drying-poles**③ outside their Neolithic Cave, but Taffy **slipped away**④ down to her Daddy quite early, and they fished. Presently she began to **giggle**⑤, and her Daddy said, 'Don't be **silly**⑥, child.'

'But wasn't it **inciting**⑦!' said Taffy. 'Don't you remember how the Head Chief **puffed out**⑧ his cheeks, and how funny the nice Stranger-man looked with the mud in his hair?'

'Well do I,' said Tegumai. 'I had to pay two deerskins—soft ones with **fringes**⑨—to the Stranger-man for the things we did to him.'

'We didn't do anything,' said Taffy. 'It was Mummy and the other Neolithic ladies—and the mud.'

'We won't talk about that,' said her Daddy, 'Let's have lunch.'

Taffy took a marrow-bone and sat **mousy-quiet**⑩ for ten whole minutes, while her Daddy scratched on pieces of birch-bark with a shark's tooth. Then she said, Daddy, I've thinked of a secret surprise. You make a noise—any sort of noise.

字母表是怎么创造出来的

① beloved /bɪˈlʌvd/ adj. 心爱的，亲爱的

② hide /haɪd/ n. 兽皮

③ drying-pole /ˈdraɪkɪŋ-pəʊl/ n. 凉衣杆

④ away /əˈweɪ/ adv. 在远处

⑤ giggle /ˈɡɪɡl/ v. 咯咯地笑；傻笑；咯咯地笑着说

⑥ silly /ˈsɪli/ adj. 愚蠢的，犯傻

⑦ incite /ɪnˈsaɪt/ v. 激励；煽动；激起

⑧ puff /pʌf/ v. 鼓起腮帮子

⑨ fringe /frɪndʒ/ n. 边缘，流苏，端

⑩ mousy-quite /ˈmaʊsi-kwaɪət/ adj. 安静的

在上个故事中，我们讲到特菲曼·梅塔柳迈（亲爱的读者，我们还是叫她特菲）出了点儿小错，所犯的错误与她爸爸的渔叉、陌生人和图画信有关。一个星期后，她又和爸爸一起去捉鱼。妈妈本想让她呆在家里，帮着她把兽皮挂起来，晾在新石器时代山洞边那个大大的晾衣杆上，但特菲一早便偷偷地溜到河下游去找爸爸。他们在一起捉鱼的时候，特菲突然咯咯地笑起来。爸爸对她说："别犯傻了，孩子。"

"那可真有意思！"特菲说，"难道你不记得首领鼓起腮帮子、那个陌生人满头泥巴的样子了吗？"

"我记得清清楚楚，"特奎曼·鲍普苏莱说，"我不得不赔给那陌生人两张带毛边的、柔软的鹿皮，以补偿我们对他所做的一切。"

"我们没做什么错事，"特菲说，"做错事的是妈妈和其他女人们——还有那些泥巴。"

"我们不说这些了，"爸爸说，"吃午饭吧。"

特菲拿起一块髓骨，安静地坐下，整整十分钟什么也没有说。这时爸爸拿着一块鲨鱼齿在桦树皮上划着道道。特菲开口说："爸爸，我想出了一个秘密的、吓人一跳的主意。你随便发出个

'Ah!' said Tegumai. 'Will that do to begin with?'

'Yes,' said Taffy. 'You look just like a carp-fish with its mouth open. Say it again, please.'

'Ah! ah! ah!' said her Daddy. 'Don't be rude, my daughter.'

'I'm not meaning rude, really and truly,' said Taffy. 'It's part of my secret-surprise-think. Do say ah, Daddy, and keep your mouth open at the end, and lend me that tooth. I'm going to draw a carp-fish's mouth **wideopen**①.'

'What for?' said her Daddy.

'Don't you see?' said Taffy, scratching away on the bark. 'That will be our little secret s'prise. When I draw a carp-fish with his mouth open in the smoke at the back of our Cave—if Mummy doesn't mind—it will remind you of that ah-noise. Then we can play that it was me jumped out of the dark and surprised you with that noise—same as I did in the beaver-swamp last winter.'

'Really?' said her Daddy, in the voice that **grown-ups**② use when they are truly **attending**③. 'Go on, Taffy.'

'Oh bother!' she said. 'I can't draw all of a carp-fish, but I can draw something that means a carp-fish's mouth. Don't you know how they stand on their heads rooting in the mud? Well, here's a **pretence**④ carp-fish (we can play that the rest of him is drawn). Here's just his mouth, and that means 'ah.' And she drew this. (1)

'That's not bad,' said Tegumai, and scratched on his own piece of bark for himself; 'but you've forgotten the **feeler**⑤ that hangs across his mouth.'

'But I can't draw, Daddy.'

'You needn't draw anything of him except just the opening of his mouth and the feeler across. Then we'll know he's a carp-fish, 'cause

① wide-open
/waɪd-ˈəʊpən/ adv
大张着

② grown-ups
/grəʊn-ʌps/ v. 大人

③ attend /əˈtend/ v. 吸引住

④ pretence /prɪˈtens/ n. 假装，

⑤ feeler /ˈfiːlə(r)/ n. 触角

声音——什么声音都可以。"

"啊！"特奎曼说，"用这个作为开头吗？"

"是的，"特菲说，"您看起来就像一只张着嘴巴的鲤鱼。请您再说一遍。"

"啊！啊！啊！"爸爸说，"女儿，不许没有礼貌。"

"我真的不是那个意思，"特菲说，"这只是我偷偷吓人一跳的主意的一部分。爸爸，说'啊'，嘴巴一直张着。把那只鲨鱼齿借给我吧，我要把鲤鱼大张着的嘴巴画下来。"

"干什么用？"爸爸问。

"您没看见吗？"特菲说，同时不停地在桦树皮上刻画着。"这将是我们秘密的小小吓人游戏。如果我在山洞后面被烟熏黑的地方画一只张着大嘴的鱼——如果这样做妈妈不介意的话——它就会提醒你，让你想起'啊'这个发音。然后我们就可以玩儿，我从黑暗中跳出来，用那个声音吓你一跳——就像我们去年冬天在河狸出没的沼泽地里玩儿的那样。"

"真的？"爸爸问，听得出这个大人被特菲的想法深深地吸引住了。"继续说下去，特菲。"

"喔，讨厌！"她说，"我没法儿画出一整条鲤鱼，但我可以画点儿什么代表鲤鱼的嘴巴。您不知道它们大头朝下栽进淤泥里的样子吗？那么，假装这是鲤鱼（假设鱼的其他部分已经画出来了），这就是它的嘴巴，代表'啊'。"她就画出了下面这个图形（1）。

"这倒不错"，特奎曼说，随手在自己的桦树皮上也画了一下，"但你忘记了它嘴边长的触须。"

"但我不会画呀，爸爸。"

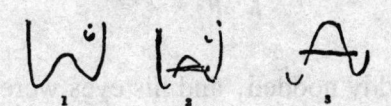

· 153 ·

the **perches**① and **trouts**② haven't got feelers. Look here, Taffy.' And he drew this. (2.).

'Now I'll copy it.' said Taffy. 'Will you understand *this* when you see it?' And she drew this. (3.)

'**Perfectly**③,' said her Daddy. 'And I'll be quite as s'prised when I see it anywhere, as if you had jumped out from behind a tree and said "Ah!"'

'Now, make another noise,' said Taffy, very proud.

'Yah!' said her Daddy, very loud.

'H'm,' said Taffy. 'That's a **mixy**④ noise. The end part is *ah*-carp-fish-mouth; but what can we do about the front part? *Yer-yer-yer* and *ah! Ya!*'

'It's very like the carp-fish-mouth noise, Let's draw another **bit**⑤ of the carp-fish and join 'em,' said her Daddy. He was quite incited too.

'No. If they're joined, I'll forget. Draw it **separate**⑥. Draw his **tail**⑦. If he's standing on his head the tail will come first. Besides, I think I can draw tails easiest,' said Taffy.

'A good **notion**⑧,' said Tegumai. 'Here's a carp-fish tail for the *yer*-noise.' And he drew this. (4.)

'I'll try now,' said Taffy. 'Member I can't draw like you, Daddy. Will it do if I just draw the **split**⑨ part of the tail, and the **sticky-down**⑩ line for where it joins?' And she drew this. (5.)

Her Daddy nodded, and his eyes were **shiny**⑪ bright with 'citement.

① perch /pɜrtʃ/ n. 河鲈

② trout /traut/ n. 鲑鱼鳟鱼

③ perfectly /'pɜrfɪktlɪ/ adv. 完全地，完整地（文中指绝对明白）

④ mix /mɪks/ n. 混合

⑤ bit /bɪt/ n. 小段，一部分

⑥ separate /' sepəreɪt/ v. 分开；

⑦ tail /teɪl/ n. 尾巴

⑧ notion /'nəʊʃn/ n. 想法，主意

⑨ split /splɪt/ v. 分叉，分开

⑩ sticky-down /'stɪkɪ-daʊn/ adj. 粘的；连接起来

⑪ shiny /' ʃaɪnɪ/ adj. 放光的，发光的

"只要在它张大的嘴上画一条线就行了。这样我们就知道这是条鲤鱼了，因为河鲈和鳟鱼没有触须。看这儿，特菲。"他又画了一笔（图2）。

"我也模仿您画一笔，"特菲说，"看到这个的时候，您会明白这是什么意思吗？"她画出了下面这个图形（3）。

"绝对明白，"爸爸说，"在哪儿看见它，我都会大吃一惊。就像你从一棵树背后跳出来大叫一声'啊'一样。"

"现在，您再发出个声音吧"，特菲说。她很为自己感到骄傲。

"呀！"爸爸大声说。

"嗯，"特菲说，"这是个混合音。后面的音是啊——鲤鱼嘴巴，前面的音我们该怎么办？'耶—耶'（ye）和'啊'（a）！呀！"

"这听起来像鲤鱼嘴代表的声音。我们再画出鲤鱼身体的另外一部分，与原来的合在一起。"爸爸也兴致勃勃地说。

"不，如果合在一起的话，我就会忘掉。分开画吧，画它的尾巴。如果鱼头朝下，那尾巴就先伸出来了。而且，我想画尾巴是最容易的。"特菲说。

"好主意，"特奎曼说，"这个是代表'耶(ye)'这个音的鲤鱼尾巴。"他画了出来。

"让我试试，"特菲说，"但爸爸，您要知道，我没办法画得像您那样好。如果我只画尾巴的分叉部位，再用一条向下的竖线与鱼身子连起来，怎么样？"她画出了图形（5）。

· 155 ·

Just So Stories

'That's beautiful,' she said. 'Now make another noise, Daddy.'

'Oh!' said her Daddy, very loud.

'That's quite easy,' said Taffy. 'You make your mouth all around like an egg or a stone. So an egg or a stone will do for that.'

'You can't always find eggs or stones. We'll have to scratch a round something like one.' And he drew this. (6.)

'My **gracious**①!' said Taffy, 'what a lot of noise-pictures we've made, carp-mouth, carp-tail, and egg! Now, make another noise, Daddy.'

'Ssh!' said her Daddy, and **frowned**② to himself, but Taffy was too incited to notice.

'That's quite easy,' she said, scratching on the bark.

'Eh, what?' said her Daddy. 'I meant I was thinking, and didn't want to be **disturbed**③.'

'It's a noise just the same. It's the noise a **snake**④ makes, Daddy, when it is thinking and doesn't want to be disturbed. Let's make the *ssh*-noise a snake. Will this do?' And she drew this. (7.)

'There,' she said. 'That's another s'prise-secret. When you draw a hissy-snake by the door of your little back-cave where you mend the spears, I'll know you're thinking hard; and I'll come in most mousy-quiet. And if you draw it on a tree by the river when you are fishing, I'll know you want me to walk most most mousy-quiet, so as not to **shake**⑤ the banks.'

'Perfectly true,' said Tegumai. 'And there's more in this game than

远古传奇

爸爸点点头,他的眼里闪着兴奋的光芒。

"太妙了,"她说,"现在您再发一个别的音,爸爸。"

"噢! (o)"爸爸大声说。

"这个太简单了,"特菲说,"您的嘴巴张得圆圆的,像个鸡蛋,也像一颗卵石。那么,鸡蛋和卵石就能代表这个声音了。"

"但你不可能总能找到鸡蛋或卵石。我们最好把这个圆圆的形状画下来。"他画了起来(6)。

① gracious /'greɪʃəs/ adj. 亲切的(文中指太棒了)

"太棒了!"特菲说,"我们创造了多少代表声音的符号啊——鲤鱼嘴巴、鲤鱼尾巴、还有鸡蛋!爸爸,现在再发出另外一种声音。"

② frown /fraʊn/ v. 皱眉; 皱眉表示

"嘶(s)!"爸爸说,而且还对着自己皱了皱眉头。但特菲太兴奋了,没有注意到。

"这可挺简单的,"她一边说,一边在树皮上划着。

③ disturb /dɪ'stɜːb/ v. 打扰; 打乱

"呃,什么?"爸爸说,"我的意思是我正在思考,并且不愿意被别人打扰。"

④ snake /sneɪk/ n. 蛇;

"这个声音正好代表这个意思。这是蛇发出来的声音,爸爸。当蛇在思考并且不愿意被人打扰时就发出这种声音。我们画一条蛇表示'嘶'(s)这个声音。这个行吗?"她画了出来(7)。

⑤ shake /ʃeɪk/ v. 摇动,动摇(文中指乱崩乱跳)

"那么,"她说,"这是另外一个秘密游戏。当你在后面小山洞的门口修理渔叉时,只要画出一条嘶嘶叫的蛇的图形,我就知道你正在认真思考着问题,就会用最轻的声音、蹑手蹑脚地走过来。如果你钓鱼时在旁边的树干上画上这个符号,我就知道你想让我最最轻声地走路,不要在河岸上乱蹦乱跳。"

"太对了,"特奎曼说,"这游戏包含的内容比

· 157 ·

you think. Taffy, dear, I've a notion that your Daddy's daughter has hit upon the finest thing that there ever was since the Tribe of Tegumai took to using shark's teeth **instead**[①] of **flints**[②] for their spear-heads. I believe we've found out the big secret of the world.'

'Why?' said Taffy, and her eyes **shone**[③] too with incitement.

'I'll show,' said her Daddy. 'What's water in the **Tegumai**[④] language?'

'*Ya*, of course, and it means river too—like Wagai-*ya*—the Wagai river.'

'What is bad water that gives you fever if you drink it—black water— swamp-water?'

'*Yo*, of course.'

'Now look,' said her Daddy. 'S'pose you saw this scratched by the side of a **pool**[⑤] in the beaver-swamp?' And he drew this. (8.)

'Carp-tail and round egg. Two noises **mixed**[⑥]! *Yo*, bad water,' said Taffy. 'Course I wouldn't drink that water because I'd know you said it was bad.'

'But I needn't be near the water at all. I might be **miles**[⑦] away, **hunting**[⑧], and still—'

'And still it would be just the same as if you stood there and said, "G'way, Taffy, or you'll get fever." All that in a carp-fish-tail and a round egg! O Daddy, we must tell Mummy, quick!' and Taffy danced all round him.

'Not yet,' said Tegumai; 'not till we've gone a little further. Let's see. *Yo* is bad water, but *So* is food cooked on the fire, isn't it?' And he drew this. (9.)

'Yes. Snake and egg,' said Taffy. 'So that means dinner's ready. If you saw that scratched on a tree you'd know it was time to come to the Cave. So'd I.'

① instead /ɪn'sted/ adv. 改为,更换,
② flint /flɪnt/ n. 燧石
③ shine /ʃaɪn/ v. 闪着

④ Tegumai 特奎曼部落

⑤ pool /puːl/ n. 沼泽地,水池;

⑥ mixed /mɪkst/ adj. 混合的,结合

⑦ mile /maɪl/ n. 英里
⑧ hunting /'hʌntɪŋ/ n. 狩猎

你能想到的要多得多。亲爱的特菲,我想自从特奎曼部落用鲨鱼齿代替燧石做渔叉头以来,是我的女儿想出了这世界上最伟大的一个主意。我相信,我们已经发现了这世界上最重大的秘密。"

"为什么?"特菲问,她的眼里也闪着兴奋的光芒。

"我会讲给你听的,"爸爸说,"在我们特奎曼部落的语言里,'水'怎么说?"

"当然是'亚'(ya),它也指河流——瓦格亚就是河。"

"那人喝了后会发烧的'脏'水——黑水、沼泽水怎么说?"

"当然是'幽'(yo)。"

"现在你瞧,"爸爸说,"假设河狸沼泽池的一边刻着这个图形。"他画了起来(8)。

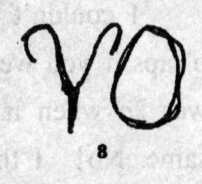

yo
8

"鲤鱼尾巴和圆圆的鸡蛋,两个发音结合在一起!'幽(yo)',脏水,"特菲说,"当然我不会喝那儿的水了。因为我知道你说那儿的水脏。"

"但我没必要就站在水边呀。我也许在几英里外的地方打猎,但还"

"如果你不站在水边这样说,它还是同样的意思啊——'快离开,特菲,否则喝了你就会发烧的'全部意思已经包括在鲤鱼尾巴和圆圆的鸡蛋里了!噢,爸爸,我们一定要把这些告诉妈妈,快点儿!"特菲围着爸爸又蹦又跳。

"等一会儿,"特奎曼说,"我们再想想。'幽'(yo)指的是脏水,但'嗖'(so)应该是指火上烹制的食物,对不对?"他画了出来(9)。

"对,蛇和鸡蛋,"特菲说,"那意思是饭做

· 159 ·

'My Winkie!' said Tegumai. 'That's true too. But wait a minute. I see a **difficulty**①. So means "come and have dinner," but *sho* means the dryingpoles where we hang our hides.'

'**Horrid**② old drying-poles!' said Taffy. 'I hate helping to hang heavy, hot, **hairy**③ hides on them. If you drew the snake and egg, and I thought it **meant**④ dinner, and I came in from the wood and found that it meant I was to help Mummy hang the two hides on the drying-poles', what would I do?'

'You'd be **cross**⑤. So'd Mummy. We must make a new picture for *sho*. We must draw a **spotty**⑥ snake that **hisses**⑦ sh-sh, and we'll play that the plain snake only hisses ssss.'

'I couldn't be sure how to put in the **spots**⑧,' said Taffy. 'And p'raps if you were in a hurry you might leave them out, and I'd think it was *so* when it was *sho*, and then Mummy would catch me just the same. No! I think we'd better draw a picture of the horrid high drying-poles their very selves, and make quite sure. I'll put them in just after the hissy-snake. Look!' And she drew this. (10.)

'P'raps that's safest. It's very like our drying-poles, **anyhow**⑨,' said her Daddy, laughing. 'Now I'll make a new noise with a snake and drying-pole sound in it. I'll say *shi*. That's Tegumai for spear, Taffy.' And he laughed.

'Don't **make fun of**⑩ me,' said Taffy, as she thought of her picture-letter and the mud in the Stranger-man's hair. 'You draw it, Daddy.'

'We won't have beavers or hills this time, eh?' said her Daddy, 'I'll just draw a **straight**⑪ line for my spear.' and he drew this. (11.)

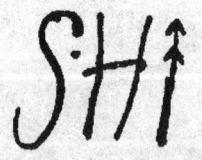

① difficulty /'dɪfɪkʌltɪ/ n. 困难；问题

② horrid /'hɒrɪd/ adj. 可恶的

③ hairy /'heərlɪ/ adj. 多毛的，长毛的

④ meant /'miːnt/ adv. 那是指

⑤ cross /krɒs/ adj. 生气的

⑥ spotty /'spɒtɪ/ adj. 多斑点的，

⑦ hiss /hɪs/ n. 嘶嘶声

⑧ spot /spɒt/ n. 斑点，

⑨ anyhow adv. 总之；无论如何

⑩ make fun of 取笑，寻开心

⑪ straight /streɪt/ n. 直线，直

好了。如果你看到树上刻画着这个符号，就知道该进山洞了。我也一样会明白它的意思。"

"天！"特奎曼说，"说得也对。但等一下，有个问题。'嗖'（so）的意思是'来吃饭'，但'收'（sho）指的却是我们晾兽皮的杆子。"

SO SHO

"可恶的破晾衣杆！"特菲说，"我讨厌帮妈妈晾晒那些沉甸甸、热乎乎、毛扎扎的兽皮。如果你画出蛇和鸡蛋，我想那是指饭做好了，就从树林里跑回来，结果却发现它指的是让我帮妈妈往晾衣杆上挂两张兽皮。我该怎么办呢？"

"那样的话，你和妈妈两个人都会生气。我们必须重新画一个'收'（sho）。我们必须画一条长着斑点的蛇，让它发'湿'（sh）的声音，普通的蛇就让它发'嘶'（si）的声音。"

"我可不知道怎么画斑点，"特菲说，"而且也许一着急忘了画，结果我把'收'（sho）当作'嗖'（so），妈妈还是一样能抓到我。不！我想，我们最好把那些可怕的晾衣杆画出来，这样就很清楚了。我让它们跟在嘶嘶叫的蛇的后面。看！"她画了出来（10）。

"这可能是最安全的办法了。无论如何，这看上去很像我们的晾衣杆，"爸爸哈哈笑着说，"现在我要再发出一种声音，把蛇和晾衣杆所代表的声音全包括进去。我说'师'（shi），这在部落语言指的是渔叉，特菲。"他笑了起来。

"别拿我开心了，"特菲说，她又想起了那封图画信和陌生人满头泥巴的样子。"爸爸，你画出来吧。"

"这次我们不画河狸或小山，呃？"爸爸说，

· 161 ·

Just So Stories

'Even Mummy couldn't mistake that for me being killed.'

'Please don't, Daddy. It makes me **uncomfy**⑪. Do some more noises. We're getting on beautifully.'

'Er-hm!' said Tegumai, looking up. 'We'll say *shu*. That means sky.'

Taffy drew the snake and the drying-pole. Then she stopped. 'We must make a new picture for that end sound, mustn't we?'

'*Shu-shu-u-u-u!*' said her Daddy. 'Why, it's just like the round-egg-sound made thin.'

'Then s'pose we draw a **thin**② round egg, and pretend it's a **frog**③ that hasn't eaten anything for years.'

'N-no,' said her Daddy. 'If we drew that in a hurry we might mistake it for the round egg itself. *Shu-shu-shu*! I'll tell you what we'll do. We'll open a little hole at the end of the round egg to show how the O-noise runs out all thin, *ooo-oo-oo*. Like this.' And he drew this. (12.)

'Oh, that's **lovely**④! Much better than a thin frog. Go on,' said Taffy, using her **shark**'s⑤ tooth.

Her Daddy went on drawing, and his hand shook with **excitement**⑥. He went on till he had drawn this. (13.)

'Don't look up, Taffy,' he said. 'Try if you can make out what that means in the Tegumai language. If you can, we've found the Secret.'

'Snake—**pole**⑦—broken-egg—carp-tail and carp-mouth,' said Taffy. '*Shu-ya*. Sky-water (rain).' Just then a **drop**⑧ fell on her hand, for the day had **clouded**⑨ over. 'Why, Daddy, it's raining. Was that what you meant to tell me?'

远古传奇

① uncomfy /ʌnˈkʌmfɪ/ adj. 不舒服的；不轻松的

② thin /θɪn/ adj. 薄的，瘦的；
③ frog /frɒɡ/ n. 蛙，青蛙；

④ lovely /ˈlʌvlɪ/ adj. 可爱的；
⑤ shark /fɑːk/ adj. 可爱
⑥ excitement /eksˈsaɪtmənt/ n. 激动；

⑦ pole /pəʊl/ n. 杆；竿
⑧ drop /drɒp/ n. 滴，落下，微量
⑨ cloud /klaʊd/ v. 乌云密布；

"我只画一条直线代表我的渔叉。"他画了起来（11）。

"这表示我被杀死了，连你妈妈都不会误解的。"

"别这样，爸爸，这让我感到很不舒服。再发出几种声音吧，我们进展得好极了。"

"呃——嗯！"特奎曼抬眼望了望，"我说'书'（shu），这指的是天空。"

特菲把蛇和晾衣杆画了出来。她停下笔，问："我们必须给那个尾音画出一张新图，对不对？"

"'书'（shu）——书（shu）——屋（u）——物（u）——物（u）！"爸爸说，"我感觉出圆鸡蛋的声音变细了。"

SHĬ Ŭ SHŬYĀ

"那就假设我们画了一个瘦瘦的鸡蛋。假设它是只青蛙，已经几年没吃一点儿东西了。"

"嗯——不，"爸爸说，"如果画得匆忙，我们也许会错画成圆圆的蛋。书（shu）——书（shu）——书（shu）！我告诉你怎么办。我们在蛋的顶端开个小洞，表示'噢'（o）音跑出来蛋变瘦了，噢噢噢（o）——噢噢噢（o），就这样。"他画了出来（12）。

"哇，好可爱呀！这比一只瘦青蛙可好玩多了。接着来吧，"特菲手里拿着鲨鱼齿说。

爸爸继续画着，手激动得直打颤。他画出了图（13）。

"别抬头看，特菲，"他说，"试试你是否能看懂用特奎曼语言画的这些东西代表什么意思。如果能看懂，我们就发现了一个秘密。"

"蛇——杆——顶端开了口的蛋——鲤鱼尾巴和鲤鱼嘴巴，"特菲念着，"书（shu）——亚（Ya），天上的水。"正在那时，一滴雨落在她的手

· 163 ·

'Of course,' said her Daddy. 'And I told it you without saying a word, didn't I?'

'Well, I think I would have known it in a minute, but that **raindrop**① made me quite sure. I'll always remember now. *Shu-ya* means rain or "it is going to rain." Why, Daddy!' She got up and danced round him. 'S'pose you went out before I was **awake**②, and drawed *shu-ya* in the smoke on the wall, I'd know it was going to rain and I'd take my beaver-skin **hood**③. Wouldn't Mummy be surprised?'

Tegumai got up and danced. (Daddies didn't mind doing those things in those days.) 'More than that! More than that!' he said. 'S'pose I wanted to tell you it wasn't going to rain much and you must come down to the river, what would we draw? Say the words in Tegumai-talk first.'

'*Shu-ya-las, ya maru.* (Sky-water ending. River come to.) what a lot of new sounds! I don't see how we can draw them.'

'But I do—but I do!' said Tegumai. 'Just **attend**④ a minute, Taffy, and we won't do any more today. We've got *shu-ya* all right, haven't we? But this *las* is a **teaser**⑤. La-la-la' and he waved his shark-tooth.

'There's the hissy-snake at the end and the carp-mouth before the snake—*as-as-as*. We only want *la-la*, said Taffy.

'I know it, but we have to make *lala*. And we're the first people in all the world who've ever tried to do it, Taffimai!'

'Well,' said Taffy, **yawning**⑥, for she was rather tired. '*Las* means **breaking**⑦ or finishing as well as ending, doesn't it?'

'So it does,' smd Tegumai. '*Yo-las* means that there's no water in the tank for Mummy to cook with—just when I'm going hunting, too.'

① raindrop /reɪn drɒp/ n. 雨滴，雨点

② awake /əˈweɪk/ v. 唤醒，使醒过来；使觉醒

③ hood /hʊd/ n. 兜帽

④ attend /əˈtend/ v. ；照顾；参加（文中指专心的）

⑤ teaser /ˈtiːzə(r)/ n. 戏弄者（文中指一个难题）

⑥ yawn /jɔːn/ v. 打哈欠，打着哈欠说

⑦ breaking /ˈbreɪkɪŋ/ n. 破坏；断线（文中指停止）

上。仰头看，头顶上乌云密布。"呀，爸爸，下雨了。这就是您想告诉我的话吗？"

"当然，"爸爸说，"而且我一个字也没说就告诉了你，不是吗？"

"嗯，我本想我一会儿就能理解它们的意思，但雨滴让我一下子就肯定下来了。我会永远记着的。'书（shu）——亚（ya）'指的是雨，或'快下雨了'。哇，爸爸！"她站起来，围着爸爸又蹦又跳。"如果你在我睡醒之前就出去了，还在墙上的烟灰上写下'书亚（shu—ya）'，我就知道快下雨了，就会戴上我的河狸皮兜帽。妈妈该多惊讶啊！"

特奎曼站起身来，又蹦又跳（那时的爸爸们可不介意这样做）。"还有更多的！更多！"他说，"如果我想告诉你雨不会再下了，而且你必须下山到河边来，我们该怎么写？先用特奎曼部落语言说一遍。"

"书亚拉斯（shu—Ya—la—si），亚玛如（yamaru）——天上的雨水停了，到河边来。这么多新的发音！我不知道怎么画出来。"

"但我知道——我知道！"特奎曼说，"再专心呆一会儿，特菲，今天就到此为止了。我们知道了书亚（shu—ya），不是吗？但这个 las 是个难题。拉（la）——拉（la）——拉（la）！"他挥舞着鲨鱼齿。

"一只尾部嘶嘶响的蛇前面有一个鲤鱼嘴巴——爱丝（as）——爱丝（as）——爱丝（as）。我们只想要拉拉"(la—la)。"特菲说。

"我知道，但我们必须创造出拉拉（la—la）。我们是这个世界上最早做这种尝试的人，特菲曼！"

"啊，"特菲打了个哈欠，她挺累的，"拉斯（las）指的是休息、停止、结束，对不对？"

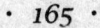

Just So Stories

'And *shi-las* means that your spear is broken. If I'd only thought of that instead of drawing silly beaver pictures for the Stranger!'

'*La! La! La!*' said Tegumai, waiving his **stick**① and frowning. 'Oh bother!'

'I could have drawn *shi* quite easily,' Taffy went on. 'Then I'd have drawn your spear all broken—this way!' And she drew. (14.)

'The very thing,' said Tegumai. 'That's *la* all over. It isn't like any of the other **marks**②, either.' And he drew this. (15.)

'Now for *ya*. Oh, we've done that before. Now for maru. *Mum-mum-mum. Mum* **shuts one**'s③ mouth up, doesn't it? We'll draw a **shut**④ mouth like this.' And he drew. (16.)

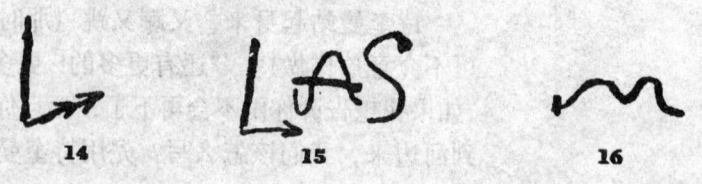

'Then the carp-mouth open. That makes *Ma-nm-ma*! But what about this rrrrr-thing, Taffy?'

'It sounds all **rough**⑤ and **edgy**⑥, like your shark-tooth saw when you're cutting out a **plank**⑦ for the **canoe**⑧,' said Taffy.

'You mean all sharp at the edges, like this?' said Tegumai. And he drew. (17.)

'Exactly,' said Taffy. 'But we don't want all those **teeth**⑨; only put two.'

'I'll only put in one,' said Tegumai. 'If this game of ours is going to be what I think it will, the easier we make our sound-pictures the

远古传奇

① stick /stɪk/ n. 棍，手杖，棒

② mark /mɑːk/ n. ；标明；标志；作记号（文中指发音图画）

③ shut /ʃʌt/ v. 关上，关闭，闭上
④ shut up v. 关闭，闭上

⑤ rough /rʌf/ adj. 粗糙的
⑥ edgy /ˈedʒɪ/ adj. 锋利的
⑦ plank /plæŋk/ n. 厚木板
⑧ canoe /kəˈnuː/ n. 独木舟

⑨ teeth /tiːð/ n. 锯齿

"是的，"特奎曼说，"幽拉斯（yo—las）的意思是'罐子里没有妈妈做饭要用的水了'——也就是我要出去打猎的时候。"

"'（施拉斯'（shi—las）指的是你的渔叉断了。如果我能想到这一点该多好！就不用给陌生人画那些傻乎乎的河狸了。"

"拉（la）！拉（la）！拉（la）！"特奎曼皱着眉头，挥舞着小棍儿，"见鬼！"

"要我写'施'（shi）可不太容易，"特菲接着说，"那我就画你的渔叉全断了的样子吧——这样子。"她画了出来（14）。

"是这东西，"特奎曼说，"'拉'（la）就是这个样子。"而且它与其他发音图画也不一样。"他画了出来（15）。

"现在轮到'亚'（ya）了。哦，我们以前画过。现在画'玛如'（ma-ru）。唔（mu）——唔（mu）——唔（mu）。说'呒'时，人的嘴就闭上了，不是吗？我们画嘴巴闭上的样子。"他画了起来（16）。

L LAS m 川
14　15　16　17　18

"然后把鲤鱼嘴巴张开。这样就成了玛（ma）——玛（ma）——玛（ma）！但特菲，日（ri）——日（ri）——日（ri）这个发音该怎么办？"

"这个音听起来又粗糙又锋利，就像你锯板条做独木舟时用的鲨鱼牙锯齿。"特菲说。

"你指的是锯齿边缘很锋利，就像这个样子？"特奎曼一边问一边画了出来（17）。

"一点儿不错，"特菲说，"但我们不需要这么多锯齿，两个就足够了。"

"我只留一个，"特奎曼说，"如果这个游戏

· 167 ·

Just So Stories

better for everybody.' And he drew. (18.)

'*Now*, we've got it,' said Tegumai, standing on one leg. 'I'll draw 'em all in a **string**① like fish.'

'Hadn't we better put a little bit of stick or something between each word, so's they won't rub up **against**② each other and **jostle**③, same as if they were carps?'

'Oh, I'll leave a **space**④ for that,' said her Daddy. And very incitedly he drew them all without stopping, on a big new bit of birchbark. (19.)

'*Shu-ya-las ya-maru*,' said Taffy, reading it out sound by sound.

'That's enough for today,' said Tegumai. 'Besides, you're getting tired, Taffy. Never mind, dear. We'll finish it all tomorrow, and then we'll be remembered for years and years after the biggest trees you can see are all **chopped**⑤ up for **firewood**⑥.'

So they went home, and all that evening Tegumai sat on one side of the fire and Taffy on the other, drawing *ya's* and *yo's* and *shu's* and *shi's* in the smoke on the wall and giggling together till her Mummy said, 'Really, Tegumai, you're worse than my Taffy.'

'Please don't mind,' said Taffy. 'It's only our secret surprised, Mummy dear, and we'll tell you all about it the very minute it's done; but please don't ask me what it is now, or else I'll have to tell.'

So her Mummy most **carefully**⑦ didn't; and bright and early next morning Tegumai went down to the river to think about new sound-pictures, and when Taffy got up she saw *Ya-las* (water is ending or running out) **chalked**⑧ on the side of the big stone water-tank, outside the Cave.

'Um,' said Taffy. 'These picture-sounds are rather a **bother**⑨!

① sting /stɪŋ/ n. 刺，针刺，（文中指串起来）
② against /əˈgenst/ prep. 相反；逆着；反对
③ jostle /ˈdʒɑs/ v. 推挤，冲撞；
④ space /speɪs/ n. 空间；空当
⑤ chop /tʃɒp/ v. 砍
⑥ firewood /ˈfaɪə(r)wʊd/ n. 木柴；柴火
⑦ carefully /ˈkeəfʊli/ adv. 小心谨慎地；警惕地
⑧ chalk /tʃɔːk/ v. 用石笔写；
⑨ bother /ˈbɒðə/ n. 麻烦，讨厌的人

能按照我们意愿发展下去的话，对所有人来说，我们所创造的发音图画越简单越好。"他画了出来（18）。

"现在我们该满意了。"特奎曼边说边做了个金鸡独立的姿势，"我把它们写成一串儿，就像用绳子把鱼穿起来一样。"

"难道我们不该在每个词之间画一小杠或别的什么符号吗？那样它们就不会像绳子上的鱼一样，你蹭我，我蹭你，互相推推撞撞的了。"

"哦，那我就在每个词之间留一个空当，"爸爸说。他非常兴奋地在一块新桦树皮上不停顿地写出了一行字（19）。"

SHUYALASYAMARU

书——亚——拉斯亚——玛如（shu—ya—lasya—maru）。"特菲一个音一个音地拼读出来。"今天就到这儿吧，"特奎曼说，"而且你也感到累了。亲爱的特菲，不要紧，明天我们就能全部完成了。你看到那些最高大的树木了吗？等它们被砍倒作为木柴后，那时人们就世世代代地记住了我们两个人。"

于是他们就回家去了。那天晚上，特奎曼和特菲分别坐在火堆的两旁，在墙上被烟熏黑的地方写下一个个亚（ya）、幽（yo）、书（shu）、施（shi）。他们一边写一边咯咯地笑，最后妈妈说："特奎曼，你还不如我的特菲，真的。"

"请别介意，"特菲说，"亲爱的妈妈，这只是我们之间的一个秘密的惊喜。完成后我会马上告诉你；但现在请不要问我，否则我就不得不说出来了。"

于是妈妈小心翼翼地不去问她。第二天一早，天大亮的时候，特奎曼就下山到河边去琢磨

Daddy's just as good as come here himself and told me to get more water for Mummy to cook with.' She went to the **spring**① at the back of the house and filled the **tank**② from a **bark**③ bucket, and then she ran down to the river and **pulled**④ her Daddy's left ear—the one that belonged to her to pull when she was good.

'Now come along and we'll draw all the left-over sound-pictures,' said her Daddy, and they had a most inciting day of it, and a beautiful lunch in the middle, and two games of **romps**⑤. When they came to T, Taffy said that as her name, and her Daddy's, and her Mummy's all began with that sound, they should draw **a sort of**⑥ family group of themselves holding hands. That was all very well to draw **once or twice**⑦; but when it came to drawing it six or seven times, Taffy and Tegumai drew it **scratchier**⑧ and scratchier, till at last the T-sound was only a thin long Tegumai with his arms out to hold Taffy and Teshumai. You can see from these three pictures **partly**⑨ how it happened. (20, 21, 22.)

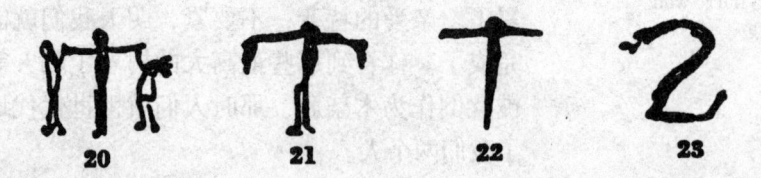

Many of the other pictures were much too beautiful to begin with, **especially**⑩ before lunch, but as they were drawn **over and over again**⑪ on birchbark, they became **plainer**⑫ and easier, till at last even Tegumai said he could find no fault with them. They turned the hissy-snake the other way round for the Z-sound, to show it was hissing **backwards**⑬ in a soft and gentle way (23); and they just made a **twiddle**⑭ for E, because it came into the pictures so often (24); and they drew pictures of the **sacred**⑮ Beaver of the Tegumais for the B-sound (25, 26, 27, 28); and because it was a **nasty**⑯, **nosy**⑰ noise, they just drew noses for

① spring /sprɪŋ/ n. 泉水
② tank /tæŋk/ n. 罐
③ bark /bɑːk/ n. 树皮
④ pull /pʊl/ v. 拉，牵，揪

⑤ romp /rɒmp/ v. 蹦蹦跳跳，喧闹地玩耍；

⑥ a sort of 一种……
⑦ once or twice 一次或两次
⑧ scratchy /ˈskrætʃɪ/ adj. 潦草的；
⑨ partly /ˈpɑːtlɪ/ adv. 部分，几分

⑩ especially /ɪˈspeʃəlɪ/ adv. 特别
⑪ over and over again 一遍又一遍后
⑫ plain /pleɪn/ adj. 简单的，平常的
⑬ backwards /ˈbækwədz/ adv. 后退 向后；往回
⑭ twiddle /ˈtwɪdl/ v. 捻弄，旋弄（文中指设计）
⑮ sacred /ˈseɪkrɪd/ adj. 神圣的；庄严的
⑯ nasty /ˈnɑːstɪ/ adj. 可恶的
⑰ nosy /ˈnəʊzɪ/ adj. 大鼻子

新的声音图形。特菲起床后看见山洞外面大石水罐上用石笔写着"亚——拉斯（ya—las）"（没有水了或水快用光了）。

"呃，"特菲说，"这声音图画可真讨厌！这就像爸爸自己站在这儿对我说，去多弄点儿水来给妈妈做饭用。"她来到家后面的泉水边，用一只树皮桶把水罐灌满，然后跑下山，来到河边，揪住了爸爸的左耳朵——爸爸允许她在表现好的时候就揪这只耳朵。

"来，我们一起把剩下的代表声音的图形画完，"爸爸说，于是他们又过了最最兴奋的一天。中午美美吃了一顿，还玩了两个蹦蹦跳跳的游戏。写到"特"（te）的时候，特菲说爸爸、妈妈和她名字的第一个发音都是"特"，所以应该把他们一家人手拉手地画在一起。这样画一两次还行，可六七次以后，父女俩就越画越潦草了，最后代表"特"（t）发音的图形只剩下细高的特奎曼伸出胳膊搂着特菲和妈妈。你可以从20、21、22这三幅图中看到这一切是怎么演变的。

刚开始的时候（特别是在午饭前），这些图形都画得非常非常美丽，但在桦树皮上画了一遍又一遍后，就变得既普通又简单，最后特奎曼认为从这些图形上已经挑不出什么缺点了。他们把嘶嘶叫的蛇左右翻了个儿，来代表"兹"（zi）的发音，形容蛇嘶嘶叫着、轻柔地向后退的样子（图23）；他们把"衣"（e）设计成漩涡的形状，因为它出现得太频繁了（图24）；他们把本地区神圣的河狸画出来代表"毕"（b）的声音（图25、26、27、28）；因为"恩"是个挺可恶的鼻音，在他们感到累之前，就画了个鼻子来表

· 171 ·

the N-sound, till they were tired (29); and they drew a picture of the big **lake-pike's**① mouth for the **greedy**② Ga-sound (30); and they drew the pike's mouth again with a spear behind it for the scratchy, **hurty**③ Ka-sound (31); and they drew pictures of a little bit of the **winding**④ Wagai river for the nice windy-windy Wa-sound (32, 33); and **so on**⑤ and so **forth**⑥ and so following till they had done and drawn all the sound-pictures that they wanted, and there was the Alphabet, all **complete**⑦.

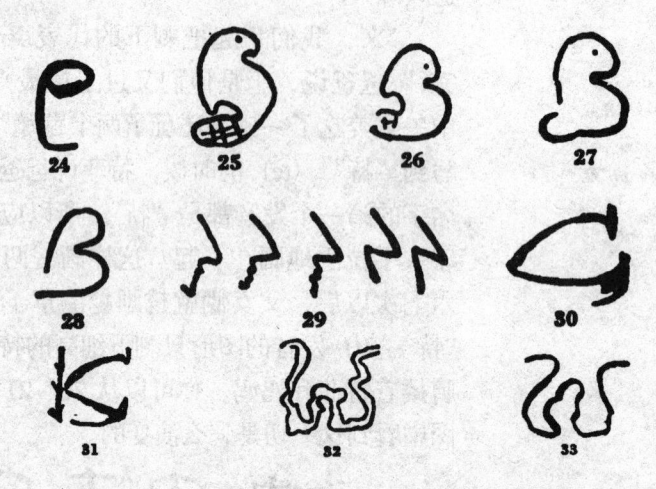

And after thousands and thousands and thousands of years, and after **Hieroglyphics**⑧ and **Demotics**⑨, and **Nilotics**⑩, and **Crypties**⑪, and **Cufics**⑫, and **Runics**⑬, and **Dorics**⑭, and **Ionics**⑮, and all sorts of other **ricks and tricks**⑯ (because the Woons, and the Neguses, and the Akhoonds, and the Repositories of Tradition would never leave a good thing alone when they saw it), the fine old easy, **understandable**⑰ Alphabet—A, B, C, D, E, and the rest of'em—got back into its proper shape again for all Best Beloveds to learn when they are old enough.

But I remember Tegumai Bopsulai, and Taffimai Metallumai and Teshumai Tewindrow, her dear Mummy, and all the days gone by. And it was so—just so—a little time ago—on the banks of the big Wagai!

① lake-pike /leɪk paɪk/ n. 大湖狗鱼
② greedy /'griːdɪ/ adj. 贪婪的
③ hurty /'hɜːtlɪ/ v. 刺痛的；使疼痛
④ winding /'waɪndɪŋ/ adj. 蜿蜒的，弯曲的
⑤ soon /suːn/ adv. 很快，马上，立刻
⑥ forth /fɔːθ/ adv. 往前；向外
⑦ complete /kəm'pliːt/ v. 完成；使完整
⑧ Hieroglyphics n. 象形文字
⑨ Demotics n. 埃及文字
⑩ Nilotics n. 尼罗河文字
⑪ Cryptics n. 隐义文字
⑫ Cufics n. 北欧文字
⑬ Runics n. 古希腊文字
⑭ Dorics n. 爱奥尼亚文字
⑮ Ionics n. 一种古老的文字
⑯ ricks and tricks n. 神秘符号
⑰ understandable /ˌʌndə(r)'stændəbl/ adj. 能懂的

示（图29）；他们画了大湖狗鱼的嘴，表示贪婪的声音"嘎"（ga）（图30）；他们又画了狗鱼的嘴，还在后面画了一只矛，表示刮擦、刺痛的声音"卡''（ka）（图31）；他们画了一小段蜿蜒曲折的瓦格河，代表那美妙的"哇''（wa）（32、33）的声音；等等，等等。最后他们把想要的声音图形全都画了出来，字母表就这样完成了。

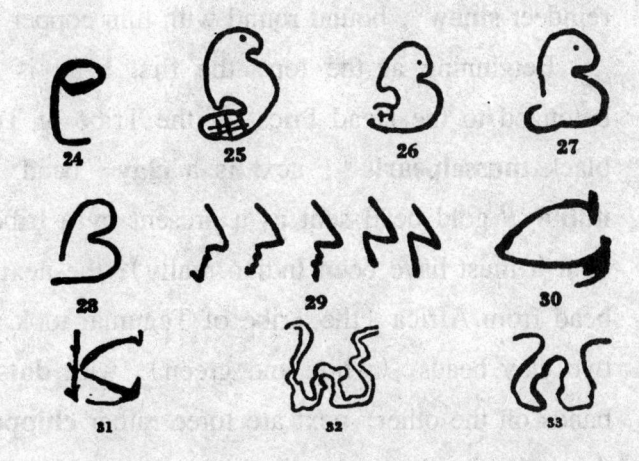

几千年后，又过了成千上万年，出现了象形文字、埃及文字、尼罗河文字、隐义文字、北欧文字、古希腊文字、爱奥尼亚文字和其他各种各样的神秘符号后（沃恩斯人、尼格人、艾克胡恩兹人和那些保守派只要看到好的东西就不放过），那些古老易懂的字母——A、B、C、D、E等等又恢复了原来的模样。小朋友们长大后，就可以利用这些字母来学习知识了。

但我还记得特奎曼·鲍普苏莱、特菲曼·梅塔柳迈和她亲爱的妈妈特舒曼·特温德鲁还有那些早已逝去的日子。而且那仿佛就发生在不久以前——在瓦格河边！

Just So Stories

One of the first things that Tegumai Bopsulai did after Taffy and he had made the **Alphabet**① was to make a **magic**② Alphabetnecklace of all the letters, so that it could be put in the Temple of Tegumai and kept for ever and ever. All the Tribe of Tagumai brought their most **precious**③ beads and beautiful things, and Taffy and Tegumai spent five whole years getting the **necklace**④ in order. This is a picture of the magic Alphabetnecklace. The **string**⑤ was made of the finest and strongest reindeer-**sinew**⑥, bound round with thin copper wire.

Beiginning at the top, the first bead is an old **silver**⑦ one that belonged to the Head Priest of the Tribe of Tegumai; then come three black **musselpearls**⑧; next is a **clay**⑨ bead (blue and gray); next a **nubbly**⑩ gold bead sent as a present by a tribe who got it from Africa (but it must have been Indian really); the next is a long flat-sided glass bead from Africa (the Tribe of Tegumai took it in a fight); then come two clay beads (white and green), with **dots**⑪ on one, and dots and bands on the other; next are three rather **chipped**⑫ **amber**⑬ beads; then three clay beads (red and white), two with dots, and the big one in the middle with a **toothed**⑭ pattern. Then the letters begin, and between each letter is a little **whitish**⑮ clay bead with the letter repeated small. Here are the letters

  A is scratched on a tooth—an **elk-tusk**⑯ I think.
  B is the Sacred Beaver of Tegumai on a bit of old **glory**⑰.
  C is a pearly **oyster**⑱-shell—inside front.
  D must be a sort of mussel-shell—outside front.
  E is a **twist**⑲ of silver wire.
  F is broken, bra what remains of it is a bit of **stag's**⑳ **horn**㉑.
  G is painted black on a piece of wood. (The bead after G is a small
    shell, and not a clay bead. I don't know why they did that.)

① alphabet /ˈælfəbɪt/ n. 字母表；
② magic /ˈmædʒɪk/ adj. 神奇的
③ precious /ˈpreʃəs/ adj. 宝贵的，珍爱的，过于精致的
④ necklace /ˈnekləs/ n. 项链
⑤ string /strɪŋ/ v. 连接
⑥ sinew /ˈsɪnjuː/ n. 肌肉，（文中指驯鹿腱）
⑦ silver /ˈsɪlvə(r)/ n. 银，银器，
⑧ mussel-pearl /ˈmʌsl pɜːl/ n. 贻贝珠
⑨ clay /kleɪ/ n. 泥
⑩ nub /nʌb/ n. 小块，
⑪ dot /dɒt/ n. 点，小圆点；
⑫ chip /tʃɪp/ v. 打磨
⑬ amber /ˈæmbə/ n. 琥珀；
⑭ toothed /tuːθt/ adj. 有…齿的，锯齿状的
⑮ whitish /ˈhwaɪtɪʃ/ adj. 发白的；带白色的
⑯ elk-tusk /elk tʌsk/ n. 麋鹿牙
⑰ glory /ˈɡlɔːrɪ/ n. 光荣（文中指象牙）
⑱ oyster /ˈɔɪstə(r)/ n. 牡蛎壳
⑲ twist /twɪst/ v.；扭弯，扭曲
⑳ stag /stæɡ/ n. 雄鹿；
㉑ horn /hɔːn/ n. 角，角质

特奎曼·鲍普苏莱和特菲创造出字母表后，特奎曼所做的第一件事就是制作一条神奇的字母表项链，这样他就能把项链放在部落的神庙里，永远地保留下去。部落的人送来了他们最宝贵的珠子和美丽的饰物，特菲和爸爸花了整整五年的时间才把项链按顺序排列好。这是一张这串神奇字母表项链的图画。他们挑选了最好、最结实的驯鹿腱，用细铜丝密密缠好，当做连接珠子的绳子。

从顶头开始，第一颗珠子是用特奎曼部落首领的一块旧银子做的；接下来是三枚黑色的贻贝珠；然后是颗泥珠（灰蓝色）；接着是另外一个部落从非洲得到的一颗金珠子，作为礼物送给特奎曼部落（但这颗珠子实际上应该产自印度）；再下面是一颗长形的平边玻璃珠，这颗珠子产于非洲，是特奎曼部落在一次战争中得到的；然后又是两颗泥珠（白绿色），一颗上面有小点，另一颗既有小点又有条纹；接下来是三颗打磨精细的琥珀珠；然后又是三颗泥珠（红白色），两颗带斑点，中间大的那颗上面画有牙齿啮合的图案。然后就开始有字母了，每两个字母之间有一个发白的泥珠，上面又把字母重复画了一遍，不过字体小多了。这些字母是：

A：刻在一颗牙齿上——我想是麋鹿牙。

B：特奎曼部落神圣的河狸，画在一块老象牙上。

C：一块珍珠状牡蛎壳——里面朝上。

D：一定是种贻贝——外面朝上。

E：一条扭曲的银丝。

F：断开了，但从残留物来看是牡鹿角。

G：在一块木板上，被涂成黑色（后面是一块小贝壳，不是泥珠。我不知道他们为什么要这

Just So Stories

H is a kind of a big brown **cowrie**①-shell.

I is the inside part of a long shell groud down by hand. (It took Tegumai three months to grind it down.)

J is a fish hook **in mother-of-pearl**②.

L is the broken spear in silver. (K ought to follow J of course, but the necklace was broken once and they mended it wrong.)

K is a thin **slice**③ of bone scratched and rubbed in black.

M is on a **pale**④ gray shell.

N is a piece of what is called **porphyry**⑤ with a nose scratched on it. (Tegumai spent five months **polihing**⑥ this stone.)

O is a piece of oyster-shell with a hole in the middle.

P and Q are missing. They were lost a long time ago, in a great war, and the tribe mended the necklace with the dried rattles of a **rattlesnake**⑦, but no one ever found P and Q. That is how the saying began, 'You must mind your P's and Q's.'

R is, of course, just a shark's tooth.

S is a little silver snake.

T is the end of a small bone, **polished**⑧ and **shiny**⑨.

U is another piece of oyster-shell.

W is a **twisty**⑩ piece of mother-of-pearl that they found inside a big mother-of-pearl shell, and sawed off with a wire dipped in sand and water. It took Taffy a month and a half to polish it and **drill**⑪ the holes.

X is silver wire joined in the middle with a raw **garnet**⑫. (Taffy found the garnet.)

Y is the carp's tail in **ivory**⑬.

Z is a bell-shaped piece of **agate**⑭ marked with Z-shaped stripes. They made the Z-snake out of one of the stripes by picking out the soft stone and rubbing in red sand and bee's-wax. Just in the

① cowrie /ˈkaʊrɪ/ n. 玛瑙贝

② mother of pearl 珠母层；珍珠母

③ slice /slaɪs/ n. 薄片，一份，切片

④ pale /peɪl/ adj. 淡灰色的 灰白的；

⑤ porphyry /ˈpɔːfɪrɪ/ n. 斑岩

⑥ polish /ˈpɒlɪʃ/ v. 打磨

⑦ rattlesnake /ˈrætl sneɪk/ n. 响尾蛇

⑧ polished /ˈpɒlɪʃd/ adj. 擦亮 光滑

⑨ shiny /ˈʃaɪnɪ/ adj. 有光泽的,发光的

⑩ twisty /ˈtwɪstɪ/ n. 扭；缠,歪歪扭扭

⑪ drill /drɪl/ v. 钻出；在…上钻孔；钻孔

⑫ garnet /ˈɡɑːnɪt/ n. 石榴石,深红色

⑬ ivory /ˈaɪvərɪ/ n. 象牙,乳白色

⑭ agate /ˈæɡət/ n. 玛瑙,

样做)。

H：一种褐色的大宝贝贝壳。

I：用于打磨的一块长形贝壳的内侧部分 (特奎曼用了三个月才把它磨好)。

J：珍珠母做的渔钩。

L：银子做的，是个断开的渔叉 (紧接着 J 本应是 K，但项链曾断开过一次，他们修理时把顺序搞错了)。

K：一块薄薄的骨头，用黑墨刻画并打磨过。

M：写在一块淡灰色的贝壳上。

N：一块斑岩石，上面刻着一只鼻子 (特奎曼用了五个月的时间来打磨这块石头)。

O：一块牡蛎壳，中间有一个洞。

P 和 Q 找不到了。很久很久以前在一次大规模的战争中就丢失了。部落里的人用晒干的响尾蛇的蛇环修理过一次，但没有找到 P 和 Q。所以有谚语说："当心你的 P 和 Q (你必须谨言善行)。"

R：当然是颗鲨鱼齿。

S：一条小银蛇。

T：一块小骨头的尾端，磨得很光滑并闪闪发光。

U：另外一块牡蛎壳。

W：他们在一块大珍珠母里找到的一小块歪歪扭扭的珍珠母，用一根蘸着沙子和水的线把它慢慢拉出来。特菲花了一个半月的时间才把它打磨光滑，并在上面钻出了一些小洞。

X：用一块毛糙的石榴石从中间把银线连接在一起 (石榴石是特菲找到的)。

Y：象牙做的鲤鱼尾巴。

Z：一块铃铛形状的玛瑙上有着 Z 形的花

mouth of the bell you see the clay bead repeating the Z-letter.

These are allthe letters.

The next bead is a small round greeny lump of copper ore; the next is a lump of rough turquoise; the next is a rough gold nugget (what they call water-gold); the next is a melonshaped clay bead (white with green spots). Then comes four flat ivory pieces, with dots on them rather like **dominoes**[①]; then come three stone beads, very badly **worn**[②]; then two soft iron beads with **rustholes**[③] at the edges (they must have been magic, because they look very common); and last is a very very old African bead, like glass—blue, red white, black, and yellow. Then comes the **loop**[④] to slip over the big silver button at the other end, and that is all.

I have copied the necklace very carefully. It weighs one pound seven and a half ounces. The black **squiggle**[⑤] behind is only put in to make the beads and things look better.

① domino /'dɒmɪnəʊ/ n. 骨牌游戏；骰子；

② worn /wɜːm/ adj. 磨损的，疲倦的

③ rusthole /rʌst həʊl/ n. 锈，生锈

④ loop /luːp/ n. 圈，环；圆环

⑤ squiggle /'skwɪɡl/ n. 弯曲的线

纹。他们选择了其中一条花纹，把上面的软石刻掉，然后用红沙和蜂蜡揉搓，这样就形成了Z形的一条蛇。你能在铃铛口处看到泥珠上把Z又写了一遍。

全部字母就都在这儿了。

下面，接着是一颗绿铜矿石，再往下是一团粗糙的绿松石；然后又是一块毛糙的金块（所谓的水金）；接着是一颗瓜形泥珠（白色带绿点）；然后是四个磨平的象牙块，上面有斑点，看起来像多米诺骨牌；接下来是三颗石珠，磨损得很厉害；然后是发软的铁珠，边缘处有锈洞（这珠子一定很神奇，因为它们看上去很普通）；最后是一颗非常非常古老的非洲珠子，看上去和玻璃一样——有蓝、红、白、黑、黄等多种颜色。然后是穿过另一端的大银扣的圆环，就到此为止了。

我非常仔细地复制了这条项链。它重达一点七磅零半盎司。后面画的波形曲线是为了突出表现珠子和饰物，使它们看上去好看一些。

Of all the **Tribe**① of Tegumai
Who cut that figure, none remain—
On Merrow Down the **cuckoos**② cry—
The silence and the sun remain.
But as the **faithful**③ years return
And hearts **unwounded**④ sing again,
Comes Taffy dancing through the **fern**⑤
To lead the Surrey spring again.
Her brows are bound with **bracken-fronds**⑥,
And golden **elf-locks**⑦ fly above;
Her eyes are bright as **diamonds**⑧
And bluer than the skies above.
In **moccasins**⑨ and deer-skin **cloak**⑩,
Unfearing⑪, free and fair she flits,
And lights her little damp-wood smoke
To show her Daddy where she flits.
For far—oh, very far behind,
So far she cannot call to him,
Comes Tegumai alone to find
The daughter that was all to him.

① tribe /traɪb/ n. 部落，部族
② cuckoo /ˈkʊkuː/ n. 杜鹃鸟；布谷鸟
③ faithful /ˈfeɪθfʊl/ n. 信徒（文中指时光）
④ unwounded /ʌnˈwuːndɪd/ adj. 未受伤的
⑤ fern /fɜːn/ n. 蕨，蕨类植物
⑥ bracken-frond /ˈbrækən frɒnd/ n. 欧洲蕨
⑦ elf-lock /elf lɒk/ n. 头发
⑧ diamond /ˈdaɪəmənd/ n. 钻石
⑨ moccasin /ˈmɒkəsɪn/ n. 鹿皮鞋
⑩ cloak /kləʊk/ n. 外套；宽大外衣
⑪ unfearing /ʌnˈfɪərɪŋ/ adj. 大无畏的；不畏惧的

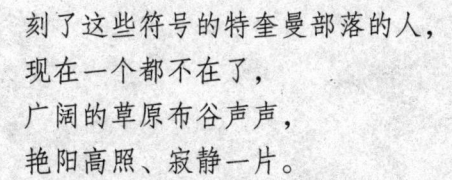

刻了这些符号的特奎曼部落的人，
现在一个都不在了，
广阔的草原布谷声声，
艳阳高照、寂静一片。

但如果时光倒流，
未受伤的心再次吟唱，
特菲在长满蕨菜的大地上飞舞着，
又引来明媚的春光。

她前额沾满蕨菜，
金色的头发纷乱飘扬，
她的眼睛如钻石般明亮，
比头上的天空还湛蓝辉煌。

她穿着鹿皮鞋、鹿皮外套，
飞舞着，
无畏，美丽，自由自在。
手中潮湿的小木块燃烧着，
让飘散的烟雾，
告诉爸爸她的去向。

远方，很远很远，
她喊爸爸的声音都听不见。
特奎曼正独自走来，
寻找他的女儿，
那个对他来说意味着一切的小姑娘。

The Crab that Played with the Sea

Before the High and **Far-Off**① Times, O my Best Beloved, came the Time of the Very Beginnings; and that was in the days when the Eldest **Magician**② was getting Things ready. First he got the Earth ready; then he got the Sea ready; and then he told all the Animals that they could come out and play. And the Animals said, 'O Eldest Magician, what shall we play at?' and he said, 'I wall show you.' He took the Elephant—All-the-Elephant-there-was —and said, 'Play at being an Elephant,' and All-the-Elephant-there-was played. He took the Beaver—All-the-Beaver-there-was-and said, 'Play at being a Beaver,' and All-the-Beaver-there-was played. He took the Cow—All-the Cow-there-was—and said, 'Play at being a Cow,' and All-the-Cow-there-was played. He took the **Turtle**③—All-the-Turtle-there-was— and said, 'Play at being a Turtle,' and All-the-Turtle-there-was played. One by one he took all the beasts and birds and fishes and told them what to play at.

But towards evening, when people and things grow **restless**④ and tired, there came up the Man (With his own little girl-daughter?)—Yes, with his own best beloved little girl-daughter sitting upon his shoulder, and he said, 'What is this play, Eldest Magician?' And the Eldest Magician said, 'Ho, Son of Adam, this is the play of the Very

与大海游戏的螃蟹

① far off 远；在远处的
远；在远处的

② magician /məˈdʒɪʃn/ n.
魔法师，

③ turtle /ˈtɜːtl/ n. 海龟；
龟；

④ restless /ˈrestlɪs/ adj. 得不到休息的，很累，疲劳

亲爱的读者，很久很久以前，世界刚诞生的时候，最古老的魔法祖师刚刚把一切准备好。他先把陆地弄好，然后又把海洋弄好。接着他告诉所有的动物可以出来做游戏了。动物们问："哦，尊贵的魔法祖师，我们应该怎样玩游戏呢？"他回答道："我会告诉你们的。"他对大象说："像大象一样玩游戏吧。"于是大象就照他的话去做了。他对河狸说："像河狸一样玩游戏吧。"于是河狸就照他的话去做了。他对母牛说："像母牛一样玩游戏吧。"于是母牛就照他的话去做了。他对乌龟说："像乌龟一样玩游戏吧。"于是乌龟也按照他的话去做了。他把飞禽和走兽一个一个地带出来，并告诉它们怎么玩游戏。

人和动物一天没休息，傍晚时分，大家都感到很累。这时，有一个人（带着他的小女儿？）来找魔法祖师。没错，他最喜爱的小女儿坐在他的肩膀上。他对魔法祖师说："尊贵的魔法祖师，这是个怎样的游戏？"大师答道："噢，亚当之子，这是创始日游戏；因为你很聪明，所以这游戏并不适合你。"这个人给大师敬了个礼，

· 183 ·

Beginning; but you are too wise for this play.' And the Man **saluted**① and said, 'Yes, I am too wise for this play; but see that you make all the Animals **obedient**② to me.'

Now, while the two were talking together, Pan Amma the Crab, who was next in the game, **scuttled**③ off **sideways**④ and stepped into the sea, saying to himself, 'I will play my play alone in the deep waters, and I will never be obedient to this son of Adam.' Nobody saw him go away except the little girl-daughter where she leaned on the Man's shoulder. And the play went on till there were no more Animals left without orders; and the Eldest Magician **wiped**⑤ the fine dust off his hands and walked about the world to see how the Animals were playing.

He went North, Best Beloved, and he found All-the-Elephant-there-was **digging**⑥ with his tusks and stamping with his feet in the nice new clean earth that had been made ready for him.

'Kun?' said All-the-Elephant-there-was, meaning, 'Is this right?'

'Payah kun,' said the Eldest Magician, meaning, 'That is quite right; and he breathed upon the great rocks and **lumps**⑦ of earth that All-the-Elephant-there-was had thrown up, and they became the great Himalayan Mountains, and you can look them out on the map.

He went East, and he found All-the-Cow-there-was feeding in the field that had been made ready for her, and she **licked**⑧ her **tongue**⑨ round a whole forest at a time, and **swallowed**⑩ it and sat down to **chew**⑪ her **cud**⑫.

'Kun?' said All-the-Cow-there-was.

'Payah kun,' said the Eldest Magician; and he breathed upon the bare **patch**⑬ where she had eaten, and upon the place where she had sat down, and one became the great Indian Desert, and the other became the Desert of Sahara, and you can look them out on the map.

① salute /səˈluːt/ v. 向...
致敬;致敬

② obedient /əˈbiːdɪənt/ adj.
服从的,听从

③ scuttle /ˈskʌtl/ v.; 逃脱
仓促逃跑,匆匆爬走

④ sideways /ˈsaɪdweɪz/
adv. 从一边;从旁边

⑤ wipe /waɪp/ v. 擦,消除

⑥ digging /ˈdɪɡɪŋ/ n. 挖掘

⑦ lump /lʌmp/ n. 土堆

⑧ lick /lɪk/ v. 舔;

⑨ tongue /tʌŋ/ n. 舌;

⑩ swallow /ˈswɒləʊ/ v. 吞
下,咽下

⑪ chew /tʃuː/ v. 嚼,嚼
碎,咀嚼

⑫ cud /kʌd/ n. 反刍的食
物

⑬ patch /pætʃ/ n. 小块土
地

说道:"是的,我很聪明,不适合玩这个游戏;但请你让所有的动物都听从我的命令。"

他们两个正说着,一只叫鲍·安玛的螃蟹(在游戏中排第二位)从一旁匆匆爬走,沉入大海中。它自言自语道:"我要在深水中自己玩游戏,决不服从亚当之子的命令。"除了斜靠在爸爸肩膀上的那个小女孩外,谁也没有注意到它已经悄悄溜走了。游戏继续进行着,最后所有的动物都得到了指令。于是,魔法祖师拍拍手上的细沙,到世界各地去看一看动物们是怎么玩耍的。

亲爱的读者,他到了北方,看到大象正在为它准备的干净整洁的新大陆上用长牙挖土,用四足踩地。

"昆?"大象问,意思是:"这样可以吗?"

"帕亚昆,"魔法祖师说,意思是:"非常好。"然后他向被大象抛起来的大石块和土堆吹了口气,它们就变成了喜马拉雅山,你可以在地图上找到这个地方。

他到了东方,看到母牛正在为它准备的田野里觅食。它在整个森林里舔食着食物并吞下去,然后卧在地上,反刍胃里的食物。

"昆?"母牛问。

"帕亚昆,"魔法祖师说。他向被母牛吃光的那一块地和卧着的那一块地吹了口气,于是前一块地变成了印度大沙漠,后一块地变成了撒哈拉大沙漠。你在地图上可以找到这些地方。

他到了西方,看到河狸正在为它准备的大河口修建河狸水坝。

"昆?"河狸问。

He went West, and he found All-the-Beaver-there-was making a beaverdam across the mouths of broad rivers that had been got ready for him.

'Kun?' said All-the-Beaver-there-was.

'Payah kun,' said the Eldest Magician; and he breathed upon the fallen trees and the still water, and they became the Everglades in Florida, and you may look them out on the map.

Then he went South and found All-the-Turtle-there-was scratching with his **flippers**① in the sand that had been got ready for him, and the sand and the rocks **whirled**② through the air and fell far off into the sea.

'Kun?' said All-the-Turtle-there-was.

'Payah kun,' said the Eldest Magician; and he breathed upon the sand and the rocks, where they had fallen in the sea, and they became the most beautiful islands of Borneo, Celebes, Sumatra, Java, and the rest of the Malay Archipelago, and you can look them out on the map!

By and by the Eldest Magician met the Man on the banks of the Perak river, and said, 'Ho! Son of Adam, are all the Animals obedient to you?'

'Yes,' said the Man.

'Is all the Earth obedient to you?'

'Yes,' said the Man.

'Is all the Sea obedient to you?'

'No,' said the Man. 'Once a day and once a night the Sea runs up the Perak river and drives the sweet-water back into the forest, so that my house is made wet; once a day and once a night it runs down the river and draws all the water after it, so that there is nothing left but mud, and my canoe is **upset**③. Is that the play you told it to play?'

'No,' said the Eldest Magician. 'That is a new and a bad play.'

'Look!' said the Man, and as he spoke the great Sea came up the

"帕亚昆,"魔法祖师说。他向倒地的树木和平静的水面吹了口气,它们就变成了佛罗里达州的大沼泽地。你可以在地图上找到这个地方。

然后他来到南方,看到海龟正在为它准备的沙滩上用鳍状肢划动着,沙子和石块在空中飞旋,落入远处的海水里。

"昆?"海龟问。

"帕亚昆,"魔法祖师说。他向那些落入海里的沙子和石块吹了一口气,它们就变成了一些最美丽的岛屿——加里曼丹岛、西里伯斯岛、苏门达腊岛、爪哇岛——形成了马来群岛。你可以在地图上找到这些地方!

最后魔法祖师在霹雳河河岸遇到了那个人,对他说:"喂!亚当之子,所有的动物都听从你的命令吗?"

"是的,"这个人回答道。

"所有的陆地都服从你的命令吗?"

"是的,"这个人回答道。

"所有的海洋都服从你的命令吗?"

"不,"这个人说,"每个白天和夜里,海水都要涌起一次,把霹雳河里的水推向森林深处,这样我的房屋就全部被水泅湿了;每个白天和夜晚,海水都要后退一次,这样就把河里的水都吸走了,只剩下泥巴。我的独木舟也不能用了。这就是你让它玩的游戏吗?"

"不是,"魔法祖师说,"听起来很新鲜,但这可是个坏游戏。"

"看!"这个人说。这时海水涌向霹雳河,河

① flipper /ˈflɪpə(r)/ n. 鳍状肢
② whirl /wɜːl/ v. 回旋,旋转

③ upset /ʌpˈset/ n. 翻倒,混乱(文中指不能用)

mouth of the Perak river, driving the river backwards till it **overflowed**① all the dark forests for miles and miles, and **flooded**② the Man's house.

'This is wrong. **Launch**③ your canoe and we will find out who is playing with the Sea,' said the Eldest Magician. They stepped into the canoe; the little girl-daughter came with them; and the Man took his kris—**a curving**④, **wavy**⑤ **dagger**⑥ with a blade like a **flame**⑦,—and they pushed out on the Perak river. Then the sea began to run back and back, and the canoe was **sucked**⑧ out of the mouth of the Perak river, past Selangor, past Malacca, past Singapore, out and out to the Island of Bingtang, as though it had been pulled by a string.

Then the Eldest Magician stood up and shouted, 'Ho! beasts, birds, and fishes, that I took between my hands at the Very Beginning and taught the play that you should play, which one of you is playing with the Sea?'

Then all the beasts, birds, and fishes said together, 'Eldest Magician, we play the plays that you taught us to play—we and our children's children. But not one of us plays with the Sea.'

Then the Moon rose big and full over the water, and the Eldest Magician said to the **hunchbacked**⑨ old man who sits in the Moon **spinning**⑩ a fishingline with which he hopes one day to catch the world, 'Ho! Fisher of the Moon, are you playing with the Sea?'

'No,' said the **Fisherman**⑪, 'I am spinning a line with which I shall some day catch the world; but I do not play with the Sea.' And he went on spinning his line.

Now there is also a Rat up in the Moon who always **bites**⑫ the old Fisherman's line as fast as it is made, and the Eldest Magician said to him, 'Ho! Rat of the Moon, are you playing with the Sea?'

And the Rat said, 'I am too busy biting **through**⑬ the line that this

① overflow /ˈəʊvə(r)fləʊ/ v. 涌出，泛滥；从…中溢出
② flood /flʌd/ v. 淹没
③ launch /lɔːntʃ/ v. 使下水，把船放进水里；（文中指划船入海）
④ curvy /ˈkɜːvɪ/ adj. 弯曲的，曲线美的
⑤ wavy /ˈweɪvɪ/ adj. 弧形锯齿形；呈波浪形的
⑥ dagger /ˈdægə/ n. 匕首
⑦ flame /fleɪm/ n. 火焰；
⑧ suck /sʌk/ v. 吸，吸入，（文中指被卷入霹雳河中）

⑨ hunchbacked /ˈhʌntʃbæktɪd/ adj. 驼背的
⑩ spin /spɪn/ v. 纺织，纺
⑪ fisherman /ˈfɪʃə(r)mən/ n. 渔夫；

⑫ bite /baɪt/ v. 咬；

⑬ through /θruː/ adv. 从头到尾，自始至终（文中指忙着做某事）

水向后退，直到冲进了几十里外的茂密森林，淹没了这个人的家。

"情况有点不对头。咱们划着独木舟，看看是谁在与大海玩游戏。"魔法祖师说。他们坐上独木舟，那个人还带上了他的小女儿和一把弧形锯齿匕首，匕首的刀片像火焰一样。他们划向霹雳河。这时河水已经开始后退了，独木舟被水流吸出了河口，像被绳子拽着一样漂离了霹雳河、雪兰莪、马六甲、新加坡，一直漂到槟榔屿。

魔法祖师站起身来，大声喊道："嘿！飞禽、走兽和游鱼们，我用双手开创了这个世界，并教给你们怎么玩儿——你们之中是谁在与大海做游戏？"

所有的飞禽、走兽和游鱼齐声回答："尊敬的魔法祖师，我们和我们的子孙们按照您教的方法玩游戏。但我们之中谁也没有与大海玩游戏。"

这时海上升起了一轮大大的满月，月亮上坐着一位驼背老人，他正在纺一根钓鱼线，希望有一天用这根渔线钓起整个世界。魔法祖师对他说："嘿！月亮渔夫，是你在与大海做游戏吗？"

"不是，"渔夫答道，"我正在纺一根线，希望有一天能用它钓起整个世界。可我没有与大海做游戏呀。"说完，他继续纺线。

月亮上还有一只老鼠，渔夫的线一纺好，它就立刻去咬线。魔法祖师对它说："嘿！月亮上的老鼠，是你在与大海做游戏吗？"

老鼠回答道："不是，我正忙着咬渔夫

old Fisherman is spinning. I do not play with the Sea.' And he went on biting the line.

Then the little girl-daughter put up her little soft brown arms with the beautiful white shell **bracelets**① and said, 'O Eldest Magician! when my father here talked to you at the Very Beginning, and I leaned upon his **shoulder**② while the beasts were being taught their plays, one beast went away **naughtily**③ into the Sea before you had taught him his play.'

And the Eldest Magician said, 'How wise are little children who see and are silent! What was the, beast like?'

And the little girl-danghter said, 'He was round and he was flat; and his eyes grew upon **stalks**④; and he walked **sideways**⑤ like this; and he was covered with strong **armour**⑥ upon his back.'

And the Eldest Magician said, 'How wise are little children who speak truth! Now I know where Pau Aroma went. Give me the **paddle**⑦!'

So he took the paddle; but there was no need to paddle, for the water flowed **steadily**⑧ past all the islands till they came to the place called Pusat Tasek—the Heart of the Sea—where the great **Hollow**⑨ is that leads down to the heart of the world, and in that hollow grows the Wonderful Tree, Pauh Janggi, that bears the magic twin **nuts**⑩. Then the Eldest Magician slid his arm up to the shoulder through the deep warm water, and under the roots of the Wonderful Tree he touched the broad back of Pau Amma the Crab. And Pau Amma **settled down**⑪ at the touch, and all the Sea rose up as water rises in a **basin**⑫ when you put your hand into it.

'Ah!' said the Eldest Magician. 'Now I know who has been playing with the Sea; and he called out, 'What are you doing, Pau Amma?'

① bracelet /ˈbreɪslɪt/ n. 手镯

② shoulder /ˈʃəʊldə(r)/ n. 肩，肩部

③ naughtily /ˈnɔːtɪlɪ/ adv. 顽皮地；淘气地

④ stalk /stɔːk/ n. 柄

⑤ sideways /ˈsaɪdweɪz/ adv. 向一边；从一边；从旁边

⑥ armour /ˈɑːmə/ n. 盔甲，铠甲

⑦ paddle /ˈpædl/ n. 桨

⑧ steadily /ˈstedɪlɪ/ adv. 稳定地，有规则地，

⑨ hollow /ˈhɒləʊ/ n. 洞；空洞

⑩ nut /nʌt/ n. 坚果，

⑪ settled down 安顿下来
⑫ basin /ˈbeɪsn/ n. 盆

纺的线呢。我没和大海做游戏。"说完，它继续咬线。

这时，那个人的小女儿伸出她那软软的褐色的小胳膊（胳膊上戴着一根漂亮的白贝壳手链），说："哦，尊敬的魔法祖师！创始日那天，我爸爸和您说话的时候，您正教动物们玩游戏的方法，当时我斜靠在爸爸的肩膀上，看到其中有一只淘气的动物在您教它之前溜进了大海里。"

魔法祖师说："这小女孩是多么聪明啊！她看到了还能保持安静！那动物长得什么样？"

小女孩答道："它身体又圆又平，两只眼睛长在肉柄上。它像这样横斜着走，背上还披着坚硬的铠甲。"

魔法祖师说："讲真话的小孩子是多么聪明啊！现在我知道鲍·安玛到哪里去了。把桨给我！"

他拿过桨。其实已经没有必要划水了，因为水已经慢慢地流过了所有岛屿，最后来到了大海的心脏——一个叫普斯特·塔塞克的地方。这里有一个空洞，直通世界的中心。空洞里生长着一棵名叫布·詹吉的神奇树，树上长满了神奇的孪生坚果。魔法祖师把胳膊伸入温暖的深水中，在神奇树的根部他摸到了螃蟹鲍·安玛巨大的后背。鲍·安玛被摸了一下后，调整了一下身体，重新坐好。于是整个海面都升高了，就像你把手伸进盆里后水面涨起来一样。

"啊！"魔法祖师说，"现在我知道是谁在与大海做游戏了。"他喊道："鲍·安玛，你在干什么？"

· 191 ·

Just So Stories

And Pau Amma, deep down below, answered, 'Once a day and once a night I go out to look for my food. Once a day and once a night I return. Leave me alone.'

Then the Eldest Magician said, 'Listen, Pau Amma. When you go out from your cave the waters of the Sea pour down into Pusat Tasek, and all the **beaches**① of all the islands are left bare, and the little fish die, and Raja Moyang Kaban, the King of the Elephants, his legs are made **muddy**②. When you come back and sit in Pusat Tasek, the waters of the Sea rise, and half the little islands are **drowned**③, and the Man's house is flooded, and Raja Abdullah, the King of the Crocodiles, his mouth is filled with the salt water.'

Then Pan Amma, deep down below, laughed and said, 'I did not know I was so important. **Henceforward**④ I will go out seven times a day, and the waters shall never be still; '

And the Eldest Magician said, 'I cannot make you play the play you were meant to play, Pan Amma, because you escaped me at the Very Beginning; but if you are not afraid, come up and we will talk about it.'

'I am not afraid,' said Pau Amma, and he rose to the top of the sea in the moonlight. There was nobody in the world so big as Pau-Amma—for he was the King Crab of all Crabs. Not a common Crab, but a King Crab. One side of his great shell touched the beach at Sarawak; the other touched the beach at Pahang; and he was taller than the smoke of three **volcanoes**⑤! As he rose up through the **branches**⑥ of the Wonderful Tree he tore off one of the great twin-fruits—the magic **double-kernelled**⑦ nuts that make people young, — and the little girl-daughter saw it **bobbing**⑧ **alongside**⑨ the canoe, and pulled it in and began to pick out the soft eyes of it with her little golden **scissors**⑩.

'Now,' said the Magician, 'make a Magic, Pau Amma, to show that you are really important.'

① beach /bi:tʃ/ n. 海滩（文中指岛屿）

② muddy /'mʌdɪ/ v. 使沾上泥污

③ drown /draʊn/ v. 淹没；

④ henceforward /ˌhensˈfɔːwə(r)d/ adv. 此后，今后

⑤ volcano /vɒlˈkeɪnəʊ/ n. 火山

⑥ branch /brɑːntʃ/ n. 树枝，

⑦ double-kernel /ˈdʌblˈkɜːnl/ n. 孪生

⑧ bobbing /ˈbɒbɪŋ/ n. 快速滚落

⑨ alongside /əˈlɒŋsaɪd/ prep. 在...旁边；沿着...的边

⑩ scissors /ˈsɪzə(r)z/ n. 剪刀

从深深的海底传来了鲍·安玛的回答："白天和夜晚我各出去一次，到外面寻找食物。白天和夜晚我各回来一次。别管我。"

魔法祖师说："鲍·安玛，你听着。你从洞里出来的时候，大海里的水就流进了普斯特·塔塞克，于是所有岛屿的岸边都光秃秃的，小鱼们死了，大象之王瑞嘉·蒙雅的腿上都是泥巴。等你回来坐在普斯特·塔塞特的时候，大海的水又涨了起来，一半的小岛被淹没在水下面，这个人的房子被大水冲了，鳄鱼之王瑞嘉·阿布杜拉的嘴里都是咸水。"

从深深的海底传来鲍·安玛的一声大笑："我不知道我有这么重要。以后我每天要出去七次，水就再没有安静的时候了。"

魔法祖师说："鲍·安玛，我不会让你想怎么样就怎么样的，因为在创始日那天你溜走了；但如果你不害怕的话，可以出来，我们谈一谈。"

"我可不怕，"鲍·安玛说。月光下它浮出水面。它身体大得无以伦比——因为它是螃蟹之王，记住它可不是普通的螃蟹，是螃蟹之王。它甲壳的一边碰到了沙捞越海滩，另一边碰到了彭亨海滩。它比火山喷发出来的烟雾还要高三倍！它从神奇树的枝叶中浮出来，碰掉了一颗大个的孪生坚果——人吃了神奇的孪生坚果，就会变得年轻。小女孩看到坚果滚落到独木舟边，就拾起来，用她的小金剪子取出里面柔软的果仁。

"现在，"魔法祖师说，"鲍·安玛，显示一下你的魔力吧，让我们看看你有多重要。"

鲍·安玛翻了翻眼珠，摆了摆爪子。但它只

Pau Amma rolled his eyes and waved his legs, but he could only **stir up**① the Sea, because, though he was a King Crab, he was nothing more than a Crab, and the Eldest Magician laughed.

'You are not so important after all, Pan Amma,' he said. 'Now, let me try,' and he made a Magic with his left hand—with just the little **finger**② of his left hand—and—lo and behold, Best Beloved, Pau Amma's hard, blue-green-black shell fell off him as a husk falls off a **cocoa-nut**③, and Pau Amma was left all soft—soft as the little crabs that you sometimes find on the beach, Best Beloved.

'Indeed, you are very important,' said the Eldest Magician. 'Shall I ask the Man here to cut you with kris? Shall I send for Raja Moyang Kaban, the King of the Elephants, to pierce you with his tusks, or shall I call Raja Abdullah, the King of the Crocodiles, to bite you?'

And Pan Amma said, 'I am **ashamed**④! Give me back my hard shell and let me go back to Pusat Tasek, and I will only stir out once a day and once a night to get my food.'

And the Eldest Magician said, 'No, Pau Aroma, I will not give you back your shell, for you will grow bigger and prouder and stronger, and perhaps you will forget your promise, and you will play with the Sea once more.'

Then Pau Amma said, 'What shall I do? I am so big that I can only hide in Pusat Tasek, and if I go anywhere else, all soft as I am now, the sharks and the dogfish will eat me. And if I go to Pusat Tasek, all soft as I am now, though I may be safe, I can never stir out to get my food, and so I shall die.' Then he **waved**⑤ his legs and **lamented**⑥.

'Listen, Pau Amma,' said the Eldest Magician. 'I cannot make you

远古传奇

能搅动海洋，因为它虽然是螃蟹之王，但也仅仅是螃蟹之王而已。魔法祖师大笑不已。

"鲍·安玛，你可一点儿也不重要，"他说，"现在让我试试吧。"他用左手——实际上是左手的小手指变了个戏法。瞧，注意看！亲爱的读者，鲍·安玛黑中透着蓝绿色的硬壳一下子就从背上掉了下来，就像咖啡豆的硬皮剥落下来一样。脱了壳的鲍·安玛浑身软绵绵的，亲爱的读者，就像小朋友们在沙滩上捡到的小螃蟹一样。

"你的确很重要，"魔法祖师说，"我可以叫那个人用匕首来砍你吗？我可以叫大象之王瑞嘉·蒙雅，让它用长牙穿破你的身体，或者让鳄鱼之王瑞嘉·阿布杜拉来咬你吗？"

鲍·安玛说："我太惭愧了！把硬壳还给我，让我回到普斯特·塔塞克去吧，我保证每个白天、每个黑夜都各只出去一次寻找食物。"

魔法祖师说："不，鲍·安玛，我不会把硬壳给你的，不然你会长得更大、更壮、更骄傲，也许还会忘记你的诺言，再次与大海玩游戏。"

鲍·安玛听了，说："那我该怎么办？原来我的身体那么庞大，只能藏在普斯特·塔塞克里；现在我的身体又这么柔软，一定会被鲨鱼或小狗鱼吃掉。而且，即使我回到普斯特·塔塞克，那里虽然安全，但我软塌塌的，不能掀起海水寻找食物，会被饿死的。"它摆动着爪子哀求着。

"鲍·安玛，你听着，"魔法祖师说，"我不会让你想怎么玩就怎么玩的，因为创始日那天你就从我面前溜走了。但如果你愿意选择的话，我会为了你和你的子孙，把大海里的每块石头、每

① stir up 激起；煽动

② finger /ˈfɪŋɡə(r)/ n. 手指；指头

③ cocoa-nut /ˈkəʊkəʊnʌt/ n. 咖啡豆

④ ashamed /əˈʃeɪmd/ adj. 惭愧的；羞耻的

⑤ wave /weɪv/ v. 使波动，使飘扬（文中指掀起海水）

⑥ lament /ləˈment/ v. 哀求；悔恨

· 195 ·

Just So Stories

play the play you were meant to play, because you escaped me at the Very Beginning; but if you choose, I can make every stone and every hole and every bunch of weed-in all the seas a safe Pusat Tasek for you and your children for always.'

Then Pau Amma said, 'That is good, but I do not choose yet. Look! there is that Man who talked to you at the Very Beginning. If he had not taken up your **attention**① I should not have grown tired of waiting and run away, and all this would never have happened. What will he do for me?'

And the Man said, 'If you choose, I will make a Magic, so that both the deep water and the dry ground will be a home for you and your children—so that you shall be able to **hide**② both on the land and in the sea.'

And Pau Amma said, 'I do not choose yet. Look! there is that girl who saw me running away at the Very Beginning. If she had spoken then, the Eldest Magician would have called me back, and all this would never have happened. What will she do for me?'

And the little girl-daughter said, 'This is a good nut that I am eating. If you choose, I will make a Magic and I will give you this pair of scissors, very sharp and strong, so that you and your children can eat cocoa-nuts like this all day long when you come up from the Sea to the land; or you can **dig**③ a Pusat Tasek for yourself with the scissors that belong to you when there is no stone or hole **near by**④; and when the earth is too hard, by the help of these same scissors you can run up a tree.'

And Pau Amma said, 'I do not choose yet, for, all soft as I am, these gifts would not help me. Give me back my shell, O Eldest Magician, and then I will play your play.'

And the Eldest Magician said, 'I will give it back, Pau Amma, for

远古传奇

个洞穴、每丛海草都变得和普斯特·塔塞克一样安全。"

鲍·安玛说："好主意，但我还不想选择。看！创始日那天就是这个人与你说话。要是那天他没有吸引你的注意力的话，我就不会等得不耐烦、最后逃走的，这一切都不会发生。他该为我做些什么？"

于是那个人说："如果你选择的话，我可以施展魔法，让你和你的子孙在深水和陆地上都能生存——这样你们既能藏在陆地上，也能生活在海水里。"

鲍·安玛说："我还不想选择。看，在创始日那天看到我溜走的就是那个小女孩。如果她当时就说出来，魔法祖师当时就可以把我叫回来，那么这一切就都不会发生了。她该为我做些什么？"

小女孩说："我吃的这个坚果味道真不错。如果你愿意的话，我可以变个戏法，让你身上长出一双锋利结实的剪刀，这样你和你的子孙从海里爬上陆地的时候，就可以整天像我这样吃可可豆了；附近没有石头或洞穴的时候，你还可以用自己这双剪子给自己挖出一个安全的洞。如果泥土太硬了挖不动，你还可以利用这双剪子爬到树上去。"

鲍·安玛说："我还是不想选择。因为我的身体太柔软了，这些礼物都帮不上忙。魔法祖师，把硬壳还给我吧，我会按照您的指示玩游戏的。"

魔法祖师说："我会还给你的，鲍·安玛。一年中有11个月你的壳是硬的，但从第12个月

① attention /ə'tenʃn/ n. 注意力

② hide /haɪd/ v. ；躲藏，隐藏

③ dig /dɪg/ v. 挖；挖掘，
④ nearby /ˌnɪr'baɪ/ adj. 附近的，近旁的

· 197 ·

eleven months of the year; but on the twelfth month of every year it shall grow soft again, to remind you and all your children that I can make magics, and to keep you **humble**①, Pan Amma; for I see that if you can run both under the water and on land, you will grow too **bold**②; and if you can climb trees and **crack**③ nuts and dig holes with your scissors, you will grow too **greedy**④, Pau Amma.'

Then Pau Amma thought a little and said, 'I have made my choice. I will take all the gifts.'

Then the Eldest Magician made a Magic with the right hand, with all five fingers of his right hand, and lo and **behold**⑤, Best Beloved, Pan Amma grew smaller and smaller and smaller, till at last there was only a little green crab swimming in the water alongside the canoe, crying in a very small voice, 'Give me the scissors!'

And the girl-daughter picked him up on the **palm**⑥ of her little brown hand, and sat him in the **bottom**⑦ of the canoe and gave him her scissors, and he waved them in his little arms, and opened them and shut them and **snapped**⑧ them, and said, 'I can eat nuts. I can crack shells. I can dig holes. I can climb trees. I can breathe in the dry air, and I can find a safe Pusat Tasek under every stone. I did not know I was so important. Kun?' (Is this right?)

'Payah-kun,' said the Eldest Magician, and he laughed and gave him his **blessing**⑨; and little Pau Amma **scuttled**⑩ over the side of the canoe into the water; and he was so tiny that he could have hidden under the **shadow**⑪ of a dry leaf on land or of a dead shell at the bottom of the sea.

'Was that well done?' said the Eldest Magician.

'Yes,' said the Man. 'But now we must go back to Perak, and that is a **weary**⑫ way to **paddle**⑬. If we had waited till Pau Amma had gone out of Pusat Tasek and come home, the water would have carried us

① humble /ˈhʌmbl/ adj. 谦卑的，谦逊的
② bold /bəʊld/ adj. 大胆的
③ crack /kræk/ v. 剥，裂开
④ greedy /ˈɡriːdɪ/ adj. 贪婪的

⑤ behold /bɪˈhəʊld/ v. 看到

⑥ palm /pɑːm/ n. 手掌
⑦ bottom /ˈbɒtəm/ n. 底；底部
⑧ snap /snæp/ v. 咬，抓，（文中指挥舞）

⑨ blessing /ˈblesɪŋ/ n. 祝福
⑩ scuttle /ˈskʌtl/ v. 急跑；逃避（文中指滑入）
⑪ shadow /ˈʃædəʊ/ n. 阴影

⑫ weary /ˈwɪrɪ/ v. 使疲倦，累
⑬ paddle /ˈpædl/ n. 桨

开始，壳开始变软，提醒你和你的子孙我是会施展魔法的，提醒你要谦卑一点，鲍·安玛。因为我知道，如果你在水中和陆地上都能跑的话就会变得很胆大；如果你能用剪刀爪上树、剥坚果，挖洞穴，会变得贪婪无比，鲍·安玛。"

鲍，安玛想了一会儿，说："我已经想好了要选什么；我接受这些礼物。"

魔法祖师用右手五个手指施展起魔法。亲爱的读者，注意，仔细看！鲍·安玛变得越来越小，最后他们只看到一只绿色的小螃蟹在独木舟边游着，用细小的声音说："把剪刀给我！"

小女孩用褐色的小手把螃蟹捡起来，放在手掌上，然后又把它放在独木舟底部，把剪刀给了它。螃蟹用小胳膊挥舞着剪刀，一开一合。它说："我能吃坚果了。我可以把壳捏碎，我可以挖洞，我可以爬树，我可以在陆地上呼吸，我甚至可以在石头下面找到安全的藏身之所。我知道我的确很重要。昆（对不对）？"

"帕亚昆，"魔法祖师说。他哈哈笑着说了几句祝福的话。小螃蟹鲍·安玛从独木舟的一侧滑进水里。它太小了，可以在陆地上一片干叶子的阴影下或海底的一只死贝壳里藏身。

"一切都没问题吧？"魔法祖师问。

"是的，"那个人说，"但现在我们必须回到霹雳河去。要是划回去的话，那可太累了。如果我们一直等到鲍·安玛从普斯特·塔塞克出来再回家的话，水流就会把我们带回去。"

"你太懒了，"魔法祖师说，"你的孩子也应该很懒惰。他们应该是世界上最懒的人，应该叫

Just So Stories

there by itself.'

'You are lazy,' said the Eldest Magician. 'So your children shall be lazy. They shall be the laziest people in the world. They shall be called the Malazy—the lazy people; and he held up his finger to the Moon and said, 'O Fisherman, here is the Man too lazy to **row**① home. Pull his canoe home with your line, Fisherman.'

'No,' said the Man. 'If I am to be lazy all my days, let the Sea work for me twice a day for ever. That will save paddling.'

And the Eldest Magician laughed and said,

'Payah kun' (That is fight).

And the Rat of the Moon stopped biting the line; and the Fisherman let his line down till it touched the Sea, and he pulled the whole deep Sea along, past the Island of Bintang, past Singapore, past Malacca, past Selangor, till the canoe **whirled**② into the mouth of the Perak river again. 'Kun?' said the Fisherman of the Moon. 'Payah kun,' said the Eldest Magician. 'See now that you pull the Sea twice a day and twice a night for ever, so that the Malazy fishermen may be saved paddling. But be careful not to do it too hard, or I shall make a magic on you as I did to Pau Amma.'

Then they all went up the Perak river and went to bed, Best Beloved.

Now listen and attend!

From that day to this the Moon has always pulled the sea up and down and made what we call the **tides**③. Sometimes the Fisher of the Sea pulls a little too hard, and then we get **spring-tides**④; and sometimes he pulls a little too **softly**⑤, and then we get what are called **neap-tides**⑥; but nearly always he is careful, **because**⑦ of the Eldest Magician.

And Pau Amma? , You can see when you go to the beach, how all

远古传奇

做马懒人（马来人）——懒惰的人。"他向着月亮举起手，说："嘿，渔夫！这个人太懒了，不想划船回家。用你的线把船拉回去吧，渔夫。"

"不，"那个人说，"如果注定我一生都懒惰的话，让大海一天为我工作两次，永远如此。这样就省却了划船的气力。"

魔法祖师笑着说：

"帕亚昆（好吧）。"

月亮上的老鼠停止咬线，渔夫把渔线垂下来，与海面接触，然后他把整个大海都拉了起来。海水经过槟榔屿、新加坡、马六甲、雪兰莪，直到载着独木舟回旋在霹雳河河口。

"昆？"月亮渔夫问道。

"帕亚昆，"魔法祖师回答说，"从现在开始，你在每个白天和夜晚，分两次拉动大海，永远如此，这样马懒（来）渔夫就不用费力摇桨了。但注意别太用力，不然我会像对鲍·安玛一样对你施加魔法的。"

亲爱的朋友们，然后他们都走上河岸，回到家里。

现在请仔细听好！

从那一天开始直到现在，月亮就一直把海水拉起拉落。我们称这种现象为"潮汐"。有时月亮渔夫用力大了一点儿,，我们就有了"大潮"；如果用力小了一些，我们就有了"小潮"。但一般来说因为魔法祖师的缘故，月亮渔夫还是很小心的。

鲍·安玛怎么样了？你去海滩的时候可以看到，它的子孙们在沙子里的每块石头和每丛海草中为自己建造了小小的安身之所——普斯特·塔

---

① row /rəʊ/ v. 划船，划

② whirl /wɜːl/ v. 回旋，急走

③ tid /taɪd/ n. 潮汐
④ spring-tid /sprɪŋ'taɪd/ n. 大潮汐
⑤ softly /'sɒftlɪ/ adj. 软的，柔和的，温和的（文中指用力小）
⑥ neap-tid /niːp'taɪd/ n. 小潮汐
⑦ because of 因为；为了……缘故

201

Pau Amma's babies make little Pusat Taseks for themselves under every stone and bunch of weed on the sands; you can see them waving their little scissors; and in some parts of the world they truly live on the dry land and run up the palm trees and eat cocoa-nuts, exactly as the girl-daughter **promised**①. But once a year all Pau Ammas must **shake off**② their hard armour and be soft—to **remind**③ them of what the Eldest Magician could do. And so it isn't fair to kill or hunt Pau Aroma's babies just because old Pau Aroma was **stupidly**④ rude a very long time ago.

Oh yes! And Pau Amma's babies hate being taken out of their little Pusat Taseks and brought home in **pickle-bottles**⑤. That is why they **nip**⑥ you with their scissors, and it serves you right!

塞克。你能看到它们到处挥舞着小小的剪刀爪。在世界上的某些地方，它们确实正如小女孩许诺的一样，生活在干燥的陆地上，能爬上棕榈树，以咖啡豆为食物。但所有的螃蟹每年都要脱一次壳，身体变得非常柔软——提醒自己记住摩法祖师的魔力。所以，如果只因为很久以前鲍·安玛又愚蠢又粗鲁就杀掉它所有子孙的话，那是不公平的。

哦，对了！鲍·安玛的子孙不喜欢被人从它们的普斯特·塔塞克安居所里拿出来，放在咸菜瓶里拎回家。这就是为什么它们用剪刀爪夹你的原因。活该！

① promise /'prɑmɪs/ v. 允诺，答应；允诺
② shake off 抖落；摆脱
③ remind /rɪ'maɪnd/ v. 提醒
④ stupidly /'stu:pɪdli/ adv. 愚蠢地
⑤ pickle-bottle /'pɪkl'bɒtl/ n. 咸菜瓶子
⑥ nip /nɪp/ n. 夹，捏

This is a picture of Pau Amma the Crab **running**① away while the Eldest Magician was talking to the Man and his Little Girl Daughter. The Eldest Magician is sitting on his magic **throne**②, **wrapped**③ up in his Magic Cloud. The three flowers in front of him are the three Magic Flowers. On the top of the hill you can see All-the-Elephant-there-was, and All-the-Cow-there-was, and All-the-Turtle-there-was going off to play as the Eldest Magician told them. The Cow has a **hump**④, because she was AH-the-Cow-there-was; so she had to have all there was for all the cows that were made afterwards. Under the hill there are Animals who have been taught the game they were to play. You can see All-the-Tiger-there-was smiling at All-the-Bones-there-were, and you can see All-the-Elk-there-was, and All-the-Parrot-there-was, and All-the-Bunnies-there-were on the hill. The other Animals are on the other side of the hill, so I haven't drawn them. The little house up the hill is All-the-House-there-was. The Eldest Magician made it to show the Man how to make houses when he wanted to. The Snake round that **spiky**⑤ hill is All-the-Snake-there-was, and he is talking to All-the-Monkey-there-was, and the Monkey is being rude to the Snake, and the Snake is being rude to the Monkey. The Man is very busy talking to the Eldest Magician. The Little Girl Daughter is looking at Pau Amma as he runs away. That humpy thing in the water in front is Pau Amma. He wasn't a common Crab in those days. He was a King Crab. That is why he looks different. The thing that looks like **bricks**⑥ that the Man is standing in, is the Big Miz-Maze. When the man has done talking with the Eldest Magician he will walk in the Big Miz-Maze, because he has to. The mark on the stone under the Man's foot is a magic mark; and down **underneath**⑦ I have drawn the three Magic Flowers all mixed up with the Magic Cloud. All this picture is Big Medicine and Strong Magic.

远古传奇

① run away 出逃；脱逃

② throne /θrəʊn/ n. 宝座
③ wrap /ræp/ v. 周围，缠绕，

④ hump /hʌmp/ n. 鼓包峰；驼背

⑤ spiky /ˈspaɪkɪ/ adj.，尖的

⑥ brick /brɪk/ n. 砖；砖块

⑦ underneath /ˌʌndə(r)ˈniːθ/ adv. 在下面

　　这幅画描述的是魔法祖师与背着小女儿的人谈话时，鲍·安码悄悄溜走时的情景。魔法祖师坐在宝座上，周围祥云朵朵。他面前有三朵神花。在小山上你可以看到大象、母牛、乌龟正离开这里，按照魔法祖师教的方法去做游戏。母牛身上有一个鼓包，因为它代表着所有的母牛，身上必须把将来母牛要长出来的东西全长出来。山下的动物们已经从魔法祖师那里学到了游戏的规则。你可以看到老虎正对着其他动物们微笑，还能看见山上的麋鹿、鹦鹉和兔子。其他动物在山的另一侧，所以我没有画出来。山上的小屋代表当时所有的房屋。魔法祖师建造了这座小屋，教人怎么盖房子，如果人想建的话。蛇盘在带尖头的小山上，它正在与猴子讲话。猴子对蛇的态度很粗鲁，蛇的态度也不好。人正忙着与魔法祖师讲话。小女孩正看着鲍·安玛逃跑。水里鼓着包的东西就是鲍·安玛。那时它可不是普通的螃蟹。它是螃蟹之王，所以看起来不一样。人脚底下踩着的像砖一样的东西是大迷宫，与魔法祖师讲话时必须站在上面，因为他不得不这样。男人脚下石头上的符号是一个神符；我在下面的祥云中画了三朵神花。整幅画就是一种神奇的药，带有巨大的魔力。

· 205 ·

Just So Stories

    This is the picture of Pau Amma the Crab rising out of the sea as tall as the smoke of three volcanoes. I haven't drawn the three volcanoes, because Pau Amma was so big. Pau Amma is trying to make a Magic, but he is only a silly old King Crab, and so he can't do anything. You can see he is all legs and **claws**①　and empty hollow shell. The canoe is the canoe that the Man and the Girl Daughter and the Eldest Magician sailed from the Perak river in. The sea is all black and **bobbly**②, because Pau Aroma has just risen up out of Pusat Tasek. Pusat Tasek is underneath so I haven't drawn it. The Man is waving his **curvy**③ kris-knife at Pau Amma. The Little Girl Daughter is sitting quietly in the middle of the canoe. She knows she is quite safe with her Daddy. The Eldest Magician is standing up at the other end of the canoe beginning to make a Magic. He has left his magic throne on the **beach**④, and he has taken off his clothes so as not to get wet, and he has left the Magic Cloud behind too, so as not to **tip**⑤ the boat over. The thing that looks like another little canoe outside the real canoe is called an **outrigger**⑥. It is a piece of wood tied to sticks, and it prevents the canoe from being **tipped over**⑦. The canoe is made out of one piece of wood, and there is a paddle at one end of it.

    这幅画描述了鲍·安玛从海中浮出来，比火山烟雾还要高三倍的样子。因为鲍·安玛太大了，我没法把火山画出来。它正企图施展魔法，但它不过是个傻傻的螃蟹王，什么大事也做不了。你可以看到，它长满了脚和爪子，硬壳里面空空的。图中独木舟上载着的那个人、小女孩和魔法祖师从霹雳河来到这里。海面很黑，都是气泡。这是因为鲍·安玛刚从普斯特·塔塞克里浮出来。普斯特·塔塞克位于海中，因此我无法画出来。那个人正向鲍·安到挥舞着他的弧形匕首。小女孩安静地坐在船的中央。她知道与爸爸在一起很安全。魔法祖师站在船的另一端，开始施展魔法。

远古传奇

① claw /klɔː/ n. 爪子

② bobbly /ˈbɒbli/ adj. 气泡的

③ curvy /ˈkɜːvi/ adj. 弯曲的,弧形的

④ beach /biːtʃ/ v. 留在上岸

⑤ tip /tɪp/ n. ；倾倒；翻倒;
⑥ outrigger /aʊtˈrɪɡə(r)/ n. 舷外支架
⑦ tipped over 防止被掀翻

他把宝座留在沙滩上，脱了衣服，这样衣服就不会湿了；他把祥云也留在了岸上，这样就不会把船碰翻了。那个看起来像另外一只独木舟的东西是舷外支架，它是钉在板条上的一块木头，防止独木舟被掀翻。独木舟是用一整块木头制作的，一边有一只船桨。

China-going P. and O.'s
Pass Pau Amma's **playground**① close,
And his Pusat Tasek lies
Near the **track**② of most B. I.'s.
U. Y. K. and N. D. L.
Knows Pau Amma's home as well
As the fisher of the Sea knows
'Bens,' M. M.'s, and Rubattinos.
But (and this is rather **queer**③)
A. T. L.'s can not come here;
O. and O. and D. O. A.
Must go round another way.
Orient④, **Anchor**⑤, Bibby, Hall,
Never go that way at all.
U. C. S. would have a fit
If it found itself on it.
And if 'Beavers' took their **cargoes**⑥
To Penang instead of Lagos,
Or a fat Shaw-Savill bore
Passengers⑦ to Singapore,
Or a White Star were to try a
Little trip to Sourabaya,
Or a B. S. A. went on
Past Natal to Cheribon,
Then great Mr. Lloyds would come
With a wire and **drag**⑧ them home!
You'll know what my **riddle**⑨ means
When you've eaten **mangosteens**⑩.
Or if you can't wait till then, ask them to let you have the outside

远古传奇

① playground /ˈpleɪgraʊnd/ n. 游乐场，操场

② track /træk/ n. 航线 行踪

③ queer /kwɪə/ adj. 奇怪的，可疑的

④ orient /ˈɔːrɪənt/ adj. 东方

⑤ anchor /ˈæŋkə/ n. 锚

⑥ cargo /ˈkɑːgəʊ/ n. 行李 货物

⑦ passenger /ˈpæsɪndʒə(r)/ n. 乘客；旅客

⑧ drag /dræg/ v. 拉，拖

⑨ riddle /ˈrɪdl/ n. 谜语；难题；

⑩ mangosteen n. 山竹果

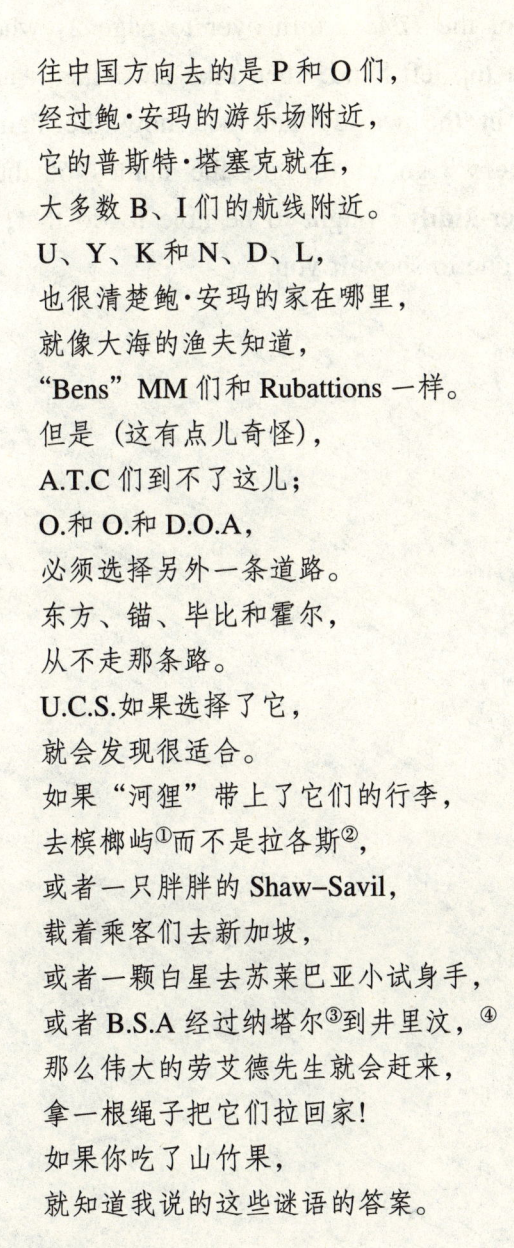

往中国方向去的是 P 和 O 们，
经过鲍·安玛的游乐场附近，
它的普斯特·塔塞克就在，
大多数 B、I 们的航线附近。
U、Y、K 和 N、D、L，
也很清楚鲍·安玛的家在哪里，
就像大海的渔夫知道，
"Bens" MM 们和 Rubattions 一样。
但是（这有点儿奇怪），
A.T.C 们到不了这儿；
O.和 O.和 D.O.A，
必须选择另外一条道路。
东方、锚、毕比和霍尔，
从不走那条路。
U.C.S.如果选择了它，
就会发现很适合。
如果"河狸"带上了它们的行李，
去槟榔屿①而不是拉各斯②，
或者一只胖胖的 Shaw-Savil，
载着乘客们去新加坡，
或者一颗白星去苏莱巴亚小试身手，
或者 B.S.A 经过纳塔尔③到井里汶，④
那么伟大的劳艾德先生就会赶来，
拿一根绳子把它们拉回家！
如果你吃了山竹果，
就知道我说的这些谜语的答案。

---

① 马来西亚马来地区西北部岛屿。译注。
② 尼日利亚首都。译注。
③ 巴西东北部港市。译注。
④ 印度尼西亚爪哇岛北岸港市。译注。

page of the *Times*; turn over to page 2, where it is marked 'Shipping' on the top left hand; then take the Atlas (and that is the finest picture-book in the world) and see how the names of the places that the **steamers**① go to fit into the names of the places on the map. Any steamer-**kiddy**② ought to be able to do that; but if you can't read, ask some one to show it you.

① steamer /ˈstiːmə (r)/ n.
轮船 汽船

② kiddy /ˈkɪdɪ/ n. 小孩

如果你实在等不及了，就请大人帮你找一份《时代周刊》的封皮，翻到第二页，左上侧标着"航海"的那一栏。然后拿出一张地图（那可是世界上最好看的图画书），在地图上找到轮船去的地方的名字。任何一个喜欢轮船的孩子都会这样做的，如果你现在还不能看懂，就请别人指给你看。

The Cat that Walked by Himself

Hear and attend and listen; for this **befell**① and **behappened**② and became and was, O my Best Beloved, when the **Tame**③ animals were wild. The Dog was **wild**④, and the Horse was wild, and the Cow was wild, and the Sheep was wild, and the Pig was wild—as wild as wild could be—and they walked in the Wet Wild Woods by their wild lones. But the wildest of all the wild animals was the Cat. He walked by himself, and all places were **alike**⑤ to him.

Of course the Man was wild too. He was **dreadfully**⑥ wild. He didn't even begin to be tame till he met the Woman, and she told him that she did not like living in his wild ways. She **picked out**⑦ a nice dry Cave, instead of a **heap**⑧ of wet leaves, to lie down in; and she lit a nice fire of wood at the back of the Cave; and she hung a dried wild-horse skin, tail-down, across the opening of the Cave; and she said, '**Wipe**⑨ your feet, dear, when you come in, and now we'll keep house.'

That night, Best Beloved, they ate wild sheep **roasted**⑩ on the hot stones, and **flavoured**⑪ with wild **garlic**⑫ and wild **pepper**⑬; and wild duck **stuffed**⑭ with wild rice and wild **fenugreek**⑮ and wild **coriander**⑯; and marrow-bones of wild **oxen**⑰; and wild **cherries**⑱, and wild **grenadillas**⑲. Then the Man went to sleep in front of the fire ever so

独来独往的猫

① befell /bɪ'fel/ n. 禽兽
② behappen /bɪ'hæpən/ v. 发生在
③ tame /teɪm/ v. 驯化,驯养
④ wild /waɪld/ adj. 野性的,野蛮的

⑤ alike /ə'laɪk/ adv. ,一样
⑥ dreadfully /'dredfʊlɪ/ adv. 极其,非常
⑦ picked /pɪkt/ adj. 找;精选的
⑧ heap /hiːp/ n. 堆
⑨ wipe /waɪp/ v. 擦
⑩ roast /rəʊst/ v. 烤,烘焙
⑪ flavour /'fleɪvə(r)/ n. 香料,调味料
⑫ garlic /'gɑrlɪk/ n. 蒜野头
⑬ pepper /'pepə(r)/ n. 胡椒
⑭ stuff /stʌf/ v. 塞满,填充
⑮ fenugreek n. 胡芦巴
⑯ coriander n. 芫荽
⑰ oxen n. 牛
⑱ cherry /'tʃerɪ/ n. 樱桃
⑲ grenadilla n. 鸡蛋果

亲爱的读者,请安静下来听好。这个故事发生在禽兽们还没有被人驯服成家禽的时候。狗是野狗,马是野马,奶牛是野奶牛,绵羊是野绵羊,猪是野猪——能多野就多野——它们在潮湿的野森林里独自行走。这其中最野的动物是猫。它独来独往,哪儿对它来说都一样,无所谓。

当然那时的男人也是野男人,而且野极了,直到他遇到女人后才渐渐文明起来。女人告诉他,她可不愿像他那样过着野人的日子。她找了一个又舒适又干燥的山洞住了下来,从此不再躺在一堆湿树叶上睡觉,还在洞的深处用木头点了一堆火。她把一张干马皮尾巴朝下地挂在洞门口,对男人说:"亲爱的,进来时把脚擦干。现在我们该管理家务了。"

那天晚上,他们吃的是在热石头上烤的羊肉,上面还撒了野蒜和野胡椒作为调料;晚餐还有野鸭,鸭肚子里填充了野米饭、野胡芦巴和野芫荽,野牛的髓骨,野樱桃,还有野鸡蛋果。饭后,男人快乐地在火堆前睡着了,而女人却坐着

· 213 ·

happy; but the Woman sat up, **combing**① her hair. She took the bone of the shoulder of **mutton**②—the big fat blade-bone—and she looked at the wonderful marks on it, and she threw more wood on the fire, and she made a Magic. She made the First Singing Magic in the world.

Out in the Wet Wild Woods all the wild animals gathered together where they could see the light of the fire a long way off, and they wondered what it meant.

Then Wild Horse stamped with his wild foot and said, 'O my Friends and O my Enemies, why have the Man and the Woman made that great light in that great Cave, and what harm will it do us?'

Wild Dog lifted up his wild nose and smelled the smell of roast mutton, and said, 'I will go up and see and look, and say; for I think it is good. Cat, come with me.'

'Nenni!' said the Cat. 'I am the Cat who walks by himself, and all places are alike to me. I will not come.'

'Then we can never be friends again,' said Wild Dog, and he **trotted off**③ to the Cave. But when he had gone a little way the Cat said to himself, 'All places are alike to me. Why should I not go too and see and look and come away at my own **liking**④.' So he slipped after Wild Dog softly, very softly, and hid himself where he could hear everything.

When Wild Dog reached the mouth of the Cave he lifted up the dried horse-skin with his nose and **sniffed**⑤ the beautiful smell of the roast mutton, and the Woman, looking at the blade-bone, heard him, and laughed, and said, 'Here comes the first. Wild Thing out of the Wild Woods, what do you want?'

Wild Dog said, 'O my Enemy and Wife of my Enemy, what is this that smells so good in the Wild Woods?'

Then the Woman picked up a roasted mutton-bone and threw it to

① comb /kəum/ v. 用梳子梳理
② mutton /'mʌtn/ n. 羊肉

③ trot /trɒt/ n. 小跑，快步

④ liking /'laɪkɪŋ/ n. 爱好，嗜好

⑤ sniff /snɪf/ v. 嗅

梳理起自己的头发。她取出一块羊肩骨——又大又宽的肩胛骨——看了看上面奇妙的符号。她又往火堆里扔了几块木头，然后开始变魔术——世界上第一个会唱歌的魔术。

在野林子里，所有的动物都聚集在远远能够看到火光的地方，想知道这一切意味着什么。

这时野马跺跺脚，说："哦，我的朋友和敌人，为什么那个男人和女人在那个山洞里点了那么大一堆火？这对我们会造成什么伤害？"

野狗伸了伸鼻子，起劲地嗅着烤羊肉的味道，说："我要走近些去看看再说。我觉得这该是件好事。猫，跟我一起去吧。"

"咪——不！"猫回答说，"我一向独来独往，哪儿对我来说都一样，无所谓。我才不去呢。"

"那以后我们可就不是朋友了。"狗说完，一溜儿小跑奔向山洞。野狗离开一会儿后，猫自言自语道："哪儿对我来说都一样。我为什么不也去看看；如果不喜欢就回来呗。"于是，它蹑手蹑脚地尾随着野狗，一听见有什么动静便躲藏起来。

野狗跑到洞口，用鼻子把马皮帘子掀开，嗅着香喷喷的烤羊肉味道。女人正盯着肩胛骨看，听到声音后大笑着说："来了第一位。野林子里的野东西，你想要什么？"

野狗说："哦，我敌人和我敌人的妻子，野林子里什么东西闻起来这么香？"

女人拿起一块烤羊骨扔给野狗，说："野林

· 215 ·

Just So Stories

Wild Dog, and said, 'Wild Thing out of the Wild Woods, **taste**① and try.' Wild Dog **gnawed**② the bone, and it was more **delicious**③ than anything he had ever tasted, and he said, 'O my Enemy and Wife of my Enemy, give me another.'

The Woman said, 'Wild Thing out of the Wild Woods, help my Man to hunt through the day and **guard**④ this Cave at night, and I will give you as many roast bones as you need.'

'Ah!' said the Cat, listening. 'This is a very wise Woman, but she is not so wise as I am.'

Wild Dog **crawled**⑤ into the Cave and laid his head on the Woman's **lap**⑥, and said, 'O my Friend and Wife of my Friend, I will help your Man to hunt through the day, and at night I will guard your Cave.'

'Ah!' said the Cat, listening. 'That is a very **foolish**⑦ Dog.' And he went back through the Wet Wild Woods waving his wild tail, and walking by his wild lone. But he never told anybody.

When the Man **waked up**⑧ he said, 'What is Wild Dog doing here?' And the Woman said, 'His name is not Wild Dog any more, but the First Friend, because he will be our friend for always and always and always. Take him with you when you go hunting.'

Next night the Woman cut great green **armfuls**⑨ of fresh grass from the water-**meadows**⑩, and dried it before the fire, so that it smelt like new-mown **hay**⑪, and she sat at the mouth of the Cave and **plaited**⑫ a **halter**⑬ out of horsehide, and she looked at the shoulder of mutton-bone—at the big broad blade-bone—and she made a Magic. She made the Second Singing Magic in the world.

Out in the Wild Woods all the wild animals wondered what had happened to Wild Dog, and at last Wild Horse stamped with his foot and said, 'I will go and see and say why Wild Dog has not returned. Cat,

① taste /teɪst/ v. 尝，尝起来
② gnaw /nɔː/ v. 啃，啃
③ delicious /dɪˈlɪʃəs/ adj. 美味的

④ guard /ɡɑːd/ v. ; 看守；守护

⑤ crawl /krɔːl/ v. 在...上爬行；爬行
⑥ lap /læp/ n. 膝盖

⑦ foolish /fuːlɪʃ/ adj. 愚蠢的，傻的

⑧ wake up 醒来
⑨ armful /ˈɑːmful/ n. 一大捧
⑩ meadow /ˈmedəʊ/ n. 草地
⑪ hay /heɪ/ n. 干草，秣
⑫ plat /plæt/ v. 把...编成
⑬ halter /ˈhɔːltə(r)/ n. 笼头

子里的野东西，自己尝尝吧。"野狗啃着骨头，觉得这是它所吃到的最好的美味。于是它说："哦，我敌人和我敌人的妻子，再给我一块肉吧。"

女人说："野林子里的野东西，如果你白天能帮助我男人打猎，夜晚能守护这个山洞的话，那么你要多少烤熟的骨头我就给你多少。"

"啊！"猫边听边说，"这个女人挺聪明，但比不上我。"

野狗爬进山洞，把头搭在女人的膝盖上，说："哦，我朋友和我朋友的妻子，我会在白天帮助你男人打猎，在夜晚守护这个山洞。"

"啊，"猫边听边说，"这狗可真笨。"它摇着尾巴独自穿过潮湿的野林子走回来。但这一切它谁也没告诉。

男人睡醒后，问："野狗在这儿干什么？"女人说："它的名字不再是'野狗'了，而是'最好的朋友'。因为它永永远远都会是我们的朋友。你打猎的时候带上它。"

第二天晚上，女人在草甸子那儿割了一大捧新鲜的绿草，在火前烤干后，散发出鲜草堆的气味，女人坐在洞口，用马皮编制了一套马笼头。她凝视着那片又大又宽的羊肩骨，开始变魔术。这是世界上第二个会唱歌的魔术。

野林子里，野兽们都很想知道野狗后来怎么样了。最后野马跺跺脚，说："我前去看看，然后告诉大家为什么野狗没回来。猫，跟我一起去吧。"

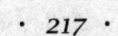

come with me.'

'Nenni!' said the Gat. 'I am the Cat who walks by himself, and all places are alike to me. I will not come.' But all the same he followed Wild Horse softly, very softly, and hid himself where he could hear everything.

When the Woman heard Wild Horse tripping and **stumbling**① on his long **mane**②, she laughed and said, 'Here comes the second. Wild Thing out of the Wild Woods, what do you want?'

Wild Horse said, 'O my Enemy and Wife of my Enemy, where is Wild Dog?'

The Woman laughed, and picked up the blade-bone and looked at it, and said, 'Wild Thing out of the Wild Woods, you did not come here for Wild Dog, but for the sake of this good grass.'

And Wild Horse, tripping and stumbling on his long mane, said, 'That is true; give it me to eat.'

The Woman said, 'Wild Thing out of the Wild Woods, **bend**③ your wild head and wear what I give you, and you shall eat the wonderful grass three times a day.'

'Ah,' said the Cat, listening, 'this is a clever Woman, but she is not so clever as I am.'

Wild Horse bent his wild head, and the Woman slipped the plaited hide halter over it, and Wild Horse breathed on the Woman's feet and said, 'O my **Mistress**④, and Wife of my Master, I will be your **servant**⑤ for the sake of the wonderful grass.'

'Ah,' said the Cat, listening, 'that is a very foolish Horse.' And he went back through the Wet Wild Woods, waving his wild tail and walking by his wild lone. But he never told anybody.

When the Man and the Dog came back from hunting, the Man said, 'What is Wild Horse doing here?' And the Woman said, 'His name is

① stumble /ˈstʌmbl/ v. 绊倒
② mane /meɪn/ n. 鬃毛

③ bend /bend/ n. 低下；弯腰

④ mistress /ˈmɪstrɪs/ n. 主妇，女主人
⑤ servant /ˈsɜrvnt/ n. 仆人

"咪——不！"猫说，"我一向独来独往，哪儿对我来说都一样，无所谓。我才不去呢。"但它还是蹑手蹑脚地尾随着野马，一听见有什么动静就赶快躲藏起来。

女人听到野马轻快的蹄音，看到它被长长的鬃毛绊得跌跌撞撞，就笑着对它说："又来了第二个。野林子里的野东西，你想要什么？"

野马说："哦，我敌人和我敌人的妻子，野狗在哪里？"

女人笑了，然后拿起肩胛骨看了看说："野林子里的野东西，你到这儿来不是为了找野狗，是为了这些美味的草料吧。"

野马被长长的鬃毛绊得趔趔趄趄，说："没错。给我点儿草吃吧。"

女人说："野林子里的野东西，低下头把我给你的东西戴上。这样你一天可以吃三顿美味的草料。"

"啊！"猫边听边说，"这女人挺聪明，但比不上我。"

野马低下头，女人把编好的笼头给它戴上。野马贴近女人的脚面说："哦，我的女主人，我主人的妻子，为了那美味的草料，我会成为您的仆人。"

"啊，"猫边听边想，"这匹马可真蠢。"它独自摇着尾巴穿过潮湿的野林子往回走。但这一切它对谁也没有说。

男人带着狗打猎回来了。男人问："这匹野马在这儿干什么？"女人回答道："它

· 219 ·

not Wild Horse any more, but the First Servant, because he will carry us from place to place for always and always and always. **Ride**① on his back when you go hunting.'

Next day, holding her wild head high that her wild horns should not catch in the wild trees, Wild Cow came up to the Cave, and the Cat followed, and hid himself just the same as before; and everything happened just the same as before; and the Cat said the same things as before, and when Wild Cow had promised to give her milk to the Woman every day in **exchange**② for the wonderful grass, the Cat went back through the Wet Wild Woods waving his wild tail and walking by his wild lone, just the same as before. But he never told anybody. And when the Man and the Horse and the Dog came home from hunting and asked the same questions same as before, the Woman said, 'Her name is not Wild Cow any more, but the Giver of Good Food. She will give us the warm white milk for always and always and always, and I will take care of her while you and the First Friend and the First Servant go hunting.'

Next day the Cat waited to see if any other Wild thing would go up to the Cave, but no one moved in the Wet Wild Woods, so the Cat walked there by himself; and he saw the Woman **milking**③ the Cow, and he saw the light of the fire in the Cave, and he smelt the smell of the warm white milk. Cat said, 'O my Enemy and Wife of my Enemy, where did Wild Cow go?'

The Woman laughed and said, 'Wild Thing out of the Wild Woods, go back to the Woods again, for I have **braided**④ up my hair, and I have put away the magic blade-bone, and we have no more need of either friends or servants in our Cave.'

Cat said, 'I am not a friend, and I am not a servant. I am the Cat who walks by himself, and I wish to come into your cave.'

① ride /raɪd/ v. 骑；骑马

② exchange /ɪksˈtʃeɪndʒ/ v. 交换；兑换

③ milking /ˈmɪlkɪŋ/ n. 挤奶

④ braid /breɪd/ v. 编成辫，梳理

的名字不再叫'野马'了，而是'最佳仆人'。因为它会把我们从一个地方载到另一个地方去，永远为我们服务。打猎的时候，你骑在它的背上。"

第二天，野奶牛来到了山洞前。它把头昂得高高的，这样头上的角就不会钩到野林子里的树枝了。猫还是像往常那样蹑手蹑脚地跟在它后面，一切照旧进行着；猫与往常一样自言自语地说着同样的话；当野奶牛允诺每天给女人提供牛奶以换取美味的草料时，猫还像往常一样，摇着尾巴穿过潮湿的野林子，而且对谁也不说。男人骑着马、带着狗打猎回来了，他提出了与往常一样的问题，这时女人回答说："它的名字不再叫'野奶牛'，而是'好食源'。它会永永远远地为我们提供白花花的温热的牛奶。在你和最好的朋友、最佳仆人外出打猎的时候，我会照顾它的。"

第二天，猫等着看是否还有其他动物到山洞那儿去。但野兽们都呆在野林子里不动。于是猫自己走了。它看见女人正在挤奶，看见山洞深处的火光，并闻到了热牛奶的香气。

猫说："哦，我敌人和我敌人的妻子，野奶牛到哪儿去了？"

女人笑着回答："野林子里的野东西，回到林子里去吧。我已经梳好了头发，还把那块神奇的肩胛骨收起来了。我们的山洞里已不再需要别的朋友或仆人了。"

猫说："我不是朋友，也不是仆人。我是只独来独往的猫，而且我希望能走进你的山洞里。"

Woman said, 'Then why did you not come with First Friend on the first night?'

Cat grew very angry and said, 'Has Wild Dog told **tales**① of me?'

Then the Woman laughed and said, 'You are the Cat who walks by himself, and all places are alike to you. You are neither a friend nor a servant. You have said it yourself. Go away and walk by yourself in all places alike.'

Then Cat **pretended**② to be sorry and said, 'Must I never come into the Cave? Must I never sit by the warm fire? Must I never drink the warm white milk? You are very wise and very beautiful. You should not be **cruel**③ even to a Cat.'

Woman said, 'I knew I was wise, but I did not know I was beautiful. So I will make a **bargain**④ with you. If ever I say one word in your **praise**⑤ you may come into the Cave.'

'And if you say two words in my praise?' said the Cat.

'I never shall,' said the Woman, 'but if I say two words in your praise, you may sit by the fire in the Cave.'

'And if you say three words?' said the Cat.

'I never shall,' said the Woman, 'but if I say three words in your praise, you may drink the warm white milk three times a day for always and always and always.'

Then the Cat **arched**⑥ his back and said, 'Now let the Curtain at the mouth of the Cave, and the Fire at the back of the Cave, and the Milk-pots that stand beside the Fire, remember what my Enemy and the Wife of my Enemy has said.' And he went away through the Wet Wild Woods waving his wild tail and walking by his wild lone.

That night when the Man and the Horse and the Dog came home from hunting, the Woman did not tell them of the bargain that she had made with the Cat, because she was afraid that they might not like it.

远古传奇

① tale /teɪl/ n. 坏话，谣言

② pretended /prɪˈtendɪd/ adj. 装出；

③ cruel /ˈkruəl/ adj. 残忍的

④ bargain /ˈbɑːɡɪn/ n. 交易

⑤ praise /preɪz/ v. 赞扬，夸奖

⑥ arched /ɑːtʃt/ adj. 弓起的

女人说："那你为什么不在第一个晚上与我们的最好的朋友一起来呢？"

猫很生气，问道："野狗跟你说我的坏话了？"

女人大笑，说："你是一只独来独往的猫，哪儿对你来说都一样，无所谓。你不是朋友也不是仆人。你自己就是这么说的。你还是离开这里，随处独行吧。"

猫装出一副遗憾的样子，问道："难道我永远也进不了山洞了吗？难道我永远也不能坐在温暖的火堆旁了吗？难道我永远也喝不到白花花的热牛奶了吗？您那么聪明，又那么有魅力。您可不能这样残忍地对待一只猫啊。"

女人说："我知道自己聪明，但我并不知道自己美丽。我们干脆做笔交易吧。只要我说出一个夸奖你的词语，你就可以走进山洞来。"

"如果你说了两个夸奖我的词语呢？"猫问。

"我不会的，"女人说，"但如果我说了两个夸奖你的词语，你就可以坐在洞深处的火堆旁。"

"如果你说出了三个呢？"猫又问。

"我不会的，"女人说，"但如果我说出了三个夸奖你的词语，你可以每天喝三顿热牛奶，永远如此。"

猫弓起身，说："现在，让洞口的帘子、洞里的火堆和火堆旁的牛奶罐记住我敌人和我敌人的妻子所说的话吧。"然后它摇着尾巴，独自穿过潮湿的野林子，离开了这里。

那天晚上，当男人带着马和狗打猎归来的时候，女人并没有把她和猫之间的交易告诉他们，因为她恐怕他们会不喜欢。

· 223 ·

Just So Stories

Cat went far and far away and hid himself in the Wet Wild Woods by his wild lone for a long time till the Woman forgot all about him. Only the **Bat**①—the little upside-down Bat—that hung inside the Cave, knew where Cat hid; and every evening Bat would fly to Cat with news of what was happening.

One evening Bat said, 'There is a Baby in the Cave. He is new and pink and fat and small, and the Woman is very **fond**② of him.'

'Ah,' said the Cat, listening, 'but what is the Baby fond of?'

'He is fond of things that are soft and **tickle**③,' said the Bat. 'He is fond of warm things to hold in lais arms when he goes to sleep. He is fond of being played with. He is fond of all those things.'

'Ah,' said the Cat, listening, 'then my time has come.'

Next night Cat walked through the Wet Wild Woods and hid very near the Cave till morning-time, and Man and Dog and Horse went hunting. The Woman was busy cooking that morning, and the Baby cried and **interrupted**④. So she carried him outside the Cave and gave him a handful of **pebbles**⑤ to play with. But still the Baby cried.

Then the Cat put out his paddy paw and patted the Baby on the cheek, and it **cooed**⑥; and the Cat rubbed against its fat **knees**⑦ and tickled it under its fat **chin**⑧ with his tail. And the Baby laughed and the Woman heard him and smiled.

Then the Bat—the little upside-down Bat—that hung in the mouth of the Cave said, 'O my Hostess and Wife of my Host and Mother of my Host's Son, a Wild Thing from the Wild Woods is most beautifully playing with your Baby.'

'A blessing on that Wild Thing whoever he may be,' said the Woman, **straightening**⑨ her back, 'for I was a busy woman this morning and he has done me a **service**⑩.'

The very minute and second, Best Beloved, the dried horse-skin

① bat /bæt/ n. 蝙蝠

② fond of 喜欢

③ tickle /ˈtɪkl/ v. 使发痒；感到痒

④ interrupt /ˌɪntəˈrʌpt/ v. 妨碍

⑤ pebble /ˈpebl/ n. 小石头

⑥ coo /kuː/ v. 咕咕地叫

⑦ knee /niː/ n. 膝；膝盖

⑧ chin /tʃɪn/ n. 下巴；下颚

⑨ straighten /ˈstreɪtn/ v. 弄直；直起来

⑩ service /ˈsɜːvɪs/ n. 服务；帮助

猫走到了一个很远很远的地方，独自在潮湿的野林子里躲藏了好长一段日子，直到女人把它忘得干干净净。只有山洞里头朝下倒挂的那只蝙蝠知道猫藏在哪里。每天晚上它都会飞到猫那里去，告诉猫最新的消息。

一天晚上，蝙蝠对猫说："山洞里有一个小宝宝。他刚出生，个头不大，白胖得像粉团儿一样。女人非常疼爱他。"

"啊，"猫边听边问，"小宝宝喜欢什么？"

"喜欢柔软、痒痒的东西，"蝙蝠回答，"睡觉时，他喜欢把暖和的东西搂在怀里。他喜欢被人逗。这些东西，他都喜欢。"

"啊，"猫边听边说，"时机到了。"

第二天夜里，猫穿过潮湿的野林子，在山洞附近躲藏起来直到天亮。男人骑着马，带着狗外出打猎了。上午，女人忙着做饭，小宝宝却在一旁不停地哭，这妨碍了她干活儿。于是女人把小宝宝抱到山洞外边，塞给他一块石头玩儿。但小宝宝还是哭个不停。

这时猫伸出毛茸茸的爪子，轻轻地摩挲着小宝宝的脸蛋，宝宝轻声咕哝起来；猫又用尾巴蹭他胖胖的膝盖，并在他的胖下巴下面搔痒。宝宝笑了起来；女人听了也笑了。

这时，那只倒挂在洞口的蝙蝠说："哦，我的女主人，我主人的妻子和主人儿子的母亲，野林子里的野东西与您的宝宝玩得好极了。"

"不论这东西是谁，愿上帝赐福于它吧。"女人挺直了背，"今天上午我简直忙坏了，是它帮了我的忙。"

就在那一刹那，洞口尾巴朝下挂着的干马皮

Curtain that was stretched tail-down at the mouth of the Cave fell down—*woosh*! — because it remembered the bargain she had made with the Cat, and when the Woman went to pick it up—lo and behold! —the Cat was sitting quite comfy inside the Cave.

'O my Enemy and Wife of my Enemy and Mother of my Enemy,' said the Cat, 'it is I; for you have spoken a word in my praise, and now I can sit within the Cave for always and always and always. But still I am the Cat who walks by himself, and all places are alike to me.'

The Woman was very angry, and shut her **lips**① tight and took up her **spinning-wheel**② and began to spin.

But the Baby cried because the Cat had gone away, and the Woman could not **hush**③ it, for it **struggled**④ and **kicked**⑤ and grew black in the face.

'O my Enemy and Wife of my Enemy and Mother of my Enemy,' said the Cat, 'take a **strand**⑥ of the wire that you are spinning and tie it to your spinning-whorl and drag it along the floor, and I will show you a magic that shall make your Baby laugh as loudly as he is now crying.'

'I will do so,' said the Woman, 'because I am **at my wits'end**⑦; but I will not thank you for it.'

She tied the **thread**⑧ to the little clay **spindle-whorl**⑨ and drew it across the floor, and the Cat ran after it and patted it with his paws and **rolled**⑩ head over heels, and **tossed**⑪ it backward over his shoulder and chased it between his **hind-legs**⑫ and pretended to lose it, and **pounced**⑬ down upon it again, till the Baby laughed as loudly as it had been crying, and **scrambled**⑭ after the Cat and **frolicked**⑮ all over the Cave till it grew tired and settled down to sleep with the Cat in its arms.

'Now,' said the Cat, 'I will sing the Baby a song that shall keep

远古传奇

"忽"地落在了地上——因为它还记得女人和猫之间达成的交易。女人把马皮捡起来的时候——嗨，你瞧！猫已经在山洞里安安静静、舒舒服服地坐着了。

"哦，我敌人和我敌人的妻子和我敌人的母亲，"猫说，"我在这儿，因为你说出了一个夸奖我的词。现在我可以永永远远地在山洞里坐下去了。但我还是那只独来独往的猫，哪儿对我来说都是一个样，无所谓。"

女人气极了。她紧紧地抿起嘴唇，拿起纺轮，开始纺线。

猫离开后，小宝宝又开始哭。女人无法让他安静下来。他又踢又蹬，四肢拼命挣扎着，连脸都变黑了。

"哦，我敌人和我敌人的妻子和我敌人的母亲，"猫说，"拿一截你纺的线系在纺线用的锭盘上，在地面上拉着它走。我给你变个戏法：你的宝宝现在用多大嗓门哭，呆会儿他就会用多大嗓门笑。"

"我会这样做的，"女人说，"我已经无计可施。但我可不会因此而感谢你。"

她把线系在一个泥制的小锭盘上，在地上拉着走。猫追着，用爪子拍打着，翻着跟头满地滚，往肩膀上又扔又抛，用后腿去抓，假装丢掉了，又跳起来，直到宝宝用刚才大哭的嗓门大笑起来，并在猫的身后爬着，在整个山洞里嬉闹着。最后他也累了，停下来搂着猫睡着了。

"现在，"猫说，"我给小宝宝唱支歌，能让

① lip /lɪp/ n. 嘴唇；
② spining-wheel /ˈspɪnhwiːl/ v. 纺轮
③ hush /hʌʃ/ n. 安静
④ struggle /ˈstrʌgl/ n. 使劲踹
⑤ kick /kɪk/ n. 踢
⑥ strand /strænd/ n. 纺线
⑦ at one's wits' end n. 无计可施
⑧ thread /θred/ n. 线，线索
⑨ spindle-whorl /ˈspɪndlwɜːl/ n. 纱锭盘
⑩ roll /rəʊl/ v. 滚，飘流
⑪ toss /tɒs/ v. 抛，投，扔
⑫ hind-leg /haɪnd-leg/ n. 后腿
⑬ pounce /paʊns/ v. 去抓
⑭ scramble /ˈskræmbl/ n. 爬行

· 227 ·

him **asleep**① for an hour.' And he began to **purr**②, loud and low, low and loud, till the Baby fell fast asleep. The Woman smiled as she looked down upon the two of them and said, 'That was wonderfully done. No question but you are very clever, O Cat.'

That very minute and second, Best Beloved, the smoke of the fire at the back of the Cave came down in clouds from the roof—*puff*! — because it remembered the bargain she had made with the Cat, and when it had cleared away—lo and behold! —the Cat was sitting quite comfy close to the fire.

'O my Enemy and Wife of my Enemy and Mother of my Enemy,' said the Cat, 'it is I, for you have spoken a second word in my praise, and now I can sit by the warm fire at the back of the Cave for always and always and always. But still I am the Cat who walks by himself, and all places are alike to me.'

Then the Woman was very very angry, and let down her hair and put more wood on the fire and brought out the broad blade-bone of the shoulder of mutton and began to make a Magic that should prevent her from saying a third word in praise of the Cat. It was not a Singing Magic, Best Beloved, it was a Still Magic; and by and by the Cave grew so still that a little wee-wee mouse crept out of a corner and ran across the floor.

'O my Enemy and Wife of my Enemy and Mother of my Enemy,' said the Cat, 'is that little mouse part of your magic?'

'Ouh! Chee! No indeed!' said the Woman, and she dropped the blade-bone and jumped upon the **footstool**③ in front of the fire and **braided up**④ her hair very quick for fear that the mouse should run up it.

'Ah,' said the Cat, watching, 'then the mouse will do me no harm if I eat it? '

① asleep /əˈsliːp/ adj. 睡熟了的
② purr /pɜː/ n. 咕噜咕噜声

他睡上一个钟头。"然后它开始呜呜地叫，声音忽高忽低，忽低忽高，直到宝宝睡熟了为止。女人微笑地看着他们，说："干得真不错。哦，猫，你很聪明，这毫无疑问。"

就在那一刹那，山洞里的火堆散发出的烟忽然从屋顶"嗖"地一声如云雾般刮了下来。因为火堆还记得女人和猫之间达成的交易。烟雾散去后——嘿，你看！猫已经安静、舒适地坐在火堆旁边了。

"哦，我敌人和我敌人的妻子和我敌人的母亲，"猫说，"我在这儿，因为你说出了第二个夸奖我的词。现在我可以永永远远地在洞深处的火堆旁坐下去了。但我还是只独来独往的猫，哪儿对来我来说都一样，无所谓。"

女人非常非常生气。她把头发披散下来，往火里又扔了些木柴，然后拿出那块宽大的肩胛骨，开始变魔术，使自己不说出夸奖猫的第三个词。这是个无声的魔术（不会唱歌）；渐渐地山洞变得非常安静，一只小老鼠从角落里爬出来在地上跑。

"哦，我敌人和我敌人的妻子和我敌人的母亲，"猫说，"这小老鼠也是你魔术的一部分吗？"

③ footstool /ˈfʊtstuːl/ n. 板凳
④ braid /breɪd/ v. 编成辫

"噢！啊！绝对不是！"女人说着，手里的肩胛骨跌落在地上。她跳到火堆前面的板凳上，飞快地梳起辫子。她害怕老鼠会顺着她的头发爬上去。

"啊，"猫看了看说，"如果我把老鼠吃了，对我不会有什么坏处吧？"

'No,' said the Woman, braiding up her hair, 'eat it quickly and I will ever be **grateful**① to you.'

Cat made one jump and caught the little mouse, and the Woman said, 'A hundred thanks. Even the First Friend is not quick enough to catch little mice as you have done. You must be very wise.'

That very moment and second, O Best Beloved, the Milk-pot that stood by the fire **cracked**② in two pieces—*ffft*—because it remembered the bargain she had made with the Cat, and when the Woman jumped down from the footstool—lo and behold! —the Cat was lapping up the warm white milk that lay in one of the broken pieces.

'O my Enemy and Wife of my Enemy and Mother of my Enemy,' said the Cat, 'it is I; for you have spoken three words in my praise, and now I can drink the warm white milk three times a day for always and always and always. But still I am the Cat who walks by himself, and all places are Mike to me.'

Then the Woman laughed and set the Cat a **bowl**③ of the warm white milk and said, 'O Cat, you are as clever as a man, but remember that your bargain was not made with the Man or the Dog, and I do not know what they will do when they come home.'

'What is that to me?' said the Cat. 'If I have my place in the Cave by the fire and my warm white milk three times a day I do not care what the Man or the Dog can do.'

That evening when the Man and the Dog came into the Cave, the Woman told them all the story of the bargain while the Cat sat by the fire and smiled. Then the Man said, 'Yes, but he has not made a bargain with me or with all **proper**④ Men after me.' Then he took off his two **leather**⑤ boots and he took up his little stone **axe**⑥ (that makes three) and he fetched a piece of wood and a **hatchet**⑦ (that is five altogether), and he set them out in a row and he said, 'Now we will

① grateful /ˈɡreɪtfʊl/ adj. 感激的

② cracked /krækt/ adj. 破碎的，声音嘶哑的

③ bowl /bəʊl/ n. 碗

④ proper /ˈprɒpə(r)/ adj. 正正经经的
⑤ leather /ˈleðə(r)/ n. 皮靴；皮革制品
⑥ axe /æks/ n. 小石斧
⑦ hatchet /ˈhætʃɪt/ n. 斧头

"没有，"女人边梳辫子边说，"快吃了它，我会感激你的。"

猫跳起来，抓住了小老鼠。女人说："100个感谢。就连最好的朋友也不能像你这样迅速地逮到老鼠。你一定非常聪明。"

就在那一刹那，火堆旁的奶罐"刷"地裂成两半——因为它还记得女人和猫之间达成的交易。当女人从凳子上跳下来时——嘿，你瞧! 猫正在舔食裂块上残留的白花花的热牛奶。

"哦，我敌人和我敌人的妻子和我敌人的母亲，"猫说，"我这样做，是因为你说出了第三个夸奖我的词。现在我可以永永远远地每天喝三次白花花的热牛奶了。但我仍旧是只独来独往的猫，哪儿对我来说都一样，无所谓。"

女人笑起来。她把一碗白花花的热牛奶放在猫的跟前，说："哦，猫，你像人一样聪明。但你得记住，你并没有和男人或狗达成交易，所以我不知道他们回来后会怎么样。"

"这跟我有什么关系?"猫说，"如果我在山洞里的火堆旁有个位置、每天能喝三次热牛奶的话，我可不管男人或狗怎么做。"

晚上，男人带着狗走进山洞，女人就把她和猫之间的交易告诉了他们，猫则微笑着坐在火堆旁边。男人说："好吧，但它可没有和我以及我以后所有正正经经的男人达成交易。"他脱下两只皮靴，拿出小石斧（共三样东西），又取来一片木头和一把短柄斧子（共五件东西），把这五件东西摆成一排，说："现在我们做个交易。如果你在山洞里不捉老鼠，那么

make our bargain. If you do not catch mice when you are in the Cave for always and always and always, I will throw these five things at you whenever I see you, and so shall all proper Men do after me.'

'Ah,' said the Woman, listening, 'this is a very clever Cat, but he is not so clever as my Man.'

The Cat counted the five things (and they looked very **knobby**①) and he said, 'I will catch mice when I am in the Cave for always and always and always; but still I am the Cat who walks by himself, and all places are alike to me.'

'Not when I am near,' said the Man. 'If you had not said that last I would have put all these things away for always and always and always; but I am now going to throw my two boots and my little stone axe (that makes three) at you whenever I meet you. And so shall all proper Men do after me!'

Then the Dog said, 'Wait a minute. He has not made a bargain with me or with all proper Dogs after me.' And he showed his teeth and said, 'If you are not kind to the Baby while I am in the Cave for always and always and always, I will hunt you till I catch you, and when I catch you I will bite you. And so shall all proper Dogs do after me.'

'Ah,' said the Woman, listening, 'this is a very clever Cat, but he is not so clever as the Dog.'

Cat counted the Dog's teeth (and they looked very **pointed**②) and he said, 'I will be kind to the Baby while I am in the Cave, as long as he does not pull my tail too hard, for always and always and always. But still I am the Cat that walks by himself, and all places are alike to me.'

'Not when I am near,' said the Dog. 'If you had not said that last I would have shut my mouth for always and always and always; but now I

远古传奇

我一看见你就朝你扔这五件东西。我以后的其他正正经经的男人也会这样，直到永远。"

"啊，"女人听了，说，"这只猫虽然聪明，但比不上我男人。"

猫数了数这五件东西（看上去有棱有角、疙疙瘩瘩的），说："我在山洞里会永远捉老鼠的，但我仍然是只独来独往的猫，哪儿对我来说都一样，无所谓。"

"我在跟前时你可不能这样，"男人说，"如果你不说最后一句，我就会把这些东西永远收起来。但现在我决定，只要看见你，我就会把两只靴子和小石斧（共三件）朝你扔去。我以后所有正正经经的男人也都会这样做！"

这时狗说："等一等，它还没有和我以及我以后所有正正经经的狗达成交易呢。"它呲着牙说："如果我在洞里的时候你对小宝宝不好，我就会追着你直到抓住你，抓到后用牙咬你，永远都会这样。我以后所有正正经经的狗也会这么做。"

"啊，"女人听了说，"这只猫很聪明，但比不上狗。"

猫数了数狗的牙齿（看上去锋利极了），说："在洞里的时候我会永远对宝宝好的，只要他不过分用力地拽我的尾巴就行。但我仍旧是只独来独往的猫，哪儿对我来说都一样，无所谓。"

"我在附近时你可不能这样，"狗说，"如果你不说最后一句话，我本来会永远闭嘴；但现在我只要遇到你，就会把你撵上树去。我以后所有正正经经的狗也会这样做！"

① knobby /ˈnɑbɪ/ adj. 多疙瘩的

② pointed /ˈpɔɪntɪd/ adj. 锋利的

am going to hunt you up a tree **whenever**① I meet you. And so shall all proper Dogs do after me.'

Then the Man threw his two boots and his little stone axe (that makes three) at the Cat, and the Cat ran out of the Cave and the Dog chased him up a tree; and from that day to this, Best Beloved, three proper Men out of five will always throw things at a Cat whenever they meet him, and all proper Dogs will chase him up a tree. But the Cat keeps his side of the bargain too. He will kill **mice**② and he will be kind to Babies when he is in the house, just as long as they do not pull his tail too hard. But when he has done that, and between times, and when the moon gets up and night comes, he is the Cat that walks by himself, and all places are alike to him. Then he goes out to the Wet Wild Woods or up the Wet Wild Trees or on the Wet Wild Roofs, waving his wild tail and walking by his wild lone.

远古传奇

① whenever adv. 不论何时，每逢（文中指从那时起）

② mice n. 老鼠

然后男人把他的两只靴子和小石斧（共三件）朝猫扔了过去，猫跑出山洞；狗在后面追它，把它撵上了树。亲爱的读者，从那一天起，五个正经男人中就有三个人一见到猫就朝它扔东西，所有正经的狗就会把它撵上树。但猫也遵守了交易规则。它捉老鼠；在屋子里的时候，只要孩子们不使劲儿拽它的尾巴，就对孩子们好。但这一切过后，在月亮升起来、夜幕降临的时候，它又成了那只独来独往的猫，哪儿对它来说都一样。那时它会走进潮湿的野林子或爬上潮湿的野树或野屋顶，摇摆着尾巴独自行走。

Just So Stories

This is the picture of the Cave where the Man and the Woman lived first of all. It was really a very nice Cave, and much wanner that it looks. The Man had a canoe. It is on the edge of the river, being **soaked**① in the water to make it **swell up**②. The **tattery**③-looking thing across the rive is the Man's salmon-net to catch salmon with. There are nice clean stones leading up from the river to the mouth of the Cave, so that the Man and the Woman could go down for water without getting sand between their toes. The things like black-**beetles**④ far down the beach are really **trunks**⑤ of dead trees that floated down the river from the Wet Wild Woods on the other bank. The Man and the Woman used to **drag**⑥ them out and dry them and cut them up for firewood. I haven't drawn the horsehide curtain at the mouth of the Cave, because the Woman has just taken it down to be cleaned. All those little **smudges**⑦ on the sand between the Cave and the river are the marks of the Woman's feet and the Man's feet.

The Man and the Woman are both inside the Cave eating their dinner. They went to another **cosier**⑧ Cave when the Baby came, because the Baby used to **crawl down**⑨ to the river and fall in, and the Dog had to pull him out.

　　首先，这是男人和女人最初居住的山洞。这洞真的很不错，虽然看上去好像挺寒冷的，实际上洞里很暖和。男人有一只独木舟，停泊在河边，浸泡在水中，于是就膨胀起来了。横在河里那些看上去破破烂烂的东西是男人用来捉鲑鱼的网子。从河边到洞口摆着一溜干净整齐的石头，这样男人和女人走到河边去的时候，脚趾缝里就不会沾上沙子了。在沙滩远处有一堆看起来像黑甲壳状的东西，其实是从对面河岸上潮湿的野林子里顺流漂下的枯死的树干。男人和女人常常把树干拽到河岸上晒干，然后劈开当木柴。我没有画洞口挂着的马皮，因为女人刚刚把它取下来，准备清洗一下。在山洞和河流

远古传奇

① soak /səuk/ v. 浸；浸泡
② swell /swel/ v. ，膨胀；使膨胀
③ tattery /'tætə(r)li/ n. 破破烂烂

④ beetle /'bi:tl/ n. 甲壳状
⑤ trunk /trʌŋk/ n. 树干
⑥ drag /dræg/ v. 拉，拖；拽

⑦ smudge /smʌdʒ/ n. 熏烟（文中指木柴）

⑧ cosy /'kəuzɪ/ adj. 舒适的，惬意的
⑨ crawl /krɔ:l/ n. 爬行

中间的沙滩上有一些小黑点，那是男人和女人的脚印。

男人和女人正在山洞里吃晚餐。有了小宝宝后，他们搬到了另外一个更舒适的山洞里住。因为小宝宝常常爬到河边掉进水里，狗不得不把他拽上岸来。

· 237 ·

Just So Stories

This is the picture of the Cat that Walked by Himself, walking by his wild lone through the Wet Wild Woods and waving his wild tail. There is nothing else in the picture except some **toadstools**①. They had to grow there because the woods were so wet. The **lumpy**② thing on the low branch isn't bird. It is moss that grew there because the Wild woods were so wet.

Underneath the truly picture is a picture of the cozy Cave that the Man and the Woman went to after the Bany came. It was their summer Cave, and they planted **wheat**③ in front of it. The man is riding on the horse to find the Cow and bring her back to the Cave to be milked. He is holding up his hand to call the Dog, who has swum across to the other side of the river, looking for **rabbits**④.

猫正摇着尾巴，独自穿行在潮湿的野林子里。除了一些伞菌外，图上没有其他东西。伞菌长在那儿，是因为那儿太潮湿了。低树枝上那一大团东西不是鸟；野林子里太潮湿了，苔藓长到了树上。

下面的小图画的是小宝宝出生后，男人和女人搬到了另外一个更舒适的山洞里。这是他们夏天的住所。他们在洞前面种了些麦子。男人正骑着马寻找母牛，好把它带回家挤奶。他举起手召唤着狗。狗游到河的对岸去找兔子。

远古传奇

① toadstool /ˈtəʊdstuːl/ n. 伞菌
② lumpy /ˈlʌpɪ/ adj. 一大团

③ wheat /hwiːt/ n. 小麦

④ rabbit /ˈræbɪt/ n. 兔

· 239 ·

Pussy① can sit by the fire and sing,
Pussy can climb a tree,
Or play with a silly old **cork**② and **string**③
To muse herself, not me.
But I like *Binkie* my dog, because
He knows how to behave;
So, *Binkie's* the same as the First Friend was
And I am the Man in the Cave.

Pussy will play man-Friday till
It's time to wet her paw
And make her walk on the window-sill
(For the **footprint**④ Crusoe saw);
Then she **fluffles**⑤ her tail and mews,
And scratches and won't attend.
But *Binkie* will play whatever I choose,
And he is my true First Friend.

Pussy will rub my knees with her head
Pretending she loves me hard;
But the very minute I go to my bed
Pussy runs out in the yard,
And there she stays till the morning-light;
So I know it is only pretend;
But *Binkie*, he snores at my feet all night,
And he is my Firstest Friend!

远古传奇

① pussy /ˈpʊsɪ/ n. 小猫，猫咪

② cork /kɔːk/ n. 软木塞，
③ string /strɪŋ/ n. 线；细绳

④ footprint /ˈfʊprɪntt/ n. 脚印；足迹
⑤ fluffy /ˈflʌfɪ/ adj. 柔软的；蓬松的

猫咪会坐在火堆旁唱歌，
会爬树，
或者用一只傻傻的旧木塞和一条绳子
逗它自己玩（而不是我）。
但我喜欢我的狗冰奇，
它知道怎么规规矩矩；
所以，冰奇就像是我的最好的朋友，
而我就是山洞里那个男人。
猫咪可以扮成"星期五"，①
直到它该洗爪子了，
或者在窗台上行走，
好留下克罗索·鲁宾孙看到的脚印。
它摇着柔软的尾巴喵喵叫，
又抓又挠不睬人。
但我可以选择和冰奇一起玩儿，
它是我真正的最好的朋友。
猫咪会用头蹭我的膝盖，
假装对我无比深爱；
但我刚上床它就一下子冲到院子里，
在那儿一直呆到第二天日出；
我知道这不过是个骗局；
而冰奇在我脚下打鼾直到天明，
它才是我最好最好的朋友！

---

① "星期五"是鲁宾孙漂流到荒岛后通过留在沙滩上的脚印发现的野人，他们成了好朋友。译注。

The Butterfly that Stamped

This, O my Best Beloved, is a story—a new and a wonderful story—a story quite different from the other stories—a story about The Most Wise Sovereign Suleiman-bin-Daoud--Solomon the Son of David.

There are three hundred and fifty-five stories about Suleiman-bin-Daoud; but this not one of them. It is not the story of the Lapwing who found the Water; or the Hoopoe who shaded Suleiman-bin-Daoud from the heat. It is not the story of the Glass Pavement, or the Ruby with the Crooked Hole, or the Gold Bars of Balkis. It is the story of the **Butterfly**[1] that Stamped.

Now attend all over again and listen!

Suleiman-bin-Daoud was wise. He understood what the beasts said, what the birds said, what the fishes said, and what the **insects**[2] said. He understood what the rocks said deep under the earth when they **bowed**[3] in towards each other and **groaned**[4]; and he understood what the trees said when they **rustled**[5] in the middle of the morning. He understood everything, from the **bishop**[6] on the bench to the **hyssop**[7] on the wall, and Balkis, his Head Queen, the Most Beautiful Queen Balkis, was nearly as wise as he was.

Suleiman-bin-Daoud was strong. Upon the third finger of the right hand he wore a ring. When he turned it once, Afrits and Djinns came out

跛脚的蝴蝶

亲爱的读者朋友，下面我要讲的是个新故事，与其他故事不同，非常神奇。它讲述了一个关于大卫之子所罗门——最聪明的君王苏雷曼宾·达奥德的故事。

有关苏雷曼宾·达奥德的故事多达 355 个，但这个故事可不在其中。它不是麦鸡找到水的故事，也不是戴胜鸟在高温下为苏雷曼宾·达奥德遮阴的故事；不是玻璃路面的故事，不是钻有曲孔的红宝玉的故事，也不是巴尔基斯女王的金条的故事。它讲的是一只跛脚的蝴蝶。

现在再请大家认真听好！

苏雷曼宾·达奥德非常聪明。他能听懂野兽、飞鸟、游鱼和昆虫的话，也能听懂地球深处岩石们彼此鞠躬致意和抱怨时说的话，还能听懂上午九十点钟树木沙沙作响时的言语。从当法官的大祭司到墙上的海索草，他无所不知。他最美丽的王后巴尔基斯几乎和他一样聪明。

苏雷曼宾·达奥德非常强壮。他右手第三个手指上戴着一枚戒指。如果他把戒指转动一次，恶魔和巨神们就会从地里钻出来，按照他的吩咐

① butterfly /ˈbʌtəflaɪ/ n. 蝴蝶
② insect /ˈɪnsekt/ n. 昆虫
③ bow /baʊ/ v. 鞠躬，鞠躬表示
④ groan /ɡrəʊn/ v. 呻吟地说 抱怨的说
⑤ rustle /ˈrʌsl/ v. 沙沙作响；
⑥ bishop /ˈbɪʃəp/ n. 法官
⑦ hyssop /ˈhɪsəp/ n. 海索草

· 243 ·

of the earth to do whatever he told them. When he turned it twice, Fairies came down from the sky to do whatever he told them; and when he turned it three times, the very great **angel**① Azrael of the Sword came dressed as a water-carrier, and told him the news of the three worlds, — Above—Below—and Here.

And yet Suleiman-bin-Daoud was not proud. He very **seldom**② **showed off**③, and when he did he was sorry for it. Once he tried to feed all the animals in all the world in one day, but when the food was ready an Animal came out of the deep sea and ate it up in three **mouthfuls**④. Suleiman-bin-Daoud was very surprised and said, 'O Animal, who are you?' And the Animal said, 'O King, live for ever! I am the smallest of thirty thousand brothers, and our home is at the bottom of the sea. We heard that you were going to feed all the animals in all the world, and my brothers sent me to ask when dinner would be ready.' Suleiman-bin-Daoud was more surprised than ever and said, 'O Animal, you have eaten all the dinner that I made ready for all the animals in the world.' And the Animal said, 'O King, live for ever, but do you really call that a dinner? Where I come from we each eat twice as much as that between meals.' Then Suleiman-bin-Daoud fell flat on his face and said, 'O Animal! I gave that dinner to show what a great and rich king I was, and not because I really wanted to be kind to the animals. Now I am ashamed, and it serves me right.' Suleiman-bin-Daoud, was a really truly wise man, Best Beloved. After that he never forgot that it was silly to show off; and now the real story part of my story begins.

He **married**⑤ ever so many wives. He married nine hundred and ninetynine wives, besides the Most Beautiful Balkis; and they all lived in a great golden palace in the middle of a lovely garden with **fountains**⑥. He didn't really want nine-hundred and ninety-nine wives, but in those

① angel /'eɪndʒəl/ n. 天使

② seldom /'seldəm/ adv. 很少，不常
③ show off v. 炫耀

④ mouthful /'maʊθfʊl/ n. 一口

⑤ married /'mærɪd/ adj. 已婚的，已娶的
⑥ fountain /'faʊntn/ n. 泉水；喷泉

——去做。如果他把戒指转动两次，仙女们就会从天上飘落下来，按照他的吩咐行事。如果他把戒指转动三次，最伟大的天使剑神艾斯瑞尔就会打扮成送水人的样子到来，把最近发生在三个世界——天上、地下和人间——的事情告诉给他。

尽管如此，苏雷曼宾·达奥德为人并不骄傲。他很少炫耀自己，否则就会感到后悔。有一次，他试图在一天内喂饱世界上所有的动物。但食物刚刚准备好的时候，从深海里来了一只动物，张开嘴巴三口就把所有的食物都吃光了。苏雷曼宾·达奥德非常惊讶，问道："哦，动物老兄，你是谁？"动物回答："哦，大王，祝您万寿无疆！我有30000个兄弟，我是最小的一个。我的家在海底，听说您要喂饱世界上所有的动物，于是哥哥们便派我来问一问这盛宴何时能准备好。"苏雷曼宾·达奥德从来没有这么震惊过，他说："哦，动物老兄，你已经把我给世界上所有动物准备的食物一扫而光了。"动物说："哦，大王，祝您万寿无疆！但您把那些东西就称为盛宴吗？在我的家乡，我们饭前饭后吃的零食比那些东西还要多一倍。"苏雷曼宾·达奥德变得没精打采，说道："哦，动物老兄！其实我举办盛宴的目的是为了显示我这个大王多么伟大富有，并不是真想对动物们表示善意。现在我很惭愧。这真是罪有应得。"亲爱的读者朋友，苏雷曼宾·达奥德是个真正明智的人。从那儿以后，他永远也不会忘记炫耀是一件多么愚蠢的事情。现在，我要讲的故事正式开始了。

他娶了好多好多位妻子，除了最美丽的巴尔基斯外，还有999位王后。她们全都住在一座宏

days everybody married ever so many wives, and of course the King had to marry ever so many more just to show that he was the King.

Some of the wives were nice, but some were simply **horrid**①, and the horrid ones **quarrelled**② with the nice ones and made them horrid too, and then they would all quarrel with Suleiman-bin-Daoud, and that was horrid for him. But Balkis the Most Beautiful never quarrelled with Suleiman-bin-Daoud. She loved him too much. She sat in her rooms in the Golden Palace, or walked in the **Palace**③ garden, and was truly sorry for him.

Of course if he had chosen to turn his ring on his finger and call up the Djinns and the Afrits they would have **magicked**④ all those nine hundred and ninety-nine **quarrelsome**⑤ wives into white **mules**⑥ of the **desert**⑦ or **greyhounds**⑧ or **pomegranate**⑨ seeds; but Suleiman-bin-Daoud thought that that would be showing off. So, when they quarrelled too much, he only walked by himself in one part of the beautiful Palace gardens and wished he had never been born.

One day, when they had quarrelled for three weeks—all nine hundred and ninety-nine wives together—Suleiman-bin-Daoud went out for peace and quiet as usual; and among the orange trees he met Balkis the Most Beautiful, very **sorrowful**⑩ because Suleiman-bin-Daoud was so worried. And she said to him, 'O my Lord and Light of my Eyes, turn the ring upon your finger and show these Queens of Egypt and Mesopotamia and Persia and China that you are the great and terrible King.' But Suleiman-bin-Daoud shook his head and said, 'O my Lady and Delight of my Life, remember the Animal that came out of the sea and made me ashamed before all the animals in all the world because I showed off. Now, if I showed off before these Queens of Persia and Egypt and Abyssinia and China, merely because they worry me, I might be made even more ashamed than I have been.'

远古传奇

① horrid /ˈhɑrəd/ adj. 极可厌的
② quarrel /ˈkwɑrəl/ v. 吵架
③ palace /ˈpælɪs/ n. 皇宫，宫殿
④ magic /ˈmædʒɪk/ n. 魔术，魔法
⑤ quarrelsome /ˈkwɑrəlsəm/ adj. 争吵不休
⑥ mule /mjuːl/ n. 骡子
⑦ desert /ˈdɪˈzɜːt/ n. 沙漠
⑧ greyhound /ˈɡreɪhaʊnd/ n. 灰狗
⑨ pomegranate /ˈpʌmɪˌɡrænɪt/ n. 石榴
⑩ sorrowful /ˈsɑrəʊfʊl/ adj. 悲伤的，焦虑的

伟的金色宫殿里。宫殿位于一个带喷泉的漂亮花园中央。其实，他本人并不需要999位妻子，但那时人们都这样做；为了证实他是国王，他不得不娶了这么多妻子。

在他这么多妻子当中，有的人很善良，有的却讨厌透顶；后者与前者吵架，结果善良的也变得令人讨厌。然后她们就都和苏雷曼宾·达奥德吵架，这让他觉得可怕极了。但最美丽的王后巴尔基斯却从来不和苏雷曼宾·达奥德吵架。她深深地爱着他。她有时在金色宫殿自己的房间里静坐，有时在花园里漫步，心里却为国王感到难过。

当然，如果他把手指上的戒指转动一下，把恶魔和神灵叫出来，他们就会用魔法把那些争吵不休的999位王后变成沙漠中的白骡子、灰狗或者石榴籽。但他认为这样做过于夸耀自己了。于是，即使王后们吵得再厉害，他也只是在花园的一个角落里独自漫步，心想要是没有出生在这个世界上该多好呀。

一天，999位王后已经在一起吵了三个星期——苏雷曼宾·达奥德又像往常一样走出去寻找和平和宁静。在桔子树丛中他遇到了最美丽的王后巴尔基斯。看到苏雷曼宾·达奥德焦虑的样子，她很伤心，说："哦，我的君王我眼睛的光芒，把你手指上的戒指转一下，向那些来自埃及、美索不达米亚、①波斯和中国的王后显示一下你是多么伟大、多么令人敬畏。"但苏雷曼宾·达奥德摇了摇头，说："哦，我的夫人我生命的

---

① 亦称"两河流域"，即底格里斯和幼发拉底两河域平原，在叙利亚东部和伊拉克境内。译注。

And Balkis the Most Beautiful said, 'O my Lord and **Treasure**[1] of my Soul, what will you do?'

And Suleiman-bin-Daoud said, 'O my Lady and Content of my Heart, I shall continue to **endure**[2] my fate at the hands of these nine hundred and ninety-nine Queens who **vex** me with their **continual**[3] quarrelling.'

So he went on between the **lilies**[4] and the **loquats**[5] and the roses and the **cannas**[6] and the heavy-scented ginger-plants that grew in the garden, till he came to the great **camphor-tree**[7] that was called the Camphor Tree of Suleiman-bin-Daoud. But Balkis hid among the tall **irises**[8] and the **spotted**[9] **bamboos**[10] and the red lilies behind the camphor-tree, so as to be near her own true love, Suleiman-bin-Daoud.

Presently two Butterflies flew under the tree, quarrelling.

Suleiman-bin-Daoud heard one say to the other, 'I wonder at your presumption in talking like this to me. Don't you know that if I stamped with my foot all Suleiman-bin-Daoud's Palace and his garden here would immediately **vanish**[11] in **a clap of thunder**[12].'

Then Suleiman-bin-Daoud forgot his nine hundred and ninety-nine bothersome wives, and laughed, till the camphor-tree shook, at the Butterfly's **boast**[13]. And he held out his finger and said, 'Little man, come here.'

The Butterfly was dreadfully frightened, but he managed to fly up to the hand of Suleiman-bin-Daoud, and **clung**[14] there, **fanning**[15] himself.

Suleiman-bin-Daoud bent his head and **whispered**[16] very softly, 'Little man, you know that all your stamping wouldn't bend one blade of grass. What made you tell that **awful**[17] **fib**[18] to your wife? —for **doubtless**[19] she is your wife.'

The Butterfly looked at Suleiman-bin-Daoud and saw the most wise King's eye **twinkle**[20] like stars on a **frosty**[21] night, and he picked up his

① treasure /ˈtreʒə(r)/ n. 金银财宝，瑰宝
② endure /ɪnˈdjʊə/ v. 忍耐，忍受；
③ vex /veks/ v. 使烦恼，恼怒
④ continual /kənˈtɪnjʊəl/ adj. 持续不断的，无休止的
⑤ lily /ˈlɪlɪ/ n. 百合，百合花
⑥ loquat n. 枇杷树；枇杷
⑦ canna n. 美人蕉
⑧ camphor-tree /ˈkæmfə trɪː/ n. 樟树，
⑨ iris /ˈaɪərɪs/ n. 鸢尾属植物
⑩ spotted-bamboo /ˈspɒtɪdbæmˈbuː/ n. 斑竹
⑪ vanish /ˈvænɪʃ/ v. 消失
⑫ a clap of thunder 一声霹雳
⑬ boast /bəʊst/ n. 自吹，大话
⑭ cling /klɪŋ/ v. 粘紧；紧贴；附着
⑮ fan /fæn/ v. 扇风
⑯ whisper /ˈhwɪspə(r)/ v. 低声说
⑰ awful /ˈɔːfʊl/ adj. 吓人的，可怕的
⑱ fib /fɪb/ v. 撒谎
⑲ doubtless /ˈdaʊtlɪs/ adv. 毫无疑问
⑳ twinkle /ˈtwɪŋkl/ v. 闪烁；闪耀
㉑ frosty /ˈfrɒstɪ/ adj. 严寒的

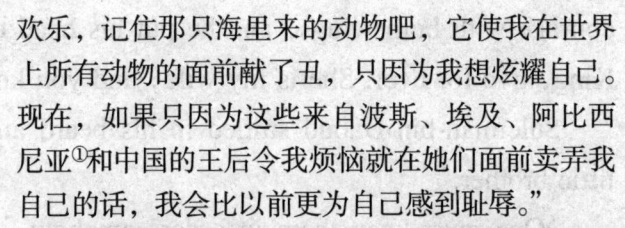

欢乐，记住那只海里来的动物吧，它使我在世界上所有动物的面前献了丑，只因为我想炫耀自己。现在，如果只因为这些来自波斯、埃及、阿比西尼亚①和中国的王后令我烦恼就在她们面前卖弄我自己的话，我会比以前更为自己感到耻辱。"

最美丽的巴尔基斯王后说："哦，我的君王我灵魂的瑰宝，那你该怎么做呢？"

苏雷曼宾·达奥德说："哦，我的夫人我心灵的全部，我的命运掌握在那999位王后手里，我要继续忍受她们无休止的争吵带给我的折磨。"

于是他继续穿行在花园里的百合、枇杷、玫瑰、美人蕉和浓香的姜类植物里，最后来到了一棵樟树面前。这棵樟树叫做苏雷曼宾·达奥德樟树。而巴尔基斯为了靠近她钟爱的苏雷曼宾·达奥德，便隐藏在樟树后高高的鸢尾花、斑竹和红色的百合花后面。

这时树下飞来两只蝴蝶，一边飞一边吵嘴。

苏雷曼宾·达奥德听到其中一只蝴蝶对另一只说："我想知道你怎么敢这么放肆地对我说话。你难道不知道，如果我跺了一下脚，苏雷曼宾·达奥德的宫殿和花园就会在一声霹雳后全部消失。"

听了蝴蝶的大话，苏雷曼宾·达奥德大笑起来，暂时忘记了他那999位令人心烦的王后，笑声震动了樟树。他伸出一根手指说："小男人，到这儿来。"

蝴蝶惊恐万分，但它还是飞到了苏雷曼宾·达奥德的手上，紧紧抓住他的手指，舞着翅膀给自己扇风。

苏雷曼宾·达奥德低下头，低声细语地说：

---
① 东非国家埃塞俄比亚的旧称。译注。

courage with both wings, and he put his head on one side and said, 'O King, live for ever. She is my wife; and you know what wives are like.'

Suleiman-bin-Daoud smiled in his beard and said, 'Yes, I know, little brother.'

'One must keep them in order somehow,' said the Butterfly, 'and she has been quarrelling with me all the morning. I said that to quiet her.'

And Suleiman-bin-Daoud said, 'May it quiet her. Go back to your wife, little brother, and let me hear what you say.'

Back flew the Butterfly to his wife, who was all of a **twitter**① behind a leaf, and she said, 'He heard you! Suleiman-bin-Daoud himself heard you!'

'Heard me!' said the Butterfly. 'Of course he did. I meant him to hear me.'

'And what did he say? Oh, what did he say?'

' Well,' said the Butterfly, fanning himself most importantly, ' between you and me, my dear—of course I don't blame him, because his Palace must have cost a great deal and the oranges are just ripening, —he asked me not to stamp, and I promised I wouldn't.'

'**Gracious**②!' said his wife, and sat quite quiet; but Suleiman-bin-Daoud laughed till the tears ran down his face at the **impudence**③ of the bad little Butterfly.

Balkis the Most Beautiful stood up behind the tree among the red lilies and smiled to herself, for she had heard all this talk. She thought, 'If I am wise I can yet save my Lord from the **persecutions**④ of these quarrelsome Queens,' and she held out her finger and **whispered**⑤ softly to the Butterfly's Wife, 'Little woman, come here.' Up flew the Butterfly's Wife, very frightened, and clung to Balkis's white hand.

远古传奇

"小男人，你知道，如果你跺脚的话，连个草片也不会压弯。为什么你要向妻子撒这种弥天大谎？——毫无疑问，它是你的妻子呀。"

蝴蝶看着眼前这最聪明的君王，他的眼睛像寒夜里闪耀的星光。于是，它用双翅鼓起勇气，歪着头说："哦，君王，祝您万寿无疆！它是我的妻子，而且你也了解妻子们通常是怎么回事儿。"

苏雷曼宾·达奥德的唇边漾起一丝微笑，说："对，小男人，我了解。"

"男人必须想办法让它们乖乖地听话，"蝴蝶说，"它已经和我吵了一上午了。我那么说是为了让它安静下来。"

苏雷曼宾·达奥德说："希望你的话能让它安静下来。小兄弟，回到你的妻子身边去吧，让我听听你怎么说。"

蝴蝶飞回妻子身边。妻子正躲在一片树叶后面抖成一团。它问道："他听见你说话了！苏雷曼宾·达奥德他自己听到的！"

"听我的！"蝴蝶说，"他当然听到了。我就是想让他听到。"

"那他是怎么说的？噢，他说了些什么？"

"嗯，"蝴蝶一本正经地扇着翅膀，"亲爱的，这是我们之间的悄悄话——当然我没有责怪他，因为他的宫殿耗资巨大；而且，桔子也快成熟了——他请求我不要跺脚，我答应了。"

"天啊！"它的妻子喊了一声，然后安静地坐下来。看到这只淘气的小蝴蝶如此厚脸皮，苏雷曼宾·达奥德笑得连眼泪都流出来了。

此时，最美丽的王后巴尔基斯站在树后红色的百合花丛中，独自微笑着，她听到了刚才对话

① twitter /ˈtwɪtə(r)/ n. 慌张；抖动

② gracious /ˈɡreɪʃəs/ adj. 天啊……

③ impudence /ˈɪmpjədəns/ n. 后脸皮的；厚颜无耻

④ persecution /ˌpɜːsɪˈkjuːʃn/ n. 困扰，烦扰

⑤ whisper /ˈhwɪspə(r)/ v. 低声说

· 251 ·

Balkis bent her beautiful head down and whispered, 'Little woman, do you believe what your husband has just said?'

The Butterfly's Wife looked at Balkis, and saw the most beautiful Queen's eyes shining like deep pools with **starlight**① on them, and she **picked up**② her courage with both wings and said, 'O Queen, be lovely for ever. You know what **men-folk**③ are like.'

And the Queen Balkis, the Wise Balkis of Sheba, put her hand to her lips to hide a smile and said, 'Little sister, I know.'

'They get angry,' said the Butterfly's Wife, fanning herself quickly, 'over nothing at all, but we must **humour**④ them, O Queen. They never mean half they say. If it pleases my husband to believe that I believe he can make Suleiman-bin-Daoud's Palace **disappear**⑤ by stamping his foot, I'm sure I don't care. He'll forget all about it tomorrow.'

'Little sister,' said Balkis, 'you are quite right; but next time he begins to boast, take him at his word. Ask him to stamp, and see what will happen. We know what men-folk are like, don't we? He'll be very much ashamed.'

Away flew the Butterfly's Wife to her husband, and in five minutes they were quarrelling worse than ever.

'Remember!' said the Butterfly. 'Remember what I can do if I stamp my foot.'

'I don't believe you one little bit,' said the Butterfly's Wife. 'I should very much like to see it done. **Suppose**⑥ you stamp now.'

'I promised Suleiman-bin-Daoud that I wouldn't,' said the Butterfly, 'and I don't want to **break my promise**⑦.'

'It wouldn't matter if you did,' said his wife. 'You couldn't bend a blade of grass with your stamping. I dare you to do it,' she said. 'Stamp! Stamp! Stamp!'

① starlight n. 星星的闪光，星光
② picked up adj. 扇动
③ men-folk /mæn fəuk/ n. 男人
④ humour adv. 迁就
⑤ disappear /ˌdɪsəˈpɪə/ v. 消失；不见
⑥ suppose /səˈpəuz/ v. 推想，猜想
⑦ break my promise 不能违背诺言

的内容。她想："如果我聪明的话，我就能使我的君王从那些吵闹不休的王后的困扰中解脱出来。"她伸出一根手指，对蝴蝶的妻子小声说道："小女人，到这里来。"蝴蝶的妻子惊恐万分地飞了过去，贴落在巴尔基斯白嫩的手上。

美丽的巴尔基斯低下头，悄声说道："小女人，你相信你丈夫刚才说的话吗"？

蝴蝶的妻子看着巴尔基斯，眼前这位最美丽的王后，她的眼睛像跳跃着星光的深潭。于是它扇动双翅鼓起勇气说："哦，王后，愿您永远这样可爱！您了解男人通常是怎么回事儿。"

王后巴尔基斯来自示巴，她非常聪明。她把手放在唇上遮掩微笑，说："小姐妹，我了解。"

"他们通常动不动就生气，"蝴蝶的妻子一边飞快地给自己扇风，一边说，"其实也没什么大不了的事儿。但是王后，我们必须迁就他们。他们所说的话一半都不能信。我丈夫说它跺一下脚，苏雷曼宾·达奥德的宫殿就会消失，要是我相信了它的话就能使它感到高兴的话，我肯定愿意这样做。明天它就会把这件事忘得一干二净。"

"小姐妹，"巴尔基斯说，"你说得对极了。但下次它如果再吹牛的话，就抓住它的话柄，让它跺脚，看看结果会怎么样。我们了解男人，不是吗？它会感到非常惭愧的。"

蝴蝶的妻子飞回到丈夫身边。五分钟过后，它们吵得比以往任何时候都要激烈。

"给我记住！"蝴蝶说，"如果我跺脚的话，会发生什么情况。"

"我一丁点儿也不相信，"它的妻子说，"我

· 253 ·

Suleiman-bin-Daoud, sitting under the camphor-tree, heard every word of this, and he laughed as he had never laughed in his life before. He forgot all about his Queens; he forgot all about the Animal that came out of the sea; he forgot about showing off. He just laughed with joy, and Balkis, on the other side of the tree, smiled because her own true love was so **joyful**①.

Presently the Butterfly, very hot and **puffy**②, came whirling back under the shadow of file camphor-tree and said to Suleiman, 'She wants me to stamp! She wants to see what will happen, O Suleiman-bin-Daoud! You know I can't do it, and now she'll never believe a word I say. She'll laugh at me to the end of my days!'

'No, little brother,' said Suleiman-bin-Daoud, 'she will never laugh at you again,' and he turned the ring on his finger—just for the little Butterfly's sake, not for the sake of showing off, —and, lo and behold, four huge Djinns came out of the earth!

'Slaves,' said Suleiman-bin-Daoud, 'when this gentleman on my finger' (that was where the impudent Butterfly was sitting) 'stamps his left front **forefoot**③ you will make my Palace and these gardens disappear in a clap of thunder. When he stamps again you will bring them back carefully.'

'Now, little brother,' he said, 'go back to your wife and stamp all you've a **mind**④ to.'

Away flew the Butterfly to his wife, who was crying, 'I dare you to do it! I dare you to do it! Stamp! Stamp now! Stamp!' Balkis saw the four vast Djinns stoop down to the four corners of the gardens with the Palace in the middle, and she **clapped**⑤ her hands softly and said, 'At last Suleiman-bin-Daoud will do for the sake of a Butterfly what he ought to have done long ago for his own sake, and the quarrelsome Queens will be frightened!'

倒很想看看这是怎么回事。你现在跺一下脚吧。"

"我答应过苏雷曼宾·达奥德不跺脚的，"蝴蝶说，"我不能违背诺言。"

"你违背了也没有什么，"它妻子说，"你跺一下脚，连个草片也压弯不了。我看你敢不敢。"它连连催促："跺！跺！跺脚！"

苏雷曼宾·达奥德正坐在樟树下，听了这些对话，放声大笑，他以前可从未这样笑过。他忘记了他的王后们，忘记了那只从海底来的动物，忘记了炫耀自己的事情，他只是快乐地笑着。而在树的另一侧，巴尔基斯看到她的心上人如此快乐，也露出微笑。

这时蝴蝶旋风般飞到樟树下。它大汗淋漓、气喘吁吁地对苏雷曼宾·达奥德说："它想让我跺脚！哦，苏雷曼宾·达奥德，它想看看会发生什么事！你知道我做不到的，现在我说的话它一个字也不相信了。它会嘲笑我的，一直到我死去！"

"不，小兄弟，"苏雷曼宾·达奥德说，"它决不会再嘲笑你了。"他把手指上的戒指转了一下——这样做是为了小蝴蝶，而不是自我卖弄——嘿，你瞧！从地里钻出四个巨神！

"我的奴隶们，"苏雷曼宾·达奥德说，"当我手上（那只厚脸皮的蝴蝶就坐在那儿）的这位绅士跺左前脚的时候，你们要在一声霹雳后使我的宫殿和花园消失；如果他再跺脚，你们就把一切恢复原状。"

"好，小兄弟，"他说，"回到你妻子身边去，想跺脚就跺脚吧。"

蝴蝶飞回妻子身边。它妻子还在大喊大叫："我看你敢不敢！看你敢不敢！跺！现在跺脚！

① joyful /ˈdʒɔɪfʊl/ adj. 快乐的笑，令人高兴的
② puffy /ˈpʌfɪ/ adj. 喘气的，肥满的
③ forefoot /ˈfɔːfʊt/ n. 前脚
④ mind /maɪnd/ v. 注意，专心于（文中指想做某事）
⑤ clap /klæp/ v. 轻拍，击

Then the Butterfly stamped. The Djinns **jerked**[1] the Palace and the gardens a thousand miles into the air: there was a most awful **thunderclap**[2], and everything grew **inky**[3]-black. The Butterfly's Wife fluttered about in the dark, crying, 'Oh, I'll be good! I'm so sorry I spoke. Only bring the gardens back, my dear darling husband, and I'll never **contradict**[4] again.'

The Butterfly was nearly as frightened as his wife, and Suleiman-bin-Daoud laughed so much that it was several minutes before he found breath enough to **whisper**[5] to the Butterfly, 'Stamp again, little brother. Give me back my Palace, most great magician.'

'Yes, give him back his Palace,' said the Butterfly's Wife, still flying about in the dark like a moth. 'Give him back his Palace, and don't let's have any more horrid magic.'

'Well, my dear,' said the Butterfly as bravely as he could, 'you see what your **nagging**[6] has led to. Of course it doesn't make any difference to me—I'm used to this kind of thing—but as a **favour**[7] to you and to Suleiman-bin-Daoud I don't mind putting things right.'

Sohe stamped once more, and that **instant**[8] the Djinns let down the Palace and the gardens, without even a bump. The sun shone on the dark-green orange leaves; the fountains played among the pink **Egyptian**[9] lilies; the birds went on singing, and the Butterfly's Wife lay on her side under the camphor-tree waggling her wings and panting, 'Oh, I'll be good! I'll be good!'

Suleiman-bin-Daoud could hardly speak for laughing. He leaned back all weak and **hiccoughy**[10], and shook his finger at the Butterfly and said, 'O great **wizard**[11], what is the sense of returning to me my Palace if at the same time you **slay**[12] me with **mirth**[13]!'

Then came a terrible noise, for all the nine hundred and ninety-nine Queens ran out of the Palace **shrieking**[14] and shouting and calling for

① jerk /dʒɜːk/ v. 猛然一动；颠簸
② thunder-clap /ˈθʌndə(r)klæp/ n. 雷声，一声霹雳
③ inky /ˈɪŋkɪ/ adj. 漆黑的
④ contradict /ˌkɒntrəˈdɪkt/ v. 否；否认（文中指再也不）
⑤ whisper /ˈhwɪspə(r)/ v. 低声说
⑥ nag /næɡ/ v. 不断唠叨；责骂不休
⑦ favourite /ˈfeɪvə/ adj. 不介意
⑧ instant /ˈɪnstənt/ n. 一刹那，瞬间
⑨ Egyptian /ɪˈdʒɪpʃn/ adj. 埃及的
⑩ hiccoughy /ˈhɪkʌpli/ v. 打嗝
⑪ wizard /ˈwɪzə(r)d/ n. 奇才，天才
⑫ slay /sleɪ/ v. 使大为高兴
⑬ mirth /mɜːθ/ n. 欢笑；高兴
⑭ shriek /ʃriːk/ n. 嘈杂声，尖声喊叫

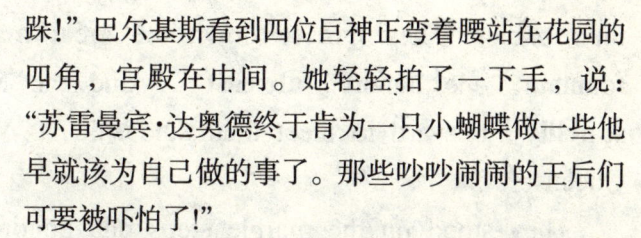

跺！"巴尔基斯看到四位巨神正弯着腰站在花园的四角，宫殿在中间。她轻轻拍了一下手，说："苏雷曼宾·达奥德终于肯为一只小蝴蝶做一些他早就该为自己做的事了。那些吵吵闹闹的王后们可要被吓怕了！"

蝴蝶跺脚了。巨神们把王宫和花园举到了1000英里高的空中：一声霹雳过后，天地间变得漆黑一片。蝴蝶的妻子在黑暗中拍打着翅膀，哭喊着："哦，今后我会乖乖听话的！我后悔说了那些话。我最亲爱的丈夫，恳求你把花园变回来吧，我今后再也不跟你对着干了。"

蝴蝶和妻子一样被吓得魂飞魄散。苏雷曼宾·达奥德捧腹大笑，几分钟后才止住笑，喘过气来低声对蝴蝶说："小兄弟，再跺一下脚，把王宫还给我吧，你这最伟大的魔术师。"

"对，把宫殿变回来吧，"蝴蝶的妻子说，它仍然像一只飞蛾那样在黑暗里乱飞。"把宫殿变回来吧，可别再要什么可怕的魔术了。"

"好吧，亲爱的，"蝴蝶尽量让自己的声音听起来很勇敢，"看到你唠唠叨叨引起的后果了吧。当然，这对我来说无所谓——我对这些把戏已经司空见惯了——但我不介意把一切再恢复原状。就当帮你和苏雷曼宾·达奥德一个忙吧。"

于是它又跺了一下脚。一刹那，巨神又把高举着的宫殿和花园稳稳地放在了地上。太阳照在墨绿色的桔叶上，喷泉在粉红色的埃及百合花的拥围下嬉戏着；鸟儿继续歌唱。蝴蝶的妻子卧在樟树下，摆动着翅膀，气喘吁吁地说："哦，我会听话的！我会学乖的！"

苏雷曼宾·达奥德笑得说不出话来。他打着

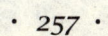

their babies. They hurried down the great **marble**① steps below the fountain, one hundred **abreast**②, and the Most Wise Balkis went **statelily**③ forward to meet them and said, 'What is your trouble, O Queens?'

They stood on the marble steps one hundred abreast and shouted, 'What is our trouble? We were living **peacefully**④ in our golden palace, as is our **custom**⑤, when upon a sudden the Palace **disappeared**⑥, and we were left sitting in a thick and **noisome**⑦ darkness; and it thundered, and Djinns and Afrits moved about in the darkness! That is our trouble, O Head Queen, and we are most extremely troubled **on account**⑧ of that trouble, for it was a **troublesome**⑨ trouble, unlike any trouble we have known.'

Then Balkis the Most Beautiful Queen—Suleiman-bin-Daoud's Very Best Beloved—Queen that was of Sheba and Sable and the Rivers of the Gold of the South—from the Desert of Zinn to the Towers of Zimbabwe—Balkis, almost as wise as the Most Wise Suleiman-bin-Daoud himself, said, 'It is nothing, O Queens! A Butterfly has made **complaint**⑩ against his wife because she quarrelled with him, and it has pleased our Lord Suleiman-bin-Daoud to teach her a lesson in low-speaking and **humbleness**⑪, for that is counted a **virtue**⑫ among the wives of the butterflies.'

Then up and spoke an Egyptian Queen—the daughter of a Pharoah—and she said, 'Our Palace cannot be **plucked up**⑬ by the roots like a **leek**⑭ for the sake of a little insect. No! Suleiman-bin-Daoud must be dead, and what we heard and saw was the earth thundering and darkening at the news.'

Then Balkis **beckoned**⑮ that bold Queen without looking at her, and said to her and to the others, 'Come and see.'

They came down the marble steps, one hundred abreast, and

远古传奇

① marble /ˈmɑːbl/ n. 大理石，雕刻品
② abreast /əˈbrest/ adv. 并肩地；并排地
③ state /steɪt/ n. 仪态；形态
④ peacefully /ˈpiːsflɪ/ adv. 平静地；和平地
⑤ custom /ˈkʌstəm/ adj. 订做的，订制的（文中指坐在那里）
⑥ disappear /ˌdɪsəˈpɪə/ v. 消失；不见
⑦ noisome /ˈnɔɪsəm/ adj. 遗弃
⑧ on account of 由于；因为
⑨ troublesome /ˈtrʌblsəm/ adj. 麻烦的，棘手的

⑩ complaint /kəmˈpleɪnt/ n. 诉苦；恳求
⑪ humbleness /ˈhʌmblnɪs/ n. 谦卑
⑫ virtue /ˈvɜːtjuː/ n. 美德
⑬ pluck /plʌk/ v. 拽
⑭ leek /liːk/ n. 韭，葱
⑮ beckon /ˈbekən/ v. 召唤；示意

嗝，虚弱地向后仰着身体，冲蝴蝶晃了晃手指，说："哦，伟大的奇才！你把王宫还给了我，同时让我快乐得要死，这到底意义何在？"

忽然传来了一阵乱哄哄的嘈杂声。999个王后战栗着跑出了王宫，大声呼唤着自己的孩子。她们每100个人一排，急忙跑到喷泉下漂亮的大理石台阶上。最聪明的王后巴尔基斯仪态万方地迎上前去，问道："王后们，你们有什么麻烦事？"

王后们每100个人一排，站在大理石台阶上，大声喊道："我们怎么了？我们在金色宫殿里像往常一样和平地生活着，忽然王宫消失了，我们坐在那里，被遗弃在黑暗中，周围嘈杂一片。一声霹雳后，恶魔和巨神就在黑暗中走动！您是王后之首，您瞧瞧，这就是我们的麻烦事。这麻烦可不同于我们所知道的麻烦，真是麻烦透了，我们感到极度不安。"

巴尔基斯是苏雷曼宾·达奥德的至爱，示巴、萨比和南部金地河畔（从津恩沙漠一直到津巴布韦要塞）的王后，她非常聪颖，几乎可以与苏雷曼宾·达奥德相媲美。巴尔基斯说："王后们，没有什么！一只蝴蝶因为妻子和它吵架而心生不满，它恳求我们的君王苏雷曼宾·达奥德给妻子一个教训，让妻子学会低声说话，举止谦卑。对蝴蝶来说，这才是妻子的美德。"

一位来自埃及的王后（法老的女儿）大叫一声："不可能就因为一只小虫子的缘故就把我们的王宫像拽韭菜一样连根拔起，不会！苏雷曼宾·达奥德一定已经死了，所以消息传来，尘世间忽然晴天霹雳，变得漆黑一片。这正是我们看到和听到的。"

对这位胆大的王后，巴尔基斯连一眼也没

· 259 ·

beneath his camphor-tree, still weak with laughing, they saw the Most Wise King Suleiman-bin-Daoud rocking back and forth with a Butterfly on either hand, and they heard him say, 'O wife of my brother in the air, remember after this, to please your husband in all things, lest he be **provoked**① to stamp his foot yet again; for he has said that he is used to this magic, and he is most **eminently**② a great magician—one who **steals**③ away the very Palace of Suleiman-bin-Daoud himself. Go in peace, little **folk**④!' And he kissed them on the wings, and they flew away.

Then all the Queens except Balkis—The Most Beautiful and **Splendid**⑤ Balkis, who stood apart smiling—fell flat on their faces, for they said, 'If these things are done when a Butterfly is **displeased with**⑥ his wife, what shall be done to us who have vexed our King with our loud-speaking and open quarrelling through many days?'

Then they put their **veils**⑦ over their heads, and they put their hands over their mouths, and they **tiptoed**⑧ back to the Palace most mousy-quiet.

Then Balkis—The Most Beautiful and Excellent Balkis—went forward through the red lilies into the shade of the camphor-tree and laid her hand upon Suleiman-bin-Daoud's shoulder and said, 'O my Lord and Treasure of my Soul, **rejoice**⑨, for we have taught the Queens of Egypt and Ethiopia and Abyssinia and Persia and India and China with a great and a **memorable**⑩ teaching.'

And Suleiman-bin-Daoud, still looking after the Butterflies where they played in the sunlight, said, 'O my Lady and Jewel of my **Felicity**⑪, when did this happen? For I have been **jesting**⑫ with a Butterfly ever since I came into the garden.' And he told Balkis what he had done.

Balkis—The tender and Most Lovely Balkis—said, 'O my Lord and Regent of my Existence, I hid behind the camphor-tree and saw it all. It was I who told the Butterfly's Wife to ask the Butterfly to stamp,

① provoke /prəˈvəuk/ v. 激怒，煽动

② eminently /ˈemɪnəntlɪ/ adv. 突出地；极好地

③ steal /stiːl/ v. 偷

④ folk /fəuk/ n. 人，家伙

⑤ splendid /ˈsplendɪd/ adj. 出色的，了不起的

⑥ displease /dɪsˈpliːz/ v. 使不高兴；不满意

⑦ veil /veɪl/ n. 面纱

⑧ tiptoe v. 踮起脚走；蹑手蹑脚地走

⑨ rejoice /rɪˈdʒɔɪs/ v. 快乐起来；使高兴

⑩ memorable /ˈmemərəbl/ adj. 永远铭记；难忘的

⑪ felicity /fɪˈlɪsətɪ/ n. ，幸福

⑫ jesting /ˈdʒestɪŋ/ adj. 玩耍；说着玩的

看，只是召唤她和其他王后："来看看吧。"

她们每100人一排，走下大理石台阶。在那棵樟树下，她们看到了最聪明的君王苏雷曼宾·达奥德，他笑得都快虚脱了，左右手各有一只蝴蝶，身体随着笑声来回晃动。她们听见他在说："哦，我飞舞在空中的小兄弟的妻子，从今往后可要记住，在各方面都要讨好你的丈夫，以免它再跺脚。因为它说它经常施展这种魔法，它是最杰出的魔术大师——它曾偷过苏雷曼宾·达奥德的王宫。平心静气地离开这里吧，小家伙！"他吻了吻它们的翅膀，两只蝴蝶飞走了。

除了最美丽、最出色的王后巴尔基斯面露微笑外，其他的王后脸色全都暗淡下来，她们说："如果蝴蝶对它妻子不满意就发生了这种事，那么我们这些天来一直在沸沸扬扬、肆无忌惮地吵架，君王困扰不堪，又该有什么事情降临到我们头上来呢？"

然后她们戴好面纱，以手掩口，悄悄踮起脚尖，回到王宫里去了。

最美丽、最出色的巴尔基斯王后穿过红色的百合花丛，走到樟树的树阴下，把手搭在苏雷曼宾·达奥德的肩上，说："哦，我的君王我灵魂的宝藏，快乐起来吧。因为我们已经深刻地教训了那些来自埃及、埃塞俄比亚、阿比西尼亚、波斯、印度和中国的王后们。想必她们会永远铭记住这一课的。"

苏雷曼宾·达奥德的目光还在追随着那两只在阳光下嬉戏的蝴蝶。他说："哦，我的夫人我幸福的宝藏，这一切是怎么发生的？因为自从踏入花园那一刻起，我就一直在与蝴蝶玩耍。"他

because I hoped that for the sake of the jest my Lord would make some great magic and that the Queens would see it and be frightened.' And she told him what the Queens had said and seen and thought.

Then Suleiman-bin-Daoud rose up from his seat under the camphor-tree, and stretched his arms and rejoiced and said, 'O my Lady and Sweetener of my Days, know that if I had made a magic against my Queens for the sake of pride or anger, as I made that **feast**[1] for all the animals, I should certainly have been put to shame. But by means of your **wisdom**[2] I made the magic for the sake of a jest and for the sake of a little Butterfly, and—behold—it has also **delivered**[3] me from the **vexations**[4] of my **vexatious**[5] wives! Tell me, therefore, O my Lady and Heart of my Heart, how did you come to be so wise?'

And Balkis the Queen, beautiful and tall, looked up into Suleiman-bin-Daoud's eyes and put her head a little on one side, just like the Butterfly, and said, 'First, O my Lord, because I loved you; and secondly, O my Lord, because I know what **women-folk**[6] are.'

Then they went up to the Palace and lived happily ever afterwards.

But wasn't it clever of Balkis?

远古传奇

把自己所做的一切都告诉给巴尔基斯。

温柔、可爱至极的巴尔基斯王后说："哦，我的君主我生命的主宰，我躲在樟树后目睹了这里发生的一切。是我让蝴蝶的妻子要它的丈夫跺脚的，因我希望借这次玩笑之机，我的君王能大展魔法，那样王后们看了就会感到害怕。"她把王后们所说、所见和所想告诉给他。

苏雷曼宾·达奥德从樟树下的座位上站起来，伸出手臂，满心欢喜地说："哦，我的夫人我生活的蜜糖，你知道如果我因为骄傲或恼怒就施展魔法，就像那次为所有的动物准备盛宴一样，我会无地自容的。这次动用魔法不过是为了开个玩笑，也为了帮助一只小小的蝴蝶。你却用自己的智慧把我从那些伤脑筋的王后们所制造的困扰中解脱出来。所以，我的夫人我心灵的归属，请你告诉我，你为什么这么聪明？"

身材颀长、容貌秀丽的巴尔基斯王后抬起头来，凝望着苏雷曼宾·达奥德的眼睛。她稍稍歪着头，就像蝴蝶那样，说："第一，君王，因为我爱你；第二，君王，因为我了解女人。"

然后，他们回到王宫，从此幸福地生活在一起。

巴尔基斯王后是不是很聪明？

① feast /fiːst/ n. 宴会，盛宴
② wisdom /ˈwɪzdəm/ n. 智慧，
③ deliver /dɪˈlɪvə/ v. 实现
④ vexation /vekˈseɪʃn/ n. 困扰，烦恼
⑤ vexatious /vekˈseɪʃəs/ adj. 伤脑筋的

⑥ woman-folk /ˈwʊmən fəʊk/ n. 女人

Just So Stories

This is the picture of the Animal that came out of the sea and **ate up**① all the food that Sulei-man-bin-Daoud had made ready for all the animals in all the world. He was really quite a nice Animal, and his Mummy was very fond of him and of his twenty-nine thousand nine hundred and ninety-nine other brothers that lived at the bottom of the sea. You know that he was the smallest of them all, and so his name was Small Porgies. He ate up all those boxes and **packets**② and **bales**③ and things that had been got ready for all the animals, without ever once taking off the lids or **untying**④ the strings, and it did not hurt him at all. The sticky-up **masts**⑤ behimd the boxes of food belong to Suleiman-bin-Daoud's ships. They were busy bringing more food when Small Porgies came ashore. He did not eat the ships. They stopped **unloading**⑥ the foods and instantly sailed away to sea till Small Porgies had quite finished eating. You can see some of the ships beginning to sail away by Small Porgie's shoulder. I have not drawn Suleiman-bin-Daoud, but he is just outside the picture, very much **astonished**⑦. The **bundle**⑧ hanging from the mast of the ship in the comer is really a package of wet dates for **parrots**⑨ to eat. I don't know the names of the ships. That is all there is in that picture.

这就是故事中提到的那只动物。它从海里钻出来，把苏雷曼宾·达奥德为全世界所有的动物准备的食物全吃光了。其实它很善良，妈妈很喜欢它和另外29999个兄弟。它们都住在海底。你知道，它是家族里最小的一个，所以它的名字叫小波吉斯。它甚至连包装盖都没有打开、绳子都没有解开就把装在盒子、箱子和大袋子里为所有动物准备的食物一扫而光。而这样的吃法对它一点伤害也没有。装食物的盒子后面竖着的东西是船上的桅杆，这些船都是苏雷曼宾·达奥德的。船正紧张的忙碌着，边运来更多的食物。这时小波吉斯出现在海岸边。它可没有吃那些船。直到小波吉斯快吃完的时候，船才停止卸货，飞快地开跑了。你可以从

① ate up 全吃光

② packet /'pækɪt/ n. 箱子
③ bale /beɪl/ n. 大袋子

④ untying v. 松开，解开
⑤ mast /mɑːst/ n. 桅杆

⑥ unload /ˌʌnˈləʊd/ v. 卸货

⑦ astonish /əˈstɒnɪʃ/ v. 使惊讶，使吃惊
⑧ bundle /ˈbʌndl/ n. 捆；包；束
⑨ parrot /ˈpærət/ n. 鹦鹉

小波吉斯的肩膀处找到那些快速开走的船。我没有把苏雷曼宾·达奥德画出来，他不在画面上。看到这一切他震惊极了。图下方角落里船桅杆上吊着的东西实际上是为鹦鹉们准备的湿枣。我不知道这些船的名字，只是把它们全画出来了。

Just So Stories

This is the picture of the four **gull-winged**① Djinns lifting up Suleiman-bin-Daoud's Palace the very minute after the Butterfly had stamped. The Palace and the gardens and everything came up in one piece like a board, and they left a big hole in the ground all full of **dust**② and smoke. If you look in the corner, close to the thing that looks like a lion, you will see Suleiman-bin-Daoud with his magic stick and the two Butterflies behind him. The thing that looks like a lion is really a lion carved in stone, and the thing that looks like a milk-can is really a piece of a **temple**③ or a house or something. Suleiman-bin-Daoud stood there so as to be out of the way of the dust and the smoke when the Djinns lifted up the Palace. I don't know the Djinns's names. They were servants of Suleiman-bin-Dauod's magic ring, and they changed about every day. They were just common gull-winged Djinns.

The thing at the bottom is a picture of a very friendly Djinn called Akraig. He used to feed the little fishes in the sea three times a day, and his wings were made of pure copper. I put him in to show you what a nice Djinn is like. He did not help to lift the Palace. He was busy feeding little fishes in the Arabian Sea when it happened.

这幅画描绘了蝴蝶跺脚的那一刻，四位长着海鸥一样翅膀的巨神把苏雷曼宾·达奥德的宫殿高举起来的情景。王宫、花园以及所有的一切像块木板一样离开了地面，地面上出现了一个大洞。一时间，尘土飞扬，烟雾四溢。图下方角落里你能看到一只像狮子一样的东西，苏雷曼宾·达奥德就站在它的附近。他手持魔棒，两只蝴蝶在他身后飞舞。狮子是用石头雕刻成的，后面牛奶罐似的东西其实是座庙，也许是房屋或其他东西。苏雷曼宾·达奥德站在那里是为了在巨神举起宫殿时避开飞扬的尘土。我不知道那些巨神的名字。他们是苏雷曼宾·达奥德的仆人，每天变幻着形象。他们只是一般的鸥翅巨神。

远古传奇

① gull-wing /gʌl-wɪŋ/ n. 海鸥一样的翅膀

② dust /dʌst/ n. 尘土；尘埃

③ temple /ˈtempl/ n. 神殿，圣堂

下面的图画画的是一位非常友善的巨神，他的名字叫阿克瑞格。过去他常常去喂海里的小鱼，一天三次。他有一双纯铜的翅膀。我把他放在这里，是为了让你看看巨神是多么讨人喜欢。四位巨神抬举宫殿时，他没有去帮忙。这一切发生时，他正在阿拉伯海里忙着喂小鱼。

There was never a Queen like Balkis,
From here to the wide world's end;
But Balkis talked to a butterfly
As you would talk to a friend.
There was never a King like Solomon,
Not since the world began;
But Solomon talked to a butterfly
As a man would talk to a man.
She was Queen of Sabaea—
And he was Asia's **Lord**①—
But they both of 'em talked to butterflies
When they took their walks **abroad**②!

远古传奇

从这里到天涯海角，
根本找不到一位像巴尔基斯那样的王后；
但巴尔基斯和蝴蝶谈话，
就像你和朋友谈话一样。

从世界伊始，
找不到一位像所罗门那样的君王。
但明君与蝴蝶谈话，
就像男人与男人谈话一样。
她是萨比的王后，
而他是亚洲之王。
但他们外出时都与蝴蝶交谈，
两个人都曾经这样。

① lord /lɔːd/ *n.* 君主；统治者，大王

② abroad /əˈbrɔːd/ *adv.* 在外面；到外面